Mending Fences, Cross Infiltration and Conflict Challenges

LINE OF ACTUAL CONTROL

Meding Fences, Cross Infiltration and Conflict Challenges

LINE OF ACTUAL CONTROL

Brig. M.N. Sarin (Retd.)

Gaurav Book Centre Pvt Ltd

Delhi

Publisher
GAURAV BOOK CENTRE PVT LTD
4832/24,Prahlad Lane,S-207 Ansari
Road, Daryaganj, Delhi-110002
Ph.: 43570976, 23278261
Email: gauravbookcentre@gmail.com

Edition: 2020

ISBN: 978-93-83316-24-3

Laser Typesetting
JEE-VEE Graphics, Delhi

Price: 1295/-

Printed
Vikas Computers, Delhi

Preface

The Line of Actual Control (LAC) is a demarcation line that separates Indian-ruled lands from Chinese-held territory. It is the effective border between India and the People's Republic of China (PRC). The LAC is 4,056-km long and traverses four Indian states: Jammu and Kashmir, Uttarakhand, Himachal, and Sikkim. On the Chinese side, the line traverses the autonomous province of Tibet. The demarcation existed as the informal cease-fire line between India and China after the 1962 conflict until 1993, when its existence was officially accepted as the 'Line of Actual Control' in a bilateral agreement.

The term "LAC" gained legal recognition in Sino-Indian agreements signed in 1993 and 1996. The 1996 agreement states, "No activities of either side shall overstep the line of actual control." The Indian government claims that Chinese troops continue to illegally enter the area hundreds of times every year. In 2013, there was a three-week standoff between Indian and Chinese troops 30 km southeast of Daulat Beg Oldi. It was resolved and both Chinese and Indian troops withdrew in exchange for an Indian agreement to destroy some military structures over 250 km to the south near Chumar that the Chinese perceived as threatening.

The state was a theatre in the 1962 Sino-Indian war, in which India had faced major losses and had to fight in extremely unprepared conditions, with almost no road connectivity. While Indian forces did manage to resist strongly at several border points the fall of Tawang and Bomdi La towns were without resistance as there was no proper supply and road infrastructure to maintain Indian army positions.

This book contains the fundamental and basic information of the subject and useful for teachers, students and researchers.

—*Author*

Contents

1

Line of Actual Control

The Line of Actual Control (LAC) is a demarcation line that separates Indian-ruled lands from Chinese-held territory. It is the effective border between India and the People's Republic of China (PRC). The LAC is 4,056-km long and traverses four Indian states: Jammu and Kashmir, Uttarakhand, Himachal, and Sikkim. On the Chinese side, the line traverses the autonomous province of Tibet. The demarcation existed as the informal cease-fire line between India and China after the 1962 conflict until 1993, when its existence was officially accepted as the 'Line of Actual Control' in a bilateral agreement. However, Chinese scholars claim that the Chinese Prime Minister Zhou Enlai first used the phrase in a letter addressed to Indian Prime Minister Jawaharlal Nehru dated 24 October 1959.

Although no official boundary had ever been negotiated between China and India, Indian government even today claims that the Johnson Line of 1865 is the effective border between China and India while the PRC government considers theMacartney-MacDonald Line of 1899 the accepted boundary.

In a letter dated 7 November 1959, Zhou told Nehru that the LAC consisted of "the so-called McMahon Line in the east and the line up to which each side exercises actual control in the west". During the Sino-Indian War (1962), Nehru refused to recognise the line of control: "There is no sense or meaning in the Chinese offer to withdraw twenty kilometers from what they call 'line of actual control'. What is this 'line of control'? Is this the line they have created by aggression since the beginning of September?

Advancing forty or sixty kilometers by blatant military aggression and offering to withdraw twenty kilometers provided both sides do this is a deceptive device which can fool nobody."

Zhou responded that the LAC was "basically still the line of actual control as existed between the Chinese and Indian sides on 7 November 1959. To put it concretely, in the eastern sector it coincides in the main with the so-calledMcMahon Line, and in the western and middle sectors it coincides in the main with the traditional customary line which has consistently been pointed out by China."

The term "LAC" gained legal recognition in Sino-Indian agreements signed in 1993 and 1996. The 1996 agreement states, "No activities of either side shall overstep the line of actual control." The Indian government claims that Chinese troops continue to illegally enter the area hundreds of times every year. In 2013, there was a three-week standoff between Indian and Chinese troops 30 km southeast of Daulat Beg Oldi. It was resolved and both Chinese and Indian troops withdrew in exchange for an Indian agreement to destroy some military structures over 250 km to the south near Chumar that the Chinese perceived as threatening. Later the same year, the BBC reported that Indian forces mistook planets for Chinese spy drones for six months. They recorded 155 such intrusions. Later the planets were identified by the Indian Institute of Astrophysics as Venus and Jupiter. In October 2013, India and China signed a border defense cooperation agreement to ensure that patrolling along the LAC does not escalate into armed conflict.

LINE OF ACTUAL CONTROL CLARIFICATION AND CBMS IMPLEMENTATION

The eight rounds of border talks demonstrated that their conflicting border versions, based on historical-legalistic arguments, could not find common ground because no mutually acceptable border treaties or agreements existed. The eight rounds of border talks raised the hope for a political solution to the border dispute.

In 1991, Premier Li peng visited India and signed the Sino-Indian Joint Communique on December 16, 1991. In the joint communiqué, they reaffirmed their independent foreign policy and the five principles of peaceful co-existence. The two sides appealed for the joint efforts for the establishment of a new international political and economic order. India reiterated its position that Tibet is an autonomous region of China and it does not allow Tibetans to engage in anti-china political activities in India.

After the two summit meetings in 1988 and 1991, China-India interactions shifted from the border dispute to the identification of a mutually acceptable lie of actual control along the China-India border. In 1993, Indian Prime Minister Rao visited China and signed an agreement on maintaining peace and tranquility along the line of actual control and reduced military forces in the border areas. This peace pact, under which both sides agreed to respect and observe the LAC, is a big step forward in exploring a lasting border solution, eliminating concerns about events such as the Sumdurong Chu incident which nearly sparked another border war in 1987. Under the LAC agreement in 1993, the two sides agreed that the boundary question shall be resolved through peaceful and friendly consultations. Neither side shall use or threaten to use force against the other by any means. Pending an ultimate solution to the boundary question, the two sides shall strictly respect and observe the LAC.

Each side will keep its military forces in the areas along the LAC to a minimum level compatible with the friendly and good-neighborly relations between the two countries. Both sides shall work out effective confidence-building measures (CBMs) in the areas along the LAC. However, the two sides agreed that references to the LAC in this agreement do not prejudice their respective positions on the boundary question.

Under this agreement, both sides agreed that each side of the China-India Joint Working Group on the boundary question shall appoint diplomatic and military experts, advising the Joint Working Group on resolution of differences on the alignment of the LAC and address issues relating to military redeployment in the border areas along the LAC. In 1996, the Chinese president Jiang Zemin visited India and both sides decided to develop a cooperative and constructive partnership, further raising political level of bilateral cooperation between the two countries. However, the Indian nuclear tests in 1998 and its leaders indicated India's nuclear tests for counter-China's nuclear threat dashed the healthy momentum of China-India relations in the late 1990s.

Apparently, China-India interactions in the 1990s focused on political and security fields. The line of actual control, the CBMs in the areas along the China-India border, and emphasis on the establishment of an international political and economic order and even India's nuclear tests are all pointed to political and security dimension of the China-India relations.

Shift Back to the Settlement of the Border Dispute in the New Century

Ushering in the new 21st century, China and India, the two Asian giants, are rising at the same time. Their bilateral relationship has its regional and global significance. As the two largest emerging powers in Asia and the world, their roles have been played far beyond the bilateral context. Certainly, their bilateral dispute, particularly the border dispute, has constrained each other's capability to play their responsible role in the regional and global affairs.

If they focused on stabilizing their relations and securing their border areas in the 1990s, they have shifted their attention to the settlement of their border dispute by developing their political and economic relations while taking concrete and substantive measures to resolve the border dispute. They understand that their bilateral problems have complicated their policy coordination and cooperation in the regional and global issues. Their bilateral differences have tended to be manipulated by other powers to serve their geostrategic interest. For the past decade, in terms of the border dispute, they have taken three substantive steps to intensify their efforts to resolve it. The first step is that India has accepted Tibet is an autonomous region of China, implying that India has given up the intention to use Tibet as a buffer zone between China and India and recognizes China's sovereignty overTibet. However, although India does not allow the Tibetans in India to engage in Anti-China political activities, it still hosts the Dalai Lama's government-in-exile. China has recognized Sikkim's status as a state of India's federation by signing the agreement on the cross-border trade with India.

The second step is that China and India signed an agreement on political parameters and guiding principles on the settlement of the China-India border dispute. This document is regarded as a big breakthrough in the joint efforts for resolving the border dispute. The third step is that the two governments have appointed their special representatives to promote the negotiations on a framework of the border settlement. The two governments have paid importance to the annual meetings of the two special representatives. The Chinese special representative is State Councilor Dai Bingguo and The Indian special representative is India's National Security adviser M. K. Narayanan.

After the two special representatives were appointed, they started to work together for a framework settlement of the border dispute according to the agreed political parameters and guiding principles. Under the current circumstances, although the two governments continue to work on the settlement of the border dispute, peace, stability, and tranquility in the border areas have remained. No armed conflicts or even skirmishes happened although some media has played up such noises of China's invasions into India's territory dozens or hundreds of times.

INDIA'S RELATIONS WITH CHINA: THE GOOD, THE BAD AND THE (POTENTIALLY) UGLY

Later this month, Indian Prime Minister Manmohan Singh will travel to Beijing. The visit will cap a year that has been full of ups and downs in India's relations with China. The tale of three trips is representative. One in May by Chinese Premier Li Keqiang, his first abroad, was intended to signal the importance Beijing placed in the Sino-Indian relationship. But it took place in the aftermath of—and some would say was overshadowed by—a border standoff between the two countries' militaries. In July, the Indian defense minister visited Beijing to rebuild trust and defense ties. Media coverage, however, focused on warnings to India issued by a PLA general, which Chinese officials had to rush to dismiss.

And Singh will be travelling from a country that is largely preoccupied domestically. When discussions do turn to China, they have focused on concerns about Indian capacity vis-à-vis that country, Indian politicians accusing the government of being soft on China and Chinese scholars labeling India's border infrastructure upgrades as provocative. These and other developments have highlighted what Indian policymakers acknowledge—that there are elements of cooperation, competition and concern in the China-India relationship.

There have been good signs for those interested in stable, cooperative Sino-Indian relations.In the spring, just after he'd formally taken office, Chinese President Xi Jinping proposed a five-point formula to improve ties between the two countries. "Positive vibes" were detected at Xi's subsequent meeting with Singh on the sidelines of the BRICS summit in Durban in March. There have been numerous public Chinese declarations of the importance of the relationship—perhaps not seen since the first half of the 1950s. The Chinese ambassador to India unusually took to the editorial pages of an Indian newspaper to emphasize, "To strengthen good-neighbourly and friendly cooperation with India is China's strategic choice and established policy which will not change." Chinese officials have indicated that greater efforts should be made toward a boundary settlement. The two countries have strategic and economic dialogues in place. They restarted their defense dialogue earlier this year and are expected to resume joint military exercises shortly. China and India also have specialized dialogues on issues like Afghanistan, Central Asia and counterterrorism. The agreement to discuss Afghanistan was considered a departure from previous Chinese policy; Beijing had earlier been reluctant to add it to the agenda because it would have likely meant talking about Chinese ally Pakistan. Along with regional discussions, China and India have also cooperated in the multilateral realm, including on issues like trade and climate change.

Premier Li chose India as his first overseas stop, with the Chinese government indicating that the choice was very deliberate. Hosting an Indian youth delegation, Li put a personal spin on the choice, noting the "the seeds of friendship sown" when he visited India 27 years ago—a trip that he said left a "lasting impact." During the May visit, he stressed the need to build trust and especially emphasized the economic benefits of greater ties.

Those economic ties have already grown. China is one of India's largest trading partners. Bilateral trade in goods has gone from less than $3 billion in 2000 to $66.57 billion in 2012. While investments haven't kept the same pace, they have also grown. In India, the interest in doing business with China is evident beyond the private sector and the central government—along with visits by a number of Indian CEOs, China has also seen visits from chief ministers of a number of Indians states, including Andhra Pradesh, Bihar, Karnataka and Madhya Pradesh. Narendra Modi, current chief minister of the state of Gujarat and prime ministerial candidate for the forthcoming national election for the BJP (India's largest opposition party), has also traveled to China. While Modi has expressed hawkish views on China on the geopolitical front, he has expressed admiration for that country's economic achievements.

The governments of both countries have reasons for wanting stable ties: the desire for a peaceful periphery in order to focus on domestic socio-economic objectives; the need for stability in South Asia, especially with the impending American drawdown of forces from Afghanistan; existing and potential economic ties; and the prospect for cooperation in the multilateral realm. For Delhi, in addition, a stable relationship with China opens up the possibility that Beijing might use its leverage with Islamabad to shape Pakistan's behavior in a way that might benefit India. For Beijing, there's desire to limit India's burgeoning relationships with the United States and Japan, as well as with other countries in what Beijing considers its backyard. Moreover, as China is preoccupied with eastern maritime disputes and the North Korean situation, stable relations on its southern and southwestern flank would also help the Chinese leadership.

This year has, however, also shown how quickly the bad in the relationship can steal the spotlight from the good—with the potential to turn ugly. In April, less than two weeks after an Indian observer commented on the "upswing in relations" between China and India, their long-standing boundary dispute flared once again. While the two countries communicated through the crisis and resolved it diplomatically, and Li's visit proceeded as planned, the border incident reinforced the mistrust that many in India feel toward China and its intentions. Furthermore, it was a reminder that despite increased engagement, bilateral differences have the potential to stall, if not reverse, progress toward more stable relations.

Differences are not restricted to the boundary dispute. Tibet remains a key source of tension between the two countries though the two countries have found a way to manage their differences on the issue for now. In addition, China's relationship with Pakistan has been a major source of concern in India. Its role in strengthening Pakistan's conventional, missile and nuclear capabilities is especially highlighted. India also disapproves of China's assistance to Pakistan in developing projects and infrastructure in area disputed between India and Pakistan.

China's growing political and economic ties with India's neighbours are also a subject of concern. Delhi watches warily increasing Chinese interactions—political and commercial—with and involvement in countries like Afghanistan, Bangladesh, Myanmar, Nepal and Sri Lanka. Concern about a military dimension being added persists. Beijing's increasing interest in operating in the Indian Ocean, which India has traditionally considered its backyard, has also not gone unnoticed. While China emphasizes that these activities have benign goals—economic development, security for its ships, etc.—some in India who tend to take a hawkish position are not convinced; others are taking a wait-and-see attitude. Even beyond the neighbourhood, there are concerns about competition with China for markets, influence and resources across the globe.

Closer to home, water is the resource that has become the subject of tension—specifically Chinese dam construction on its side of the Brahmaputra River. Indian officials have publiclycalled for Beijing to reassure India on this matter. Domestic critics, however, perceive the Indian government as being too tolerant of the construction. They argue that China has not respected information sharing agreements on this front and warn of more ambitiousChinese river diversion plans.

Economic ties, which many envisioned as the driver of good Sino-Indian ties, have also not escaped trouble. Bilateral trade in goods actually fell almost 10 percent from 2011 to 2012. In India there's much concern about the trade imbalance. The overall trade deficit has gonefrom $28 billion in 2010-2011 to $40.8 billion in 2012-2013. While investments have grown, they remain limited compared to the investment relationships that both China and India have with other countries. In India, there have also been complaints about market access in China and the treatment of Indian labor there, concern about Chinese investment in "strategic" sectors in India, accusations about visa abuses by Chinese companies and restrictions on Chinese labor. Indian companies also privately express concerns about cyber-espionage. Overall, reports of cyber attacks on Indian government and military networks—allegedly emanating from China—have done nothing to decrease distrust that persists, especially among the public.

There is also an overall sense that China does not respect India and/or that it will seek to prevent India's rise. As evidence, critics point not only to China's relationship with Pakistan, which is seen as driven by a desire to keep India tied up in South Asia, but also note China'sreluctance to endorse India's demand for a permanent seat on the U.N. Security Council or its objections to India being given membership in the Nuclear Suppliers Group.

Another overarching problem: the lack of trust in China and its intentions. This is especially evident among the public. According to a Pew poll last year, more Indians have an unfavorable view of China than a favorable view. In a more recent Lowy Institute poll, China ranked only second to Pakistan in terms of countries that people considered threatening to India, with 60 percent indicating China would be a major threat over the next decade (an additional 22 percent identified it as a minor threat). 73 percent of those surveyed identified "war with China" as a big threat over the next ten years. Almost three-quarters believed that China wants to dominate Asia. 58 percent felt that China's growth had not been good for India. This reinforces what the Pew poll found last year. In that poll, two-thirds of urbanites who expressed an opinion on the subject believed that China's growing economy was a bad thing.

Overcoming this mistrust continues to be a major obstacle. The legacy of history remains a problem. Every time there is a border incident it reinforces the narrative that has prevailed in many quarters in India since the 1962 China-India war: that China only understands strength; that while Beijing's leaders say China and India "must shake hands," they cannot be trusted—that one hand held out might just be a precursor to the other stabbing one in the back. This problem is made worse by limited connectivity and communications, and little knowledge about the other country—even though these have improved. Media coverage about China and the relationship can also get quite heated, with a tendency to focus on the negative. All these problems are exacerbated by the lack of transparency when it comes to Chinese decision-making. This has led to uncertainty about Chinese behavior and motivations, which was evident in the debate about why the border incident in April occurred—and this uncertainty exists even among policymakers.

Thus, Indian governments have tried to follow a multi-pronged strategy. The emphasis might have differed somewhat, but for the last two governments in India—one a coalition led by the BJP and the current one led by the Congress—the general approach towards China has been to co-operate, if possible, and to compete, if necessary. Indian officials have joined with Chinese counterparts to increase ties, build trust and improve communications. Simultaneously, policymakers note that competition in and of itself is not all bad. As former Indian Prime Minister Vajpayee noted in Beijing, "a sense of competition between two close and equal neighbours" might indeed be natural. There is also, however, a realization that beyond cooperation and competition, there is a potential for conflict. Thus, while hoping and working for the best, there has been some attention on planning and preparing for the worst—i.e. the possibility that China will emerge as an explicit threat. There is a desire to do this cautiously, however, with policymakers quite conscious of the potential for provocation, miscalculation and exacerbation of the security dilemma.

In practice, this overall approach has meant increasing engagement with China—political, economic and even military-to-military—at the bilateral, regional and multilateral levels. Simultaneously, this approach has translated to a series of actions including strengthening India's military, as well as its border infrastructure and border regions, maintaining a nuclear deterrent, and consolidating or expanding ties and influence in India's near abroad.

India has also tried to step up its game in China's neighbourhood. Indian policymakers underplay the strategic aspects and goals of India's "Look East" policy—which the Indian foreign ministry describes as "oriented towards deepening India's engagement with the countries of East and Southeast Asia"—and emphasize its cultural and economic aspects. However, these elements and the link to China have not been entirely missing in action. The Indian government and companies are increasingly interested and engaged in the region, especially focusing on countries like Indonesia, Japan, Singapore, Thailand and Vietnam. In recent months, India-Japan ties have probably been in the spotlight the most, with another round of the U.S.-India-Japan trilateral dialogue and Singh's visit to Japan in May. India has also sought to be more engaged with multilateral fora in the region. Officials from some Southeast Asian countries, however, want India to do much more. Channeling some of their frustrations, Hillary Clinton, when she led the State Department, called for "India not just to look east, but to engage East and act East as well."

Another key aspect of India's approach has been the pursuit of closer relations with the United States. Of course, these ties with the United States are not solely driven by China. India indeed has no desire to make a choice between its relations with China and the United States. However, the United States plays a useful role as an offshore balancer. Furthermore, Indian policymakers believe that a strong U.S.-India relationship gives them leverage with China and sends a signal to that country. Some also note that China takes India more seriously because the United States does. India, however, still has doubts about U.S. reliability as a potential partner, especially given the level of Sino-U.S. engagement, and prefers to maintain a diversified portfolio of partnerships.

So, where do India's relations with China go from here? In the near term, during the Prime Minister's visit, the two sides might sign a border defense cooperation agreement. The accord would essentially be a way to manage rather than resolve the boundary question, which the Indian foreign secretary has noted continues to be "a particularly difficult issue." The trans-border rivers question is also likely to be discussed. In addition, given the two countries' priorities, bilateral and global economic and financial issues will be high on the agenda. Potentially, there also might be agreements that could facilitate greater people-to-people ties, including a cultural and visa pacts. Regionally, developments vis-à-vis Afghanistan and the Middle East that concern both governments are likely to be discussed. Finally, on the multilateral front, trade and climate change issues might be on the agenda, given upcoming international summits in those two areas.

As for the longer term, the scenarios usually outlined are deepening cooperation, increasing competition that might lead to conflict, or continuity with both competition and cooperation in evidence. There is a debate in India—inside and outside government—about China, which scenario might prevail, the future of the relationship and what approach to take with China. The differences are evident in the Lowy poll—almost equal numbers of those surveyed believe that India "should join with other countries to limit China's influence" and "should cooperate with China to play a leading role in the world together."

How the relationship plays out will depend on a number of internal, bilateral, regional and global factors. In the meantime, Shyam Saran, a former foreign secretary and currently chairman of the National Security Advisory Board, has called for India to manage relations with China "with prudence but firmness." An air force chief described the way forward as "play cool and continue to develop capabilities."

2

Line of Actual Control in the India-China Border Areas

The Government of the Republic of India and the Government of the People's Republic of China (hereinafter referred to as the two sides).

Believing that it serves the fundamental interests of the peoples of India and China to foster a long-term good-neighbourly relationship in accordance with the 'five principles of mutual respect for sovereignty and territorial integrity, mutual non-aggression, non-interference in each other's internal affairs, equality and mutual benefit and peaceful co-existence.

Convinced that the maintenance of peace and tranquillity along the line of actual control in the India-China border areas accords with the fundamental interests of the two peoples and will also contribute to the ultimate resolution of the boundary question.

Reaffirming that neither side shall use or threaten to use force against the other by any means or seek unilateral military superiority.

Pursuant to the Agreement between the Government of the Republic of India and the Government of the People's Republic of China on the Maintenance of Peace and Tranquillity along the Line of Actual Control in the India-China Border Areas, signed on 7 September, 1993.

Recognizing the need for effective confidence building measures in the military field along the line of actual control in the border areas between the two sides. Noting the utility of confidence building measures already in place along the line of actual control in the India-China border areas. Committed to enhancing mutual confidence and transparency in the military field, Have agreed as follows :

ARTICLE I

Neither side shall use its military capability against the other side. No armed forces deployed by either side in the border areas along the line of actual control as part of their respective military strength shall be used to attack the other side, or engage in military activities that threaten the other side or undermine peace, tranquillity and stability in the India-China border areas.

ARTICLE II

The two sides reiterate their determination to seek a fair, reasonable and mutually acceptable settlement of the boundary question. Pending an ultimate solution to the boundary question, the two sides reaffirm their commitment to strictly respect and observe the line-of actual control in the India-China border areas. No activities of either side shall overstep the line of actual control.

ARTICLE III

The two sides agree to take the following measures to reduce or limit their respective military forces within mutually agreed geographical zones along the line of actual control in the India-China border areas:

(1) The two sides reaffirm that they shall reduce or limit their respective military forces within mutually agreed geographical zones along the line of actual control in the India-China border areas to minimum levels compatible with the friendly and good neighborly relations between the two countries and consistent with the principle of mutual and equal security.

(2) The two sides shall reduce or limit the number of field army, border defence forces, paramilitary forces and any other mutually agreed category of armed force deployed in mutually agreed geographical zones along the line of actual control to ceilings to be mutually agreed upon. The major categories of armaments

to be reduced, or limited are as follows : combat tanks, infantry combat vehicles, guns (including howitzers) with 75 mm or bigger calibre, mortars with 120 mm or bigger calibre, surface-to-surface missiles, surface-to-air missiles and any other weapon system mutually agreed upon.

(3) The two sides shall exchange data on the military forces and armaments to be reduced or limited and decide on ceilings on military forces and armaments to be kept by each side within mutually agreed geographical zones along the line of actual control in the India-China border areas. The ceilings shall be determined in conformity with the requirement of the principle of mutual and equal security, with due consideration being given to parameters such as the nature of terrain, road communication and other infrastructure and time taken to induct/deinduct troops and armaments.

ARTICLE IV

In order to maintain peace and tranquillity along the line of actual control in the India-China border areas and to prevent any tension in the border areas due to misreading by either side of the other side's intentions:

(1) Both sides shall avoid holding large scale military exercises involving more than one Division (approximately 1 5,000 troops) in close proximity of the line of actual control in the India-China border areas. However, if such exercises are to be conducted, the strategic direction of the main force involved shall not be towards the other side.

(2) If either side conducts a major military exercise involving more than one Brigade Group (approximately 5,000 troops) in close proximity of the line of actual control in the India-China border areas, it shall give the other side prior notification with regard to type, level, planned duration and area of exercise as well as the number and type of units or formations participating in the exercise.

(3) The date of completion of the exercise and deinduction of troops from the area of exercise shall be intimated to the other side within five days of completion or deinduction.

(4) Each side shall be entitled to obtain timely clarification from the side undertaking the exercise in respect of data specified in Paragraph 2 of the present Article.

ARTICLE V

With a view to preventing air intrusions across the line of actual control in the India-China border areas and facilitating overflights and landings by military aircraft:

(1) Both sides shall take adequate measures to ensure that air intrusions across the line of actual control do not take place. However, if an intrusion does take place, it should cease as soon as detected and the incident shall be promptly investigated by the side operating the aircraft. The results of the investigation shall be immediately communicated, through diplomatic channels or at border personnel meetings, to the other side.

(2) Subject to Paragraphs 3 and 5 of this Article, combat aircraft (to include fighter, bomber, reconnaissance, military trainer, armed helicopter and other armed aircraft) shall not fly within ten kilometers of the line of actual control.

(3) If either side is required to undertake flights of combat aircraft within ten kilometers from the line of actual control, it shall give the following information in advance to the other side, through diplomatic channels:

(a) Type and number of combat aircraft;

(b) Height of the proposed flight (in meters);

(c) Proposed duration of flights (normally not to exceed ten days);

(d) Proposed timing of flights; and

(e) Area of operations, defined in latitude and longitude.

(4) Unarmed transport aircraft, survey aircraft and helicopters shall be permitted to fly up to the line of actual control.

(5) No military aircraft of either side shall fly across the line of actual control, except by prior permission. Military aircraft of either side may fly across the line of actual control or overfly the other side's airspace or land on the other side only after obtaining

the latter's prior permission after providing the latter with detailed information on the flight in accordance with the international practice in this regard.

Notwithstanding the above stipulation, each side has the sovereign right to specify additional conditions, including at short notice, for flights or landings of military aircraft of the other side on its side of the line of actual control or through its airspace.

(6) In order to ensure flight safety in emergency situations, the authorities designated by the two sides may contact each other by the quickest means of communications available.

ARTICLE VI

With a view to preventing dangerous military activities along the line of actual control in the India-China border areas, the two sides agree as follows:

(1) Neither side shall open fire, cause bio-degradation, use hazardous chemicals, conduct blast operations or hunt with guns or explosives within two kilometers from the line of actual control. This prohibition shall not apply to routine firing activities in small arms firing ranges.

(2) If there is a need to conduct blast operations within two kilometers of the line of actual control as part of developmental activities, the other side shall be informed through diplomatic channels or by convening a border personnel meeting, preferably five days in advance.

(3) While conducting exercises with live ammunition in areas close to the line of actual control, precaution shall be taken to ensure that a bullet or a missile does not accidentally fall on the other side across the line of actual control and causes harm to the personnel or property of the other side.

(4) If the border personnel of the two sides come in a face-to-face situation due to differences on the alignment of the line of actual control o any other reason, they shall exercise self-restraint and take all necessary steps to avoid an escalation of the situation. Both sides shall also enter into immediate consultations through diplomatic and/or other available channels to review the situation and prevent any escalation of tension.

ARTICLE VII

In order to strengthen exchanges and cooperation between the military personnel and establishments in the border areas along the line of actual control, the two sides agree:

(a) To maintain and expand the regime of scheduled and flag meetings between their border representatives at designated places along the line of actual control;

(b) To maintain and expand telecommunication links between the border meeting points at designated places along the line of actual control;

(c) To establish step-by-step medium and high-level contacts between the border authorities of the two sides.

ARTICLE VIII

(1) Should the personnel of one side cross the line of actual control and enter the other side because of unavoidable circumstances like natural disasters, the other side shall extend all possible assistance to them and inform their side, as soon as possible regarding the forced or inadvertent entry across the line of actual control. The modalities of return of the concerned personnel to their own side shall be settled through mutual consultations.

(2) The two sides shall provide each other, at the earliest possible, with information pertaining to natural disasters and epidemic diseases in contiguous border areas which might affect the other side. The exchange of information shall take place either through diplomatic channels or at border personnel meetings.

ARTICLE IX

In case a doubtful situation develops in the border region, or in case one of the sides has some questions or doubts regarding the manner in which the other side is observing this Agreement, either side has the right to seek a clarification from the other side. The clarifications sought and replies to them shall be conveyed through diplomatic channels.

ARTICLE X

(1) Recognizing that the full implementation of some of the provisions of the present Agreement will depend on the two sides arriving at a common understanding of the alignment of the line of actual control in the India-China border areas, the two sides agree to speed up the process clarification and confirmation of the line of actual control. As an initial step in this process, they are clarifying the alignment of the line of actual control in those segments where they have different perceptions. They also agree to exchange maps indicating their respective perceptions of the entire alignment of the line of actual control as soon as possible.

(2) Pending the completion of the process of clarification and confirmation of the line of actual control, the two sides shall work out modalities for implementing confidence building measures envisaged under this Agreement on an interim basis, without prejudice to their respective positions on the alignment of the line of actual control as well as on the boundary question.

ARTICLE XI

Detailed implementation measures required under Article I to Article X of this Agreement shall be decided through mutual consultations in the India-China Joint Working Group on the Boundary Question. The India-China Diplomatic and Military Expert Group shall assist the India-China Joint working Group in devising implementation measures under the Agreement.

ARTICLE XII

This Agreement is subject to ratification and shall enter into force on the date of exchange of instruments of ratification. It shall remain in effect until either side decides to terminate it after giving six months' notice in writing. It shall become invalid six months after the notification.

This Agreement is subject to amendment and addition by mutual agreement in writing between the two sides.

Signed in duplicate in New Delhi on 29 November, 1996 in the Hindi, Chinese and English languages, all three texts being equally authentic. In case of divergence, the English text shall prevail.

TO ENGAGE WITH CHINA, INDIA MUST STOP PEDDLING MYTHS ABOUT THE LINE OF ACTUAL CONTROL

Political commentators have been gushing over the possibilities of strengthened economic and strategic relations between China and India, but the unresolved border dispute remains alive and can always play spoiler in the future. A border is, after all, more than a line on the map or a series of military posts on the ground; it is a reflection of how the political elite of a nation-state thinks about its security.

Chinese-controlled Aksai Chin is claimed by India as part of Jammu and Kashmir, and Indian-controlled Arunachal Pradesh is claimed by China. The only feasible solution is to accept the status quo and transform the Line of Actual Control into an international boundary. There have been several rounds of talks since the 1990s, but a resolution remains distant. Despite its parliamentary majority, Prime Minister Narendra Modi's government will be unable to sell a permanent boundary settlement without being accused of ceding territory in Aksai Chin, though in reality it will only be giving up its claim over a territory India never controlled.

This raises a pertinent question: what precisely is the border upon which India and China cannot agree?

New neighbours

Through history, China and India have not been neighbours. The current de facto border has its genesis in a line drawn on a map by Henry McMahon during a secret treaty between Britain and Tibet in March 1914. Both entities, British India and Tibet, are no more: one has been transformed into postcolonial India and the other was occupied and colonised by communist China. Yet India and China, both of whom have overthrown the mantle of Western imperialism, are jostling over the same imperialists' line – and have completely militarised and destroyed the traditional zone of contact that the border regions were.

The border is a legacy of a few dynamics, including the expansionist policies of the British in the Himalayan regions of India, the disappearance of the traditional Tibetan state, which had political and sacral hegemony over much of the region, and the modern nationalisms in postcolonial India and revolutionary China, which are keen on implementing a rigid notion of sovereignty in the border regions and legitimising the primacy of militarised security over the religious, cultural and human rights of the people inhabiting the region.

Stuck in the middle

The primary loser in the dispute is neither India nor China but Tibet. China has occupied most of Tibetan territory, while India has occupied the Tawang tract, which was historically part of Tibet. The Tibetan state had given up the Tawang region to British India in 1914 on the understanding that they would get friendship and assistance to protect their independence from China. When China went on to occupy Tibet in 1949-'50, India reneged on that understanding, preferring the diplomatically attractive Hindi-Chini-bhai-bhai rhetoric over a strategically sound and morally defensible Indo-Tibetan friendship.

Despite reluctantly hosting the Tibetan exile community today, India did not offer any tangible help to the Tibetans in their struggle for independence. Today, as Modi and Xi plan collaborations on various fronts, Tibetans are reminded that in this world of realpolitik, morality and human rights are subservient. Tibetans are perceived as strategic assets or liabilities in bargaining with China, not people of an occupied land for whom India should raise its voice. For India, it is the border that matters, not the border inhabitants.

Myths peddled by India

The popular as well as strategic approach of many in India towards the border dispute is jaundiced by the myths the Indian state peddled about the humiliating war of 1962. After the 1962 defeat, there was no credible reflection at the policy level in India. Indians accepted as real the myths that Indian territorial claims were legitimate and sacrosanct, and that the Chinese were duplicitous and stabbed gullible India in the back. The reality could not be further from this. The first Survey of India Map in 1950 showed the boundary as undefined in Aksai Chin and as undemarcated in the north east. It was only in the summer of 1954 that Jawaharlal Nehru gave personal orders for all old maps to be withdrawn and destroyed and to remove qualifiers and show the McMahon Line in bold, as if that was the de jure boundary.

Nehru later claimed innocence, insisting that there was no boundary disagreement and that Chinese claims were surprising. Since 1959, India rejected all the diplomatic overtures of Zhou Enlai and said negotiations could only take place if China withdrew from Aksai Chin, though India would not offer anything in return. Since 1961, the Indian military followed a "forward policy" in the border regions that was not only provocative but based on the assumption that China would not retaliate.

A great unresolved mystery from the time is why the best Indian minds working in intelligence, military and diplomacy accepted this assumption without a murmur of protest. It can be explained by Nehru's hubris in his own capacity as a statesperson, bureaucracies subservient to him, and the inability of the civilian and military elite to be independent-minded. Macho posturing was the order of the day. The Indianisation of the top brass in the military occurred only after independence in 1947, so they were inexperienced as leaders. Faced with an army that had its genesis in revolutionary wars, the Indian army, which had been servant to an imperial power, failed to perform its basic duty of protecting the country.

Henderson Brooks report

The post-war military report is still confidential, though an excerpt from it was leaked online earlier this year by Neville Maxwell. This Henderson Brooks Report shows that the Indian military barely put up a fight in the north east. There was a total failure of command and control at every level. The only thing that saved India from losing more territories was the unilateral ceasefire declared by China and the Chinese withdrawal back to the prewar LAC. Had China not withdrawn, India could not have done much.

Rather than reflect upon its own follies, India embarked on militarisation and refused to negotiate. While the fantasists may be waiting for China to collapse one day, the fact is that China is here to stay and India has an option of either being sincere in negotiations or letting the dispute fester. It took the border dispute and a revolt in Tibet and the exile of the Dalai Lama in 1959 to destroy the camaraderie of early 1950s. Unless China manages to put an end to the Tibet issue by reaching a settlement with the Tibetans led by the Dalai Lama, and both India and China resolve their disagreements over the border, the newfound bonhomie could unravel once again.

CHINESE INTRUSIONS ACROSS THE LINE OF ACTUAL CONTROL TELL INDIA

A number of Chinese border intrusions across the Line of Actual Control have been reported in recent months. One such event near Mount Gya in the Chumar sector of Ladakh saw Chinese troops intruding 1.5 kilometres inside Indian territory and writing "China" on the rocks with red paint. The intrusion was first noticed by an Indian patrol team on July 31, 2009. An earlier incident of Chinese intrusion in this area reportedly took place on June 21st, when two Chinese M1 helicopters violated the Indian airspace and air dropped canned food at Chumar. While admitting that such an intrusion has indeed taken place, Army Chief General Deepak Kapoor played down the episode saying that the intrusion might have taken place because of navigational error. He also went on to state that such intrusions are not new and have been taking place for years. Minister of External Affairs, S. M. Krishna, also said that the border between India and China in the Ladakh sector is 'most peaceful' and such cases of intrusion would be sorted out through the 'inbuilt mechanism'.

This 'inbuilt mechanism' is the Border Personnel Meetings/ Flag Meetings, which take place at regular intervals. The establishment of this mechanism for resolving such border transgressions can be traced to the Agreement on the Maintenance of Peace and Tranquillity along the Line of Actual Control in the China-India Border Areas of 1993. As far as the recent case of intrusion is concerned, it is reported that the regiment posted in the area under 14 Corps had taken up the matter with their Chinese counterparts during such a border meeting in August and had also lodged a formal protest.

The Chinese side, however, denied the charges and maintained that border patrols by Chinese troops were 'strictly conducted according to the law' and they had never violated India's land or air space. Despite Chinese denials, the fact remains that China has been intruding inside the Indian territory all along the LAC. The Indian Army has reportedly recorded 270 border violations and nearly 2,300 cases of "aggressive border patrolling" by Chinese soldiers last year. The point to note is that earlier such intrusions were frequently reported from Arunachal Pradesh, while lately incidences of Chinese border transgression are increasingly being reported from Sikkim and Ladakh, hitherto considered as peaceful sectors of the LAC.

The reason behind the heightened Chinese incursions has been falsely attributed by many to the on-going strengthening of Indian military capability along the LAC – the deployment of Sukhoi-30 MKI fighter jets in Tezpur, raising of two additional mountain divisions for the defence of Arunachal Pradesh, the landing of AN-32 transport plane at Daulat Begh Oldhi, the proposed deployment of an AWACS (airborne warning and control systems) plane as 'force multiplier' in the Ladakh sector, and the construction of 27 strategic roads along the India-China border. It is being argued that Chinese border intrusions are a reaction to these developments. The reality is, however, quite different. China does not need any of these excuses to transgress the LAC. It has been doing so in the past and will continue to do so in future. The unsettled border and these incursions are nothing but a manifestation of the uneasy relationship which the two countries share. The slow and steady emergence of India as a strong power in Asia is not looked upon favourably by China. And this sentiment also adversely impacts on the attempts to resolve the border dispute amicably.

China has had serious border disputes with many of its neighbours, and it chose to resolve those disputes only when it felt that the concerned neighbour was weak or when the latter acknowledged China's superior status. In the early 1960s, in a bid to demonstrate to the world that it was a responsible country and a good neighbour, China concluded border agreements with Burma, Nepal, Afghanistan and Pakistan.

These countries were militarily weak neighbours and did not have any serious ideological or political differences with China. Notably, many of those border agreements were preceded by Chinese propaganda and border incursions by Chinese troops. At this time, however, China did not settle its borders with India, Bhutan, Soviet Union, Vietnam and Laos. It even engaged in wars with India in 1962, Soviet Union in 1969 and Vietnam in 1979.

As is often said, the best indication of strained relation between two countries is tensions across their shared borders. In the case of India, China felt threatened by India's standing in the international forums and especially by its leadership role among the third world countries.

This feeling of unease was compounded by the Khampa rebellion in Tibet and the subsequent flight of the Dalai Lama to India in 1959. The strained relations between the two countries were manifested by Chinese territorial claims and increased skirmishes along the border, which culminated in the border war of 1962.

As regards the Soviet Union, the ideological split and China's attempt to supplant the USSR as the leader of the communist movement led to deteriorating relations, heightened border tensions and border clashes in 1969. Vietnam's closer affinity for the Soviet Union gradually led to the souring of relations with China, which eventually culminated in the 1979 border war. China could not settle its borders with Bhutan and Laos, which chose to be guided by India and Vietnam, respectively, on the border issue.

The second phase of Chinese border settlements with its neighbours started with the break-up of the Soviet Union in 1991. Negotiations to settle the border with Moscow began in 1987, and

China and Russia concluded the border agreement in 1991. China also negotiated separate border agreements with Tajikistan, Kyrgystan and Kazakhstan. Border negotiations with Vietnam had resumed almost immediately after the 1979 border war, and a final agreement on their land border was signed on December 30, 1999. Incidentally, the text of the Land Border Treaty is not available in the public domain. China also signed a border agreement with Laos in 1992. The point to note is that all these border settlements resulted only in minor territorial changes, despite China's extravagant territorial claims.

Now, India and Bhutan are the only two countries with which China is yet to settle its border. In the case of Bhutan, news reports hinted that during the border talks in July 2005, Bhutan might have relented to Chinese pressure tactics and accepted a package deal. In 1996, Beijing had proposed the exchange of the 495 square kilometre area of Pasamlung and Jakarlung valleys in the northern borders of central Bhutan (which China claims) for Sinchulumpa, Dramana and Shakhtoe with an area of 269 sq km in north-west Bhutan. China has also been applying pressure tactics like large scale intrusions by Tibetan herdsmen and also by the PLA to keep Bhutanese border guards in tenterhooks and has also resorted to construction of roads inside Bhutanese territory. It appears that Bhutan is under pressure both from China and its own people to arrive at a final solution to the festering border problem, but till now there is no indication that it has been successful at arriving at an acceptable solution.

Intrusions by Chinese troops into Indian territory are signals meant to assert China's growing political and military stature as well as means to test India's resolve. Given India's gradual emergence as a powerful military and economic power in Asia, China is unlikely to be keen on settling the border issue till such time India slumps into a period of weakness. Thus, for the foreseeable future, the India-China border is likely to be characterised by tensions, incursions and skirmishes, interspersed with endless border negotiations. Given this, India needs to be prepared for any eventuality and calibrate its responses to Chinese intrusions.

TIERED BORDER DEFENCE AGAINST CHINA

On balance, the prospects of Sino-Indian conflict remain. What appears certain is that China's aggressive stance and the initiation of conflict will be aimed at undermining India's status as a regional power. If India fails to respond adequately, she will be projected as a 'Soft State' susceptible to coercion. Simultaneously, the Chinese aim would be to keep India embroiled in fighting internal/regional conflicts. In doing so, China may be expected to virtually abrogate any agreements such as Border Peace and Tranquility Agreement and Confidence Building Measures and BDCA leading to incremental build up and conflict.

Lack of development of border infrastructure on the Indian side is the main reason why the Chinese could intrude freely...

A decade ago the US Department of Defense (DoD) and the global strategic community had warned that China would begin flexing muscles 2010 onwards and that India should settle the border disputes with China before this; but little was done to even plug gaps in our defences. Improvement of border infrastructure has not really taken off despite colossal Chinese military upgrades in the Tibet Autonomous Region (TAR) including nuclear missile deployments and massive exercises by the People's Liberation Army Air Force (PLAAF) and Chinese Airborne Corps in proximity to the Line of Actual Control (LAC). Chinese aggression has been on the rise, nibbling away at Indian territory consistently. The gap between the capabilities of the PLA and the Indian military has been widening. There is a need to take stock and rapidly institute a tiered border defence against China to safeguard our territorial integrity and meet the challenges of the mounting threat.

Current Scenario: Border Defence

With unity of command having been compromised, our border defence has been woefully inadequate. Reportedly, some 400 sq.km. of territory has been lost in Ladakh over and above the Aksai Chin. Responsibility of border defence is divided between the Ministry of Defence (MoD) and the Ministry of Home Affairs (MHA), with the Central Armed Police Force (CAPF) deployed in sensitive areas without placing them under the command of the Army. This facilitates smuggling of narcotics, fake currency, goods and even illegal immigration with indicators that some of these activities are institutionalised. Chinese goods are being smuggled into India also through the India-Myanmar border. Not only is the ULFA hierarchy located at Ruli on Chinese soil but China is also pumping in weapons and communication equipment through the Kachen rebels in Myanmar to the PLA in Manipur and onwards to the Maoists in India. Deployment of the Indo-Tibetan Border Police (ITBP) in sensitive areas of Ladakh without placing them under the command of the local Army formation is a folly that has been capitalised by the Chinese who have made deep intrusions without qualms.

Border Infrastructure

Despite the Border Road Organisation (BRO) being directly under the MoD, border infrastructure has been severely neglected. In February 2014, NDTV reported that out of the 26 border roads sanctioned in recent years, only one has been completed. China, on the other hand, has developed excellent infrastructure that permits quick mobilisation and vehicular movement. This includes construction of a ten-kilometre road in Pangong Tso area. In 1970, at Nathu La, the Chinese could ply a five-tonne vehicle vis-à-vis a one-tonne vehicle of ours. Today, over four decades later, the status remains the same. Lack of development of border infrastructure on the Indian side is the main reason why the Chinese could intrude freely and our security forces are unable to react effectively and in time.

Intrusions

Similar is the story with our poor response to Chinese intrusions. Criticism and shame had to be faced in wake of deep intrusions such as the one at Raki Nala in Depsang during April 2013 when even the MEA admitted that the intrusion was five to seven kilometres beyond the line of Chinese claim. It is a wonder how a 1.2 million strong army could permit 20 Chinese soldiers to sit 19 km deep inside Indian territory for 25 days. Ironically, Chinese troops had reportedly intruded into the same area on earlier occasions albeit this time the media got wise.

Such intrusions have been occurring at many places along the LAC despite the 1993 India-China Agreement on Maintenance of Peace and Tranquility Along the Line of Actual Control in the India-China Border Areas, Agreement on Confidence Building Measures in the Military Field Along the Line of Actual Control in the India-China Border Areas, 2005 Protocol on Modalities for the Implementation of Confidence Building Measures in the Military Field Along the Line of Actual Control in India-China Border Areas, and the 2012 Agreement on Establishment of a Working Mechanism for Consultation and Coordination on India-China Border Affairs.

Now, even after signing the China-drafted Border Defence Cooperation Agreement (BDCA) in 2013, the Chinese intruded into Depsang and Chumar on December 19 and 20. Then, in the first week of January 2014, intrusions took place in the Takdip area where incursions had been spotted in December 2013 as well. Now, China has proposed a Code of Conduct to be introduced along the border. Obviously China wants to play at signing agreement after agreement without changing her aggressive stance. Chinese occupation of the Depsang plains in conjunction with her presence in Gilgit-Baltisatn would threaten India's deployments in Siachen and sever the approach to Karakoram Pass. India has also lost substantial territory in the India-China-Myanmar tri-juncture area; China is also staking claims to the Tatu Bowl, loss of which would enable the Chinese to easily roll down the plains. POK is already a strategic objective of China that provides her access to the warm waters of the Indian Ocean, to Afghanistan and the CARs.

Prospects of Conflict

Much has been talked of about the possibilities of future Sino-Indian conflict from the Chinese gameplan to place India in the vice-like grip of a python to gobble up what the former wants, active defence to short swift offensive even using tactical nuclear weapons to force India to surrender territory, acupuncture warfare and the like. China's 'active defence' doctrine is a transformation from Mao's large scale people's land-centric war to high intensity, short duration localised war under informationised conditions. In this context, the chances of conflict remain.

Despite the progressing economic relations, China's focus in the Indian Ocean Region (IOR) remains a cause for concern. China has been making every possible effort to find her way to the Indian Ocean through Myanmar and Pakistan along the land routes. Her strategic interests clash with the US and her allies in the Asia-Pacific; China desperately needs another oceanic front and a strong India is hardly to her liking. Besides, for Chinese Carrier Battle Groups (CBGs) to operate effectively in the IOR, China needs land-based air and missile support. This is one reason why China is deploying missiles in the Gilgit-Baltistan area of Pakistan and developing or planning to develop ports in countries such as Myanmar, Thailand, Bangladesh, Pakistan, Maldives, Sri Lanka and Seychelles in the IOR.

Not only has China colluded with Pakistan on a conventional and nuclear front but also in the sub-conventional field by waging a collusive asymmetric war against India including through irregular forces and proxies. With China's aggression on the rise, the collusive China-Pakistan threat has multiplied exponentially with both countries following a policy of ambiguity, denial and deceit, what with repeated Chinese intrusions, claim to entire Arunachal Pradesh as "South Tibet" and now demanding a Code of Conduct for forward troops, indicating the futility of the recently signed Border Defence Cooperation Agreement (BDCA).

In the prevailing environment of global conflict, the first tier of defence must necessarily be deep inside enemy backyard...

On balance, the prospects of Sino-Indian conflict remain. What appears certain is that China's aggressive stance and the initiation of conflict will be aimed at undermining India's status as a regional power. If India fails to respond adequately, she will be projected as a 'Soft State' susceptible to coercion. Simultaneously, the Chinese aim would be to keep India embroiled in fighting internal/regional conflicts. In doing so, China maybe expected to virtually abrogate any agreements such as Border Peace and Tranquility Agreement and Confidence Building Measures and BDCA leading to incremental build up and conflict.

Should the US get more involved in the Middle East or in new and likely hotspots such as Ukraine and the CAR, Chinese adventurism in India can be expected to escalate. The US may have announced the Asia Pivot in recent months but China already has in place a globally deployable military force with nuclear/non-nuclear allies/proxies in North Korea, Pakistan, Iran, Libya, Sudan and Syria as a countermeasure even if one discounts China not resorting to the employment of large scale nuclear force.

LET FACTS SPEAK FOR THEMSELVES ON INDIA-CHINA BORDER

For almost 11 months now, the Indian Government has put a lid on the Himalayan border situation with China. Ever since several senior Government figures last September spoke out against the media coverage of Chinese border incursions, sources of information have dried up and newspapers and television networks have carried little news. It is not that the Chinese cross-border forays have ended or even abated. It is just that Indian media organisations have little information to report, even though the incidence of Chinese incursions remains high.

Beijing can only be pleased with the way New Delhi has managed to gag its own media over the border incidents. The unwitting message that this sends is that when the world's biggest autocracy builds up pressure, the world's largest democracy is willing to tame its own media.

Just as China has sought to pass off military incursions into Bhutan as instances of Chinese troops "losing their way", soldiers of its People's Liberation Army "lost their way" into Indian territory 270 times in 2008 alone — the last full year for which official figures are available. In addition, there were 2,285 instances of "aggressive border patrolling" by the PLA in 2008. Such a pattern of aggressive patrolling and intrusions has persisted to this day.

The plain fact is that the continuing border tensions reflect a growing strategic dissonance between China and India, which represent competing political and social models of development. Tibet has emerged at the centre of escalating Himalayan tensions. China has resurrected its long-dormant claim to Arunachal Pradesh — almost three times as large as Taiwan — and stepped up military pressure along the 4,057-km frontier with India.

As the resistance to its rule in Tibet has grown, Beijing has sought to present Tibet as a core issue to its sovereignty. Tibet now holds as much importance in Chinese policy as Taiwan. But in spotlighting the Arunachal issue, Beijing seems to be drawing another analogy, even if unwittingly:

Arunachal is the new Taiwan that must be "reunified" with the Chinese state.

Tibet, however, has always been the core issue in Sino-Indian relations. After all, China became India's neighbour not owing to geography but guns — by annexing buffer Tibet in 1951. Today, Beijing is ever ready to whip up diplomatic spats with western nations that extend hospitality to the Dalai Lama. But India remains the base of the Tibetan leader and his government-in-exile.

The key instigation in the more-muscular Chinese stance towards India clearly has come from the US-Indian strategic tie-up, unveiled first in 2005. As President George W. Bush declared in his valedictory speech, "We opened a new historic and strategic partnership with India".

Since then, the official Chinese media has started regurgitating the coarse anti-India rhetoric of the Mao Zedong era, with commentators warning New Delhi not to forget the lesson of 1962, when China humiliated India in a 32-day, two-front war. The Chinese Communist Party's mouthpiece, the People's Daily, earlier charged India with pursuing a foreign policy of "befriending the far and attacking the near", while a commentary by the China Institute of International Strategic Studies — a PLA think-tank — cautioned India "not to requite kindness with ingratitude" and not to "misjudge the situation as it did in 1962".

Against that background, India's interests will be better served by letting the facts on the border situation with China speak for themselves.

In recent years, China has opened pressure points against India across the Himalayas, with border incidents occurring in all the four sectors. Chinese forces are intruding even into Uttarakhand (although the line of control in this middle sector was clarified in 2001 through an exchange of maps) and into Sikkim (whose 206 km border with Tibet is not in dispute and indeed is recognised by Beijing). Yet, Indian officials have said the incursions are the result of differing perceptions about the line of truth. That may be so about Arunachal Pradesh and Ladakh, but can that be true about Sikkim and Uttarakhand? It speaks for itself that Beijing hasn't offered this lame excuse.

Even in the pre-1962 period, India sought to play down China's aggressive moves along the border. The result was "the stab in the back" in 1962, as Jawaharlal Nehru called it.

In fact, there are important parallels between the situation pre-1962 and the situation now. Border talks are regressing, Chinese claims on Indian territories are becoming publicly assertive, Chinese cross-border incursions are rising, and India's China policy is becoming feckless.

Indeed, what stands out in the history of Sino-Indian disputes is that India has always been on the defensive against a country that first moved its frontiers hundreds of miles south by annexing Tibet, then furtively nibbled at Indian territories before waging open war, and now lays claims to additional Indian territories. By contrast, on neuralgic subjects like Tibet, Beijing's public language still matches the crudeness and callousness with which it sought in 1962, in Premier Zhou Enlai's words, to "teach India a lesson".

The irony is that by laying claims to additional Indian territories on the basis of their purported ties to Tibet, China blatantly plays the Tibet card against India, going to the extent of citing the birth in Tawang of one of the earlier Dalai Lamas, a politico-religious institution it has systematically sought to destroy. Yet India remains coy to play the Tibet card against China. The net result of failing to use Tibet as a bargaining chip has been that India first lost Aksai Chin, then more territory in 1962 and now is seeking to fend off Chinese claims to Arunachal Pradesh.

Beijing openly covets Arunachal Pradesh as a cultural extension to Tibet — a classic attempt at incremental annexation. Just because the 6th Dalai Lama was born in the 17th century in Arunachal's Tawang district, Beijing claims that Arunachal belongs to Tibet and thus is part of China. By that argument, it can also lay claim to Mongolia as the 4th Dalai Lama was born there in 1589. The traditional ecclesiastical links between Mongolia and Tibet indeed have been closer than those between Arunachal and Tibet. What makes China's claim more untenable is that, as part of its gerrymandering of Tibet, it has hived off the birthplaces of the 7th, 10th, 11th and present Dalai Lama — the 14th in line — from Tibet. Before seeking Arunachal, shouldn't it be asked to first return the traditional Tibetan areas of Amdo and eastern Kham to Tibet?

3

China and Arunachal Pradesh Border

ARUNACHAL PRADESH'S BORDER ROADS

The state of Arunachal Pradesh in India's northeastern frontier has been appearing quite regularly in the Indian national security and strategic imagination for some years now. Strident Chinese territorial claims, particularly over the Tawang hill tract, have managed to unsettle New Delhi and the Indian strategic community. Against this backdrop and given that Arunachal is the largest state in India's northeastern region in terms of territory, it becomes important to assess the border roads infrastructure and connectivity in this strategically-crucial frontier state.

The state was a theatre in the 1962 Sino-Indian war, in which India had faced major losses and had to fight in extremely unprepared conditions, with almost no road connectivity. While Indian forces did manage to resist strongly at several border points the fall of Tawang and Bomdi La towns were without resistance as there was no proper supply and road infrastructure to maintain Indian army positions.

Air dropped supplies sometimes, fell into the hands of the Chinese who had occupied Tawang. This was 50 years ago but the road infrastructure and connectivity in Arunachal Pradesh still leaves a lot to be desired in terms of strategic preparedness for the Indian Army and for the general economic development of the state.

The need to construct proper roads in Arunachal Pradesh dawned on the Indian government only after it suffered in the war against the Chinese, and a skeletal network of roads was built subsequently in this difficult terrain mostly aimed at maintaining military posts and supplies in various strategic parts of the state. This was the first layer of work done on roads in the state, and only fed specific sectors such as Bhalukpung-Bomdi-La-Tawang, Itanagar-Ziro-Along-Mechuka, and the eastern sector which included a maze of roads with no inter-connectivity. The Assam government has four-laned the Stilwell Road in its territory but on the Arunachal side, the Road remains perennially under construction.

Internal connectivity within Arunachal Pradesh remains one of the pressing problems which need urgent attention-to travel to five different towns in Arunachal Pradesh, one has to cross back into Assam as many times. Air dropping of essential civil and military supplies in remote areas of Arunachal Pradesh is the prevailing norm and a number of AN-32 transport aircraft are used on a daily basis from the Guwahati, Jorhat and Dibrugarh supply bases in Assam. The road that leads to the central part of Arunachal Pradesh, particularly to its capital Itanagar, falls mostly in Assam and has been over the years ill-maintained and is prone to annual floods. The Border Roads Organisation which is in charge of maintaining these crucial roads have done a decent job, keeping in mind the difficult terrain, high rainfall and frequent landslides which sometimes sweep entire stretches of roads away, but overall, the effort is woefully inadequate..

The Trans-Arunachal Highway project which was announced by Prime Minister Manmohan Singh in 2008, has failed to pick up pace with preliminary feasibility studies still being conducted in many parts of the state. The Highway project comes very late, as the pressure on the existing road infrastructure has already increased manifold given the burden of civil supplies as also the massive convoys of army supplies and movement which has become necessary due to the current policy of trying to match Chinese army mobilization across the border. The need for a second network of border roads in Arunachal Pradesh is almost 10-15 years late, and will certainly take another 10-15 years, if not more, to come to fruition. It has been noted that in many parts of Northeast India, the second layer of road connectivity and infrastructure development has begun only when the pressure on the current infrastructure has become enormously high, often compounding implementation woes; the consistent and painful delays in project implementation, can be attributed to a clear policy planning failure on the part of both the central and state governments.

Similarly, the Bogibeel project for a bridge over the river Brahmaputra in Dibrugarh in Assam, was mooted more than a decade back, but saw work begin only just some years ago, and is now estimated to be completed only in the year 2030. This bridge has the potential to connect the middle and eastern parts of Arunachal Pradesh and save on traveling time, as these areas are now dependent on the Kaliabhoomoora Bridge across the Brahmaputra in Tezpur.

The central government still seems to be sleeping on major bottlenecks in terms of road infrastructure and connectivity as is evident in various parts of Northeast India. Major road expansion work is overdue in critical stretches such as Numaligarh-Kohima-Imphal and Guwahati-Shillong-Silchar-Aizawl, which has resulted in clogging the streets of major state capitals like Kohima, Shillong and Aizawl. The Trans-Asian Highway too, has made little progress. There needs to be greater urgency in policy implementation in order to serve the needs of not just Arunachal but the Northeast and the nation as a whole in terms of economic development and strategic military preparedness.

CHINA'S CLAIMS ON ARUNACHAL ABSURD: CHIEF MINISTER DORJEE KHANDU

The Chief Minister of Arunachal Pradesh Dorjee Khandu, termed China's claims to Arunachal Pradesh as its territory as "simply absurd". "I have been telling repeatedly that Arunachal Pradesh is an integral part of India and that Chinese claims are simply absurd.

"We are the only state in the northeast where Hindi is the link language among various tribes who speak different dialects,"

Khandu said after his swearing in. "Now, we are all set to welcome the Dalai Lama who is visiting the state from November 8."

He also said his government's topmost priority would be to work for the overall economic uplift of the state, especially focusing on developing infrastructure and boosting education and health sectors. "Now, after the people have given us a thumping victory in the elections, we need to work even harder to achieve accelerated pace of development and growth in the state," Khandu said.

"Social sectors, health, education, roads and infrastructure are the areas that we are going to give maximum thrust and focus to this time."

ARUNACHAL PRADESH TERRITORIAL DISPUTE BETWEEN INDIA AND CHINA

International law never supports a country or a state which attempts to plunder the territory from other countries or states by threatening or warfare. Article 2 of The UN Charter clearly defines that "all Members shall refrain in their international relations from the threat or use of force against the territorial integrity or political independence of any state" (Reynolds 2004.) It is so-called a territorial dispute, which is "a disagreement over the possession or control of land between two or more countries" ("Territorial Dispute.") What leads the territorial dispute is not only relevant to the possession or control of natural resources such as oil, coals, fertile land or rivers, but also culture and religion. In addition, it has been said that "in many cases territorial disputes result from vague and unclear language in a treaty that set up the original boundary" ("Territorial Dispute".) Consequently, many territorial disputes possibly generate some conflicts between countries, and even worse, they can become a primary cause of wars and/or terrorism.

A long time ago, before the territorial dispute between China and India emerged in Arunachal Pradesh, the first ancestors of the tribal groups migrated from Tibet during pre-historic period. Even though ancestors were there, little is known about the history of Arunachal Pradesh. Recorded history is only available in the Ahom chronicles from the sixteenth century: the British Christened, originally known as northeast Frontiers Agency (NEFA,) took administrative control of Arunachal Pradesh and it remained under this rule until 1948. Arunachal Pradesh is northeast India's largest and remotest state, as it has railways and air services connecting only three of its town. Natives in Arunachal Pradesh used to eat "their food in uncooked condition ignorant about the discovery of fire" (WebDigitech.) They were really isolated and not aware of the development and revolution which was occurring in this globalized world. The major cause of China-India territorial dispute, which deprived peace from Arunachal Pradesh, is from immediately after Chinese Revolution in 1911. At that time, Qing Dynasty, the last Chinese Dynasty, fell and the Emperor of Qing Dynasty resigned. As a result, China, Tibet and Mongolia became equal and separate countries. In these three countries, Tibet and Mongol tried to be approved internationally as independent states, and undertook to international society. However, on the other hand, Han Chinese Republicans started small war to subjugate reins of government of Tibet and Mongol. Therefore, they could not be independent states at that time.

In 1912-13, the British Raj made agreements with tribal leaders that defined the area that was known as NEFA. British rule could have very small impact on the isolated, self-sufficient in terms of economy and militarily uncontrollable tribal peoples. In order to arrange this conflict, in 1913 and 1914, the British administrator, Sir Henry McMahon, drew up the 550-mile McMahon Line as the border between India and China in Shimla, during a conference which also discussed the Tibetan and Chinese borders ("McMahon Line.") This conference is called Shimla Conference. Regardless of this reconciliation, the McMahon Line was rejected by the Chinese government in 1947 ("Arunachal Pradesh.")

Following this dispute, the Chinese troops crossed the McMahon Line on the August 26th, 1959 ("Arunachal Pradesh.") They abandoned this in 1961, but in October 1962 crossed the line once again with force ("McMahon Line.") As a result, Sino-Indian War broke out. The Chinese extended their frontier as they intruded deeper and deeper. However, this war did not go on for a long time. In 1963, the Chinese agreed to withdraw back to the McMahon Line, and also returned Indian prisoners of this war at that time.

Environment Aspects

By losing Arunachal Pradesh located on the northeastern tip of India, bordering Bhutan on the west, China on the north, Myanmar on the east and the states of Assam on the south, either China or India would receive some damage in terms of economy. Both China and India are able to run good business because Arunachal Pradesh is a very good place for tourists from all over the world to visit. Evergreen forest, which covers more than 60 percent of the state area, certainly makes people feel comfortable to stay there.

From this fact, Arunachal Pradesh is known for its forest resources. Forest products and industries are considered as a lifeline in Arunachal Pradesh. In fact, 75 percent of its total workforce is engaged in agriculture (mainly shifting cultivation.) Therefore, if either China or India could obtain Arunachal Pradesh, it would be able to improve its economy by taking advantage of agriculture and tourism.

In addition to it, there are many fairs and festivals there such as Losar, the New Year's Celebration of the Monpas. Another famous festival there is called Reh, which is associated with the Idu Mishmis, the six-day celebrations' special attraction is the Priest dance. Fairs or festivals are held every month, thus tourists can visit there any time for sightseeing.

Conflict Aspects

In 1962, the Chinese had a claim on what India deemed its own territory called Arunachal Pradesh. China sent many well-trained and well-armed troops to the disputed region. On the other hand, India had only ill-equipped troops there, which made them more difficult to beat Chinese troops.

The Sino-Indian (Indo-China) War was started by China on October 16, 1962 on account of the territorial dispute against India. Chinese attacked India on October 20, 1962 because it was unable to reach political accommodation on disputed territory along the 3,225-kilometer-long Himalayan border. The Chinese did not invade farther, and on November 21, 1962 declared a unilateral cease-fire. They had accomplished all of their territorial objectives, and any attempt to press farther into the plains of Assam would have stretched their logistical capabilities and their lines of communication to a breaking point. Finally, the Chinese defeated India in 1962, which as a result led to the retreat of Indian Army in terms of doctrine, training, organization and equipment from the disputed area.

Environment and Conflict Overlap

Arunachal Pradesh dispute was classified as a territorial dispute, but both China and India had big enough territories on their own. Thus, this dispute was not really caused by a decline of resources (territory.) Therefore, the dispute is direct more likely than not even it has been argued for about one century long.

China and India had a direct conflict over the fertile land which certainly supports their economy by agriculture. Major crops in the area are, for example, rice, maize, ginger and potato. These major crops yielded 134,807, 48,346, 34,890 and 32,434 in hectare respectively (Gov't of Arunachal Pradesh.)

Because Sir Henry McMahon, the British administrator, clearly established the McMahon Line as the border, which could establish buffer zones around its colony in South Asia, between British India and Tibet in 1913-14, the British have also something to do with Arunachal Pradesh dispute in terms of strategic interest.

China is also relevant to the territorial dispute. On account of various disagreements with the British, China refused to accept the terms imposed by Britain. As a result, China did not recognize the validity of the McMahon Line. China probably was mostly concerned about the loss of their essential resources such as land from losing Arunachal Pradesh. Therefore, British India and China were major countries in this territorial dispute with respect to strategic interest.

Even though both India and China found a peaceful solution to the border dispute in late 1980s, officials from two countries have met more than 15 times to argue the Arunachal Pradesh.

Chinese Foreign Ministry spokesman Kong Quan said that "As far as the incident mentioned, after investigations, we have found that the Indian side crossed the eastern sector of the Line of Actual Control (LAC).

At the request of the Chinese side, the Indian people who crossed the LAC, returned to the Indian side of the LAC" (Joseph 2003.) Thus, China still claims that "90,000 square kilometers of land in Arunachal Pradesh and does not recognize the northeastern state as part of Indian Territory" (Joseph 2003.)

Outcome of Dispute: Compromise

Arunachal Pradesh was part of the state of Assam until 1987 and was previously called NEFA. However, Arunachal Pradesh finally could gain statehood status on Feb. 20th, 1987 after making allowances for the security consideration in the east and Sino-Indian tensions ("Arunachal Pradesh.") India was satisfied with this outcome of dispute while China still does not admit the result.

Smoothening the India-China Border Wrinkles

The 17th round of India-China border talks (Feb. 10-11) in New Delhi passed off without any "free and frank" exchanges, that is, there was no disagreement. The first meeting was at the joint secretary level with military experts on both sides.

The situation on the border was reviewed and apparently was found satisfactory. The meeting it appears, was constructed by both sides to ensure no negative vibration emerged.

The main meeting, the 17th round of talks between the Special Representatives (SRs) of the two sides was much wider in scale because matters outside the border issue were discussed. The Indian Ministry of External Affairs (MEA) statement said the talks were held in a "candid, friendly and constructive atmosphere". Mr. Shivshankar Menon, the Indian SR and Mr. Yang Jiechi, the Chinese SR are veterans in the foreign policy game and India-China relations. On the Chinese side they know the stakes they are playing with. They have in their pocket "something to give" on the border issue if need be. But no one can say for sure what that is.

It must be kept in mind that the old Chinese position "if India makes concessions in the east" has not become irrelevant. In China's foreign policy dealings, nothing once stated becomes irrelevant unless it is stated so officially.

The three-step process agreed to by both sides to resolve the boundary question was reiterated. The process has arrived at step-2 to reach a framework for a resolution of this question. This will be based on the Agreement on the Political Parameters and Guiding Principles for the settlement of the India-China Boundary Question. The SRs discussed possible additional Confidence Building Measures (CBM).

Other issues discussed, according to the MEA release included areas of mutual interest including cooperation in the East Asia Summit process as well as developments in West Asia and Afghanistan. Pakistan should have figured in the discussions, but it appears that the Chinese do not want it to be seriously included in the "India-China strategic partnership and co-operation". It is too sensitive a subject.

China made its general position on the border clear when reacting to Indian President Pranab Mukherjee's visit to Arunachal Pradesh in November last year. Chinese foreign ministry spokesman Qin Gang urged *(Xinhua, Nov.30 2013)* India not to indulge in acts that complicate the boundary issue and work with China to create conditions for talks and preserve peace and tranquility on the border.

The *Xinhua* commentary went on to say "The so-called Arunachal Pradesh was established largely on three areas of China's Tibet-Monyul, Loyul and Lower Tsayul currently under Indian illegal occupation. These three areas, located between the illegal MacMahon Line and the traditional customary boundary between China and India, have always been Chinese territory." The commentary added that in February 1987, Indian authorities declared the founding of the so-called Arunachal Pradesh.

Before further meetings on the border issue the Chinese side drew the lines. That is, the basic Chinese position that the border lay along the northern banks of the river Bramhaputra; India set up Arunachal Pradesh illegally; and if India did not work with China and on its directions, China could revert to a hard-line position. This is China's position on the eastern sector of the India-

China border. It is, therefore, not surprising that even Chinese incursion into India's Depsung area in the western sector last year was generally kept outside the main agenda.

The focus is now testing out the Border Defense cooperation agreement signed during Prime Minister Manmohan Singh's visit to China last October. With national elections in India barely two months away and opinion surveys emphatically suggesting that UPA government led by the Congress has little or no hope to return to power for the third time in a row, it was only right for Prime Minister Singh and National Security Advisor (NSA) Menon to take no new initiatives on the border and analyze the efficacy of Border Defence Agreement signed between the two countries last October.

The new hierarchy in New Delhi will be well advised to consider relations with China on a much bigger canvas. While getting played by China on the boundary question, New Delhi must not lose sight of other strategic interests regionally and globally.

The Chinese leadership including the People's Liberation Army (PLA) are full of hubris as the next global super power. On the India-China border, the Chinese attained confidence of military superiority, and would continue to play mind games. The Border Defence Agreement was proposed by China, and India agreed to it only after some critical amendments. China went through with it but was not satisfied. The agreement could not put the Indian forces and border development in a strait jacket. It is going to come up with more CBMs on the border in due course. This is something Indian experts must look out for.

There was some speculation that because of support to Uighur separatists from extremist elements in Pakistan, China-Pakistan relations was becoming weaker. True, the Chinese were furious with Pakistan especially during the 2008 Beijing Olympics. But weak relationship? Emphatically no. Beijing is determined to crush the Uighur separatists as evidenced by the hard crackdown in Xinjiang.

Pakistan is of immense importance to China. It concerns Chinese interests in the Gulf and the Middle East with Pakistan being a Muslim nation. Afghanistan now looms on the horizon, but it is a tricky issue. Certainly, China is discussing Afghanistan with India but all its cards on the burning issue remain hidden. China's support to Pakistan on Pakistan's issues with India continues to be as strong as ever. On Kashmir, there has been no change in position though statements are deliberately muted. It has done nothing and said nothing on Pakistan sponsored and Pakistani based terrorism against India. Yet it high profiles the so-called "three evils" terrorism, separatism and religious extremism. China's cooperation against terrorism and extremism across the world remains a hollow trumpet till date.

A new worrisome development has taken place. The BBC reported recently that Pakistan had manufactured nuclear weapons exclusively for Saudi Arabia. There were denials but not convincing enough. It is well known that China had supplied Saudi Arabia CSS-2 nuclear capable missiles in the 1980s. Obviously, these were meant for regional use. But nuclear capable missiles without nuclear warheads is an incongruous military doctrine. China has been modernizing Pakistan's nuclear weapons capability and fissile material production facilities. The three countries tie up very nicely as the Saudis remain the mainstay not only of Pakistan's economy but of its military modernization. After all Pakistan, a Sunni majority country like Saudi Arabia, owns the "Islamic bomb"!

The above scenario is not an idle thought. The world is aware of the Pakistani nuclear scientist Dr. A. Q. Khan's nuclear trade network leading to major proliferation. China was a self-effasive but root player in this. The west let both China and Pakistan off lightly for their own geostrategic reasons. After Saudi Arabia and the US differed on the approach to the Syrian crisis the Saudis are moving back to engage China and Pakistan with more resolve. The Saudi crown prince was in Pakistan recently and his agenda included defence cooperation.

On the other end of the Indian Ocean is the issue of freedom of navigation in the South China Sea. China is increasingly trying to force control of the international maritime route through which around 50 percent of global trade passes. Using vague historical evidence mainly manipulated, China claims sovereignty of the

Spratly group of Islands in the South China Sea. It is using the naval flag march here to intimidate other claimants. India is likely to get into conflict with China on its oil exploration with Vietnam in Vietnam's waters claimed by China. There are a whole range of issues that are likely to come up in India-China interface in the next five years. The new dispensation in New Delhi will have to deal with them.

How these issues are dealt with is another question. Prime Minister Manmohan Singh made non-conflict and warm relations with China and Pakistan his top priorities. He failed because such a relationship does not exist in the minds of either of these two countries. In the course of his policies, Dr. Singh bent over too much.

The foregoing are only illustrative examples of issues that India will come to face. It is not suggested that India should adopt aggressive postures against China. But at the same time, India should get out of the habit of rolling over to achieve what is not achievable. Firmness on issues of national and strategic importance is imperative. Prime Minister Singh did this in the case of the nuclear deal with the US at the Nuclear Suppliers Group (NSG) despite China's opposition till the last moment. Unfortunately, the Chinese official criticism on President Pranab Mukherjee's visit to Arunanchal Pradesh did not elicit a suitable demarche from India.

CHINA'S ARUNACHAL PRADESH FIXATION

China has been stepping up claims to territories abutting its borders, land, sea and now air. One of the more recent additions to its interests is Arunachal Pradesh, a northeast Indian state that China recognizes as "South Tibet." Indian President Pranab Mukherjee's visit to the state in late November and his speech calling the area an "integral and important part of India" have generated an angry response from Beijing. This came barely one month after an agreement to resolve border disputes peacefully was signed by Indian Prime Minister Manmohan Singh and Chinese Premier Li Keqiang. Beijing's increasing assertiveness and growing territorial claims raise important questions about China's intentions and strategic direction.

China has a long-standing border dispute with India in the eastern sector of the Himalayas along India's north-east and China's south-western boundaries. The impenetrability of these terrains along with undefined, ambiguous borders has resulted in overlapping claims of ownership from the two Asian giants. The 1962 Sino-Indian war was the first salvo in what has become a troubled history. Since then, relations between India and China have tended to concentrate on maintaining the status-quo on the borders, leaving the onus for resolving these disputes on future generations. However, with China's growing assertiveness in territorial disputes in recent years, the border has once again become a battleground for the testing of wills and resilience.

China's claims initially extended only to Tawang, a part of Arunachal Pradesh, where the sixth Dalai Lama was said to have been born. Since the 2000s, however, China has been claiming Arunachal Pradesh in its entirety, a surprising claim given that independent India has been exercising sovereignty over it since 1955 (it became a union territory in 1972 and a state in 1987). It is worth noting that China's stance is directly motivated by its desire to put a lid on Tibetan nationalism (which it believes is fueled by support from India). Arunachal Pradesh is also strategically located at the confluence of the international borders of the PRC, Myanmar and Bhutan, giving it strategic importance. This extension of territorial claims and increasing aggression indicate a concerted strategy of widening the PRC's ambit of influence and control, consistent with its stance on the East and South China Sea disputes. Beijing's border disputes with India thus represent a wider strategic shift in its thinking, far removed from Deng Xiaoping's "keep your head down" policy, through which it seeks to revive its ancient glory as the Middle Kingdom.

The latest military standoff between China and India ensued in April this year when Chinese troops stationed themselves in India-controlled Daulat Old Begdi, more as a means to test the battle-readiness and response of the Indian establishment than as a serious onslaught. The issuance of stapled visas of athletes from Arunachal Pradesh in October was yet another provocation that spurred the Indian government to retaliate by not signing a scheduled memorandum of understanding to simplify visa procedures during Singh's Beijing visit that week. Meanwhile, the Congress-led UPA government in New Delhi is facing severe criticism from the nationalist BJP over India's meek response to Chinese provocations. With national elections around the corner and a strong likelihood of a more assertive BJP-led government at the center, provocations from China may begin to elicit more active responses from India in the future.

CHINESE INCURSIONS IN ARUNACHAL, REVEAL LOCALS

The land of rising sun has turned into the land of Chinese incursions. Arunachal Pradesh has been witness to several intrusions with the latest being last month. Headlines Today/Aaj Tak is the first channel to reach Chaglagam, the last village on the Indo-China border in Anjaw district of Arunachal Pradesh. This sleepy hamlet saw the Chinese Army arrive, stay and leave - all with a lot of imposition with it. Around 12th August they not only entered almost 40kms into India but also held a few porters hostage for several hours.

42-year-old porter Kamthalam Thapa recounts his rendezvous with the Chinese army, "We met the Chinese army on 12th August. We were held captive for several hours and released later. This doesn't happen usually but it happened this year with us."

Kamthalam is not the only one kept in Chinese custody for several hours. He along with others met the Chinese when they were very much in Indian territory. The Chinese incursion this time has been documented with the help of evidence provided by these porters who travel on this route for a living. Some of them go to the forest to collect wood and cultivate poppy.

His companion Chamba Thapa, a porter, dressed in traditional attire also had similar things to say, "We were caught on our way by the Chinese army. We had no option but to return back to the base. The Chinese went away so they left us."

The Indian government has maintained a stoic silence on the Chinese incursion but Aaj Tak/Headlines Today has evidence of the intrusion.

Moreover, the porters story is not the only tale. There is more evidence than just the porters that the Chinese army was here.

The Chinese have left wrappers of eatables in the Indian boundary and not just once but several times.

A regular porter with the army, Ambalam Chapa has stood witness to this several times. "We are porters. When we go with Army we find a lot of Chinese items littered here and there, from packets of biscuits and other eatables to other items. This is not the first time but I have seen this earlier also in past two three years. There also times when we have seen Chinese flags in the Indian region," says Ambalam.

So are these visits by the Chines timed and planned?

"Porters tell us that almost every year in July or August they see the Chinese army. We need to make roads on this side, the porters have to travel for days together. Even when the Army goes for patrolling, the locals of Chaglagam go for help," says Mailu Tega, a local Congress leader.

For social activist Ritemsu Manyu, it is an everyday fight. "Chinese entering the Indian territory is not for the first time. They come beyond the border line many times. The Indian Army sees this during its patrolling in the area. The road conditions are so bad here that several times it is locked from rest of the country for several months."

Chaglagam, the last village on the Indo-China border in Anjaw district of Arunachal Pradesh is a sleepy village with around fifty families living here. Most of them survive on local cultivation or serving as porters for the forces deployed on the border.

Chaglagam has no power supply or gas supply. There is an ITBPF camp from which villagers get local stuff for daily use. Besides this, it is a border town with just one telephone in the village for communication, forget about mobile phones.

The locals have to walk to the nearest village to get fresh supply of food and vegetables. The bad road conditions makes plying of vehicles very difficult on this route and the Border Road Organization is still far from providing motorable roads.

Even the nearest village to fetch daily requirements and vegetables is 50kms away.

State BJP President Tai Tagak echoes the concerns of the locals. "The BRO maintains this road but they are in very bad condition. The roads close down and there are no medical supplies also in the region. The government should take care of the basic facilities in the region."

On the contrary, the locals who have been there have much to share about the life beyond the barbed wire, rather the mountains.

The Mac Mohan Line, formidable boundary between India and China has left some families divided. According to Kamthalum Thapa, "The elder brother of my father lives there so we go regularly. There are very good roads in China upto the border. They are making more roads but this side of the border has a lot of problems. We have to cross dense forest."

Mailu Tega, too has similar sentiments, "There have been so many instances when China has entered into our region. They do not follow rules and they enter the farms of the locals and write that it is our area. We do not know when will we get a proper border line like the Indo-Pak border or Indo-Bangladesh border."

INDIAN SOVEREIGNTY IN ARUNACHAL PRADESH SOLIDIFY CHINESE CLAIMS IN TIBET

Foreign Minister Wang Yi's June 8 visit to New Delhi has brought up the stapled visa issue again, but with a new twist. The Chinese now argue that the stapled visa for the residents of Arunachal Pradesh is a "goodwill" gesture to facilitate the "outbound and overseas travel" of the people in the region. This position, though articulated officially for the first time, is not entirely new. Chinese scholars, primarily at think-tanks, have for some time posited the view that the stapled visa issue is to address the disputed border primarily with regard to the people of China. They argue that with rising nationalism and public awareness of the border dispute in Arunachal Pradesh, the government has adopted the policy of issuing stapled visas so as to convince the Chinese people that China has not made any concession to India on the border, and thereby sovereignty over Arunachal Pradesh, which they call "South Tibet."

Indeed, the stapled visa issue raises the question of sovereignty for Arunachal Pradesh for India. Applying the same logic, the Chinese government has issued stapled visas to the residents of Jammu and Kashmir (J&K). The issuance of stapled visas to Kashmiris questions not only India's sovereignty over J&K, but also shows China's support for Pakistan on the Kashmir issue. In effect, by using the stapled visa argument, the Chinese have not only kept up pressure on the Arunachal Pradesh border issue; they have also infringed on India's internal matters related to Kashmir.

However, despite China's intransigence on their shared border and Kashmir, India has leverage to pressure China on Tibet. By inviting Lobsang Sangay, the Prime Minister of the Tibetan Exiled Government in Dharamsala, to Prime Minister Narendra Modi's swearing in ceremony, India has taken a decisive step in addressing the stapled visa issue. Quite notably, the invitation to Modi's swearing in was not to the Dalai Lama, the spiritual leader of Tibet, but to the democratically elected leader of the entire Tibetan community. It is worth recalling that the worldwide Tibetan community participates in the election of the Tibetan prime minister. Clearly, the recognition accorded to Sangay at Modi's swearing in ceremony questions China's sovereignty in Tibet.

If China questions India's sovereignty over Kashmir and Arunachal Pradesh, and claims that the stapled visa issue "has been going on for relatively a long period of time," India is justified in shedding the appeasement policy of the earlier UPA government, and raising the question of sovereignty in Tibet, thereby establishing a quid pro quo on the border.

The roots of the India-China border dispute arguably rest in Tibet. With the Chinese occupation of Tibet in 1950, the question of China's legitimacy in Tibet loomed large. Beijing's vulnerability on Tibet was particularly pronounced at that juncture, since it was the Republic of China in Taiwan that had international recognition and representation at the United Nations. It was precisely its desire to gain legitimacy in Tibet that drove China to reach out to India and sign the 1954 Sino-Indian Agreement on Tibetan Trade. By signing the 1954 agreement, India not only surrendered all extraterritorial rights and privileges it had inherited in Tibet from the British Indian government, but also recognized Tibet as "a region of China." However, it should be noted that the legitimacy that China acquired in Tibet was only a bilateral arrangement with India.

It is pertinent to point out that the border problem is indeed one of history's leftovers, precisely because both India and China were civilizational states with no notions of bounded and demarcated territories. With the departure of the colonial British power from India, and the establishment of a Communist regime after the Chinese Civil War, the two new nascent countries were confronted with the task of establishing modern states with clear boundaries. In this task of nation-building, it was natural for them to confront the problem of disputed boundaries. This problem however, took a very different course with the Chinese invasion of Tibet, which not only gave the two countries a shared border for the first time in their histories, but also brought the issue of Tibetan identity and independence to the international stage in the post-Second World War era.

Entwined in the occupation of Tibet are two broad issues that continue to concern China, but without a clear solution: the border issue with India and the Tibetan issue of independence. In fact, the India-China bonhomie achieved through the 1954 agreement was a fragile peace that soon floundered after the 1962 Sino-Indian War. The 1962 war was essentially caused not by India's intransigence over the British-drawn borders, but China's failure to honor the 1954 gentleman's agreement, whereby Chinese sovereignty over Tibet rested on its reciprocity of Indian claims (albeit unstated) around the McMahon line border. More importantly, the principal result of the 1962 war was that although China defeated India, it could not settle the Tibetan issue. Clearly, Tibet is disputed territory.

Wang Yi's emphatic position on the stapled visa issue actually comes on the heels of the invitation of Sangay to Modi's swearing in ceremony. In fact, it clearly links the border issue with Tibet.

For quite some time, China had been steadfast in keeping the two separate, but Modi's invitation has successfully brought attention to the Tibetan issue, as the primary source of India-China tensions. It also establishes the reality that Tibet cannot be treated as an internal Chinese matter, and is essentially disputed. Hence, it is time for China to restore the true essence of the 1954 agreement by recognizing India's sovereignty in Arunachal Pradesh, in return for China's sovereignty in Tibet.

THE INDIA-CHINA DIVIDE

The Chinese Communist Party's (CCP) dislike for the 'hardline Hindu nationalist' Bharatiya Janata Party (BJP) is no secret. The shifts in India's China policy since May 1998, as evidenced in the nuclear and missile arena, military spending, and pro-Tibet and pro-Taiwan views expressed by some ministers, are said to have undermined the key assumptions underlying China's India policy. Conversations with officials and strategic analysts reveal that the Chinese are concerned over the rise of BJP as a major political force in Indian politics and its implications for China's strategic objective of supremacy in Asia. Before Pokhran II, China's India-watchers had convinced themselves that there would be 'no significant or fundamental changes' in the BJP-led Government's nuclear policy and that BJP-led India would not take any major strategic initiative (such as overt nuclearisation, strategic alliance with the United States, or support to Tibetan independence).

Although the aspirations for major power status are held by almost all Indian political parties (barring the Communists who fear provoking their Chinese masters), the BJP covets that status most ardently and is the most willing to assert it through military policy. Beijing would prefer a non-BJP weak government like the left-dominated United Front (UF) government before Pokhran II, and the successive Congress governments that preceded it, which had fine-tuned Sino-Indian bilateral relations by playing second fiddle to an assertive China. A policy paper prepared for the Chinese leadership has recommended 'targeting the BJP' as its policies have eroded Beijing's leverage against New Delhi. One analyst compared India with Nazi Germany and Iraq arguing that since the end of the Cold War, India had become too powerful and ambitious (for example, demanding a permanent seat on the UN Security Council) and warned that if India does not wish to suffer the fate of Japan in the 1940s or Iraq in the 1990s, it should give up its ambition for regional hegemony and take concrete steps to improve relations with China.

The main objective of China's Asia policy has always been to prevent the rise of an Asian rival or peer competitor to challenge its status as the Asia-Pacific's sole 'Middle Kingdom'. As an old Chinese saying goes, 'one mountain cannot accommodate two tigers'. That China does not want India to emerge as an equal is evident from its staunch opposition to India's membership of the P-5 (UN Security Council), N-5 (Nuclear Club), ASEM (Asia-Europe Summit), and APEC (Asia-Pacific Economic Cooperation). (India was made the ARF (ASEAN Regional Forum) member in December 1995 despite Beijing's opposition to it.) Speaking at the Munich Security Conference in February 1999, India's National Security Advisor, Brajesh Mishra, hinted at the BJP government's much broader political ambition by predicting that 'in the 21st century a new security order is likely to arise in the Asia-Pacific region in which India should be granted as much respect and deference by the United States and others as is China today.' Beijing's India-watchers believe that only a firm policy based on absolute strength and proactive containment of India will force the BJP-led government to act soberly towards China. Beijing knows that while China's emergence as a great power has been accepted by Western and Asian nations, India's claim to great power is yet to be accepted. So it is in the CCP's interests to keep the BJP out of power. Beijing has been blamed by India's intelligence agencies, media and some politicians for the overthrow of the BJP-led government in April 1999.

Strange as it may seem, the CCP has more in common with its bete noire, BJP, than its counterpart in India, the Communist Party of India-Marxist (CPM). In the BJP, the CCP has met its match, the latter's 'communist' pretensions notwithstanding. Contrary to the popular conception of the CCP and the BJP occupying opposite ends of the political spectrum, the BJP is the

CCP's mirror image. Just as the CCP believes in the superiority of the Han race, Han civilisation and the Han culture while displaying patronising and condescending attitude towards minorities such as Tibetans, Mongols and Muslims and downplaying the repeated colonisation of the Han race first by Inner Asian tribes such as Mongols, Manchus and Hsingnus and then by the Europeans, the BJP believes in the superiority of the Hindu race, Hindu civilisation and Hindu culture while downplaying the repeated colonisation of India by Greek, Muslim and European invaders as a result of Hindu disunity and their contributions to Indian culture. What is more, the CCP's goal of a unified 'Greater China' is not much different from the RSS/BJP's dream of 'Akhand Bharat' (United India). Just as the Chinese Communists lay claim to territories annexed by non-Chinese Mongol and Manchu empires (such as Tibet, Eastern Turkestan, Mongolia), the 'Akhand Bharat' concept includes territories (such as Burma and Sri Lanka) brought under control by the British. Much like the CCP, the BJP wants India to be an economic and military superpower in order to 'stand up' to great powers' bullying and coercion. Both have long nurtured the belief that as the two oldest civilisations and once great powers which were subjected to centuries of foreign domination, they must acquire the full spectrum of economic, technological and military (conventional, nuclear and information warfare) capabilities in order to be dominant regionally and influential globally.

Furthermore, the BJP's slogan of 'prosperous and powerful country' bears remarkable resemblance to the CCP's national goal: 'rich country, strong military' (fuguo qiangbing). Interestingly, both are courting the United States to help balance their relationships with each other until they are strong enough to do so on their own. Both want a new international status that is commensurate with their size, strength and potential. Historically and civilisationally, while China was the 'Middle Kingdom' of eastern Asia, India was the 'Middle Kingdom' of southern Asia.

The two parties are thus manifestation of the growing nationalism in India and China. Both also share remarkable similarity in economic outlooks and rhetorical excess. The BJP-led government is as aggressive in the pursuit of national interests as the CCP. Nor is it shy of flexing muscles and warning neighbours with 'serious consequences' if they don't behave-just as the Chinese Communists have always done! Although both the CCP and BJP have been labelled 'fascist', 'militarist' and 'ultra-natonalist' parties by their critics, the reality is that both are nationalist parties deeply conscious of their countries' history, culture and civilisational heritage to humankind and committed to restoring their countries' great power status. Both China after a century and India after a millenium of decline are keen to assume the great power roles they believe to be their historical and civilisational right.

Both remain suspicious of each other's long-term agenda and intentions, and are attempting to fill any perceived power vacuum or block the other from doing so. At the heart of Sino-Indian antagonism is the familiar Indian suspicion, which has now matured into a certainty, that China is seeking to deny India its proper stakes in the game of international politics. Both see themselves as newly rising great Asian powers whose time has finally come. This means that BJP's resurgent India will face CCP's rising China which will ensure a conflict of interests between the two giants unless their power competition is managed carefully. Their underlying power rivalry and their self-images as natural great powers and centres of civilisation and culture will continue to drive them to support different countries and causes. India versus China, not India versus Pakistan, has always been the main game in Asia. However, post-colonial Asia has not experienced both a strong China and a strong India at the same time. The BJP-CCP clash is borne not out of conflicting, but complementary, visions for their respective countries.

INDIA-CHINA BORDER DISPUTE

On assuming power, the People's Republic of China (PRC) renounced all prior foreign agreements as unequal treaties imposed upon it during the "century of humiliation" and demanded renegotiation of all borders. The Sino-India border remains the only major territorial dispute, other than South China Sea disputes, that China has not resolved. China's growing assertiveness in its territorial claims, especially on Arunachal Pradesh, and its relentless development of infrastructure in Tibet will shape the prospects of Sino-India relations.

The territory stretching from the jungles of northern Myanmar, westward to the Karakoram Range, and northward to the edge of the Tibetan plateau can be seen as a single geopolitical system referred to as the Himalayan-Tibetan massif. The ruggedness of this terrain makes movement of men and materiel extremely difficult, thus preventing Indian and Chinese civilizations from intermingling or projecting military power in these remote areas effectively. Not until 1962 did the Chinese and Indian armies fight each other over these desolate heights, thus altering the geopolitics of the region significantly.

Chinese President Hu Jintao met with Indian Prime Minister Manmohan Singh in Sanya City, south China's Hainan Province, April 13, 2011. Hu said China is willing to further push forward negotiations on border issues on the basis of peace and friendliness, equal consultation, mutual respect and understanding. The two sides should consider setting up a consultation and coordination mechanism on border issues so as to achieve consensus as soon as possible and to better maintain peace and stability at the border regions before the issues are solved.

China wants India to put behind the 1962 war as an "unfortunate" thing of the past and that the two countries should strengthen their military ties including formalising a border management pact under which their troops will not fire at each other. The Chinese assessment was conveyed to the Indian defence ministry team which visited Beijing on 14-15 January 2013 for the third round of the annual defense dialogue between the two countries.

Border tensions between China and India flared after New Delhi claimed a contingent of 30 to 50 PLA soldiers crossed about 12 miles beyond the Line of Actual Control between the two countries on 15 April 2012 and stayed there for three weeks. According to New Delhi, PLA soldiers frequently conduct border incursions (more than 600 times over the last three years) but do not usually cross more than a few miles over the Line of Actual Control nor stay there longer than several hours.

Beijing denied Chinese troops had crossed into Indian territory. A Chinese Ministry of Foreign Affairs spokesperson said, "China has always acted in strict compliance with relevant agreements and protocols between the two countries on maintaining peace and tranquility in the Line of Actual Control area along the border... Chinese patrol troops have never crossed the line."

Chinese Premier Li Keqiang attempted to downplay the incident and the risk of conflict. During a state visit to India, he insisted that "a few clouds in the sky cannot shut out the brilliant rays of our friendship." Premier Li did not directly address the alleged Chinese incursion, though he said "both sides believe we need to improve various border-related mechanisms that we have put into place and make them more efficient, and we need to appropriately manage and resolve our differences."

President Xi Jinping met Indian Prime Minister Manmohan Singh at the BRICS Summit in Durban, South Africa, 29 March 2013. Xi urged both sides to use special representatives to strive for a fair, rational framework that can lead to a solution to the border issue as soon as possible.

India will abide by political guidelines set by both sides and seek a solution to the border issue with a commitment to safeguarding peace, Singh said. Since 2003, more than a dozen rounds of talks had been launched to resolve the border disputes. But ties have still been occasionally strained by the issue and overshadowed by closer India-US relations amid Washington's accelerating Asia "pivot" policy.

Beijing and New Delhi resolved the April border impasse in May after a series of talks and agreed to pursue a formal agreement to build trust and confidence between the border troops. The two sides signed the agreement during the Indian prime minister's trip to China in October 2013. China and India concluded a border defense cooperation pact 24 October 2013, making it a highlight of Indian Prime Minister Manmohan Singh's visit to the Asian neighbor. The Indian Express newspaper said the pact also puts no restrictions on India developing border infrastructure or enhancing military capabilities along the border. It quoted India's Ambassador to China S. Jai Shanker as saying: "This principle allows both countries to take appropriate measures according to their own security needs."

Nevertheless, the potential for periodic low-level confrontations between border patrols to escalate likely will persist. Indian media have reported several additional albeit briefer incursions by Chinese troops since the April standoff. Furthermore, both China and India continue to boost their militaries' capabilities on the border, adding to mutual suspicion. This has left both sides sensitive to each other's border activities and disposed toward worst-case perceptions of the other sides' intentions and activities. Ely Ratner and Alexander Sullivan of the Center for a New American Security, warn: "more intense strategic competition between India and China would reverberate throughout the continent, exacerbating tensions in Central Asia, the Indian Ocean, and Southeast Asia. Disruptions to the Asian engine of economic growth caused by these tensions could debilitate the global economy."

4

Sino-Indian Territorial Problems

In terms of "the rise of China" and its "implications for India", the title of this book, the Sino-Indian territorial dispute represents an immediate arena in which India is having to face the uncomfortable implications from having an increasingly stronger neighbour. For India, the ability of China to deny India's hopes of territorial settlement on India's terms has become ever clearer in the wake of China's rise in military power in and around their disputed territory, which remains the biggest amount of land still in dispute in Asia. As such, "the 4,056—kilometre (2,520 miles) frontier between India and China, one of the longest inter-state borders in the world, remains ... not defined, let alone demarcated, on maps or delineated on the ground".

Here, the judgement over a century ago of Lord Curzon, British Viceroy of India 1898-1905 still seems relevant; the most urgent work of Foreign Ministers and Ambassadors ... is now the conclusion of Frontier Conventions in which sources of discord are removed by the adjustment of rival interests or ambitions at points where the territorial borders adjoin", for "frontiers are indeed the razor's edge on which hang suspended the modern issues of war or peace, of life or death to nations". Admittedly, the territorial issue has been officially decoupled from the wider Sino-Indian relationship; as with the PRC rhetoric that "China and India have already reached consensus on the border issue.

Before it is completely resolved, both countries will endeavour to maintain peace and stability in the border areas and will not let the border issue affect the general picture of China and India's cooperation". However, in reality their territorial issues do affect their wider relationship, in PRC terms "the existence of immense territorial disputes between China and India".

In dispute terms, this chapter argues that, in International Relations (IR) theory terms, the territorial disputes between India and China involve *classical geopolitics* entwined with *critical geopolitics*. Each strand of geopolitics, in their different ways, both involve the respective "position" that India and China hold for themselves and for each other in their immediate and extended neighbourhood. Whilst each side argues from history, the chapter argues that in reality the evidence from history is rather ambiguous and inconclusive for both sides' territorial claims. Indeed, history is a sterile area to argue from, as one Indian commentator put it, "can we go beyond history to look at solutions which do not hark back to the past?" The chapter argues that, from the outside, resolution of the issue seems feasible enough in terms of simple seeming territorial trade offs involving Arunachal Pradesh and Aksai Chin; but is complicated by smaller geographic issues surrounding Tawang, and wider geopolitical issues surrounding Tibet and indeed the balance of power in Asia between India and China.

The two main areas of dispute along this Himalayan frontier are the *Western Sector* (Aksai Chin, around 37,250 square kilometres/ 14,380 square miles); and the *Eastern Sector* (Arunachal Pradesh, around 83,740 square kilometres/ 32,330 square miles). On the one hand, Arunachal Pradesh is inhabited by over a million people, Indian citizens, and includes important Buddhist centres like Tawang. On the other hand, Aksai Chin is a virtually uninhabited bleak barren plateau with no permanent settlements. It is the place "where not a blade of grass grows" as Jawaharlal Nehru once dismissively said; but where China's National Highway 219 runs through Aksai Chin as a key geopolitical infrastructure link for the PRC between its provinces of Tibet and Xinjiang. One further complication is China's occupation of the Shaksgam valley; around

5,180 sq kilometres/1,930 square miles, to which Pakistan relinquished its Baltistan-related claims in 1963, but over which India maintains its own Kashmir-derived claims. Smaller pockets of disputed territory are found, the *Middle Sector* fringes of Himachal Pradesh and Uttar Pradesh. Elsewhere along the Himalayas, lingering uncertainty over China's recognition of Sikkim's incorporation into India in 1975 is entwined with continuing PRC claims to the "Finger Area" in the north of Sikkim, with 71 supposed incidents reported of Chinese troop "incursions" in 2008. Nearby territorial disputes between China and Bhutan around the Chumbi Valley triangulation point with India are of further concern to New Delhi, given the Chumbi Valley's location looking down onto the India's sensitive Siliguri corridor which links India's northeastern states with the rest of India.

Wider nuances arise with India's Foreign Secretary (2004—2006) Shyam Saran, and his comments about *the logic of geography*. In front of one audience, it was a question for Saran of "geopolitical reality" in which "I would like to focus particularly on Asia, where the interests of both India and China intersect. It is said that the logic of geography is unrelenting. Proximity is the most difficult and testing among diplomatic challenges a country faces", where "to those who harbour any skepticism about this fact, it would suffice to remind that we share one of the longest [and disputed] land borders in the world with China. In front of another audience, it was again a question that "it is said that the logic of geography is unrelenting and proximity is the most difficult and testing among diplomatic challenges a country faces"; with the following gloss that "frontiers with neighbours are where domestic concerns intersect with external relationships. This is where domestic and foreign policies become inextricable and demand sensitive handling", and in which "it is important for us to look at the [disputed] boundary question from the long-term and strategic perspective of India-China relations, rather than as a mere territorial issue.

The territorial issues between India and China form one of the biggest land disputes in Asia, and are of significance not only for the size of area under dispute, but also because the two disputants are the big countries most evidently on the rise in Asia. Alongside this *logic of geography*, there is then what Neville Maxwell called "the logic of power"; a *logic of power* whereby powerful states "in their expansive phases push out their frontiers until they meet the resistance of a strong neighbour or reach a physical barrier which makes a natural point of rest". In geopolitical terms, the current point of rest is along the Himalayas/Karakoram range, but in the long term where exactly is the "natural" point of rest between them? Amidst talk of mutual IR *security dilemma* dynamics, China's strengthening of military forces and related infrastructure in Aksai Chin and Arunachal Pradesh zones is now a spur to India's own more halting augmentation of military forces and related infrastructure. Meanwhile, both countries are seeking to expand their wider strategic space at a time when their immediate mountain borders remain unresolved.

NEGOTIATING STRATEGIES

One repeated emerging criticisms of India's negotiating strategy is that "unilateral concessions" have been made too often by India, without similar concessions being made by China. When PRC military forces started moving into Tibet in 1950, the Republic of India quickly moved to (a) give up the Forward Rights inherited from the das of British India, which stemmed from the Simla Convention and Anglo-Tibetan Agreement of 1904; and (b) instead recognise Chinese control over Tibet in stronger terms than the hitherto used term "suzerainty". In effect, a "Tibet Card" was there to be played at a time of PRC uncertainties. A robust Indian intervention might have maintained Tibet as an effective buffer between India and China, or at least enabled concessions to be won by India on the Himalayan—Karakoram borders.

This is the reverse logic behind recent Indian comments that "China has failed to appreciate that if Arunachal is claimed to be the southern part of Tibet Autonomous Region (TAR), India cannot accept Tibet to be within China. India's formal position on Tibet articulated in 1954 and 2003 is therefore a tentative and unilateral diplomatic offer that can only be sustained and the circle completed once China recognizes Arunachal as part of India". Reinvoking such a "Tibet Card" has been floated in some Indian circles in the past few years.

Having lost that opportunity, the next criticism of Indian negotiating strategy is that, faced with an immediate PRC military presence in Tibet and renewed Chinese claims over Aksai China and Arunachal Pradesh, Nehru ignored the chance of a trade-off seemingly offered by China in 1960; whereby Aksai China would have gone to China and Arunachal Pradesh would have gone to India. Instead, India refused to engage in sovereignty negotiations in the 1950s, maintained its claims to the fullest, neglected to build up its own military forces, yet still engaged in adventurist forward probing movements in the late 1950s. At the time, Nehru rejected the idea of territorial trade-off; India "will not concede one piece of territory in return for another in the same manner as a similar dispute between China and Burma was settled this year"; for "there is no question of barter in these matters ... facts are facts". His formal position was, in the formal *Indian Note* of June 16 1962; quite simply that "this boundary is well known and well recognized and has been so for centuries and cannot be the subject of any negotiations". The trouble was the precise boundaries were not well known, were not well recognized, and had not been in shape for centuries. The irony is that the territorial agreement reached between Burma and China in 1960 involved China following the MacMahon Line alongside other mutual concessions and swapping of territory; as did the 1963 Agreement between China and Pakistan with regard to mutual concessions over claims and territory in the Karakoram reaches.

Nehru might have said "facts are facts" but the fact of the matter is that China's military superiority and continuing occupation of Aksai Chin created a very different subsequent set of facts in the wake of India's military defeat at the hands of China in 1962. The problem for consideration of negotiated resolution of the territorial dispute is that demands and offers have shifted. From the outside, an obvious trade off would be between the *Western* Sector and the *Eastern Sector*; which is where Noorani argued that "there is no territorial dispute which has been, and still is, more susceptible to a solution than India's boundary dispute with China. Each side has its non-negotiable vital interest securely under its control. India has the McMahon Line; China has Aksai Chin" In other words, China's *de facto* control of Aksai Chin could be reflected in agreed *de jure* sovereignty for China, and India's *de facto* control of Arunachal Pradesh could in turn be reflected in agreed *de jure* sovereignty for India. This had been Zhou Enlai's seeming suggestion in 1960, and was the "Package Plan" floated by Deng Xiaoping during 1980. The problem is that the Indian government has never taken up such trade-off offers, with Chinese comments made about the weakness of the Indian governments in taking any compromise deal to the Indian public. The separate *sector-by-sector* approach advocated by India when discussions resumed in the 1980s, rather than *overall package* trade-off deals suggested by China, has not worked, it has merely led the PRC to maintain its particular claims in all Sectors.

Another possible example of unilateral concessions was Rajiv Gandhi's visit to Beijing in 1988. Various concessions were made by him. He agreed that the settlement of the border dispute no longer was necessary as a precondition for improvement of bilateral relations, secondly he agreed that some members of the Tibetan community in India were engaged in anti-China activities, and thirdly he agreed that Tibet was an internal affair for China. Ganguly considered the results were "clearly asymmetric" as no support on the Kashmir issue was received from China, which "underscored the stark debility of India's negotiating capabilities vis-à-vis China". On the other hand, the earlier unequivocal support for Pakistan's case in Kashmir was moderated by a more neutral position by the 1990s, the PRC eventually announcing it was "not taking sides on Kashmir".

A final example of "unilateral concessions" came in the 2003 *Declaration on Principles for Relations and Comprehensive Cooperation between India and China,* in which India explicitly recognised the sovereignty of China over Tibet. A careful look at the text shows one-way agreement, one-way obligations, one-way concessions. On the one hand, it stated that "The Indian side recognizes that the Tibet Autonomous Region is part of the territory of the People's Republic of China and reiterates that it does not allow Tibetans to engage in anti-China political activities in India"; before going on to immediately say, on the other hand, "The Chinese side expresses its appreciation for the Indian position and reiterates that it is firmly opposed to any attempt and action aimed at splitting China and bringing about "independence of Tibet". As can be seen, there was no recognition of Indian territory (Arunachal Pradesh?) by China; not even return recognition by China of India's sovereignty claims over Sikkim, the Princely State reincorporated into the Republic of India in 1975, an incorporation which China had refused to recognise. Indian commentators may have read the accompanying *Trade Memorandum* designating Natu La as a border trade post as recognition by China of India's sovereignty over Sikkim, but that was implied rather than explicit, *de facto* rather than *de jure*.

Meanwhile, New Delhi has refused to lay out its formal position, other than the reiteration of its full claims of the Indian Parliament in November 1962, a unanimous vote to get China to vacate all Indian-claimed territories that China occupied. Specific territorial negotiations involving sensitive political climb downs or concessions might well be conducted in private out of the public gaze, yet there seems no indications of this either. India could then indicate some sort of territorial trade-off, short of this maximalist reiteration of its full claims which China is unlikely to accept. Of course, India indicating a territorial trade-off would not necessarily meet with Chinese acceptance, given Indian suspicions that China is happy enough to avoid definitive frontier settlement; but at least it would clarify the issue, and in such an eventuality enable India to more straightforwardly strengthen her own presence and power towards China along the border. In IR terms, if *engagement* proved unsuccessful in leading to territorial settlement, then India could go for a degree of *internal balancing* through building up its military presence and power in Arunachal Pradesh and Ladakh. Some Indian commentators have suggested that "when the Agni-III is finally ready for deployment, it is likely that the Chinese will come down to the table for negotiations and there is likely to be further progress on the border dispute". It could also go for a degree of *external balancing* with others vis-à-vis China but that is a much wider issue. It could try adjusting its bigger policy on Tibet, in effect playing a "Tibet Card" to engineer geopolitical shifts in the future; though would be a much more high risk strategy immediately bringing it up against China's perceived "core interest" of averting internal fragmentation.

If India's strategy over the disputed territories has been hesitant, this has been exacerbated by the very opaqueness, the "Chinese whispers" coming from Beijing. What exactly does China really want, what is its bottom line? For example, are PRC reiterations of claims over the whole of Arunachal Pradesh, re-invoked with greater vigour since the 1990s, just a maximalist initial tactic to end up with the Tawang pocket, thereby strengthening its control over Tibet, a line of argument by Chinese commentators like Ma Jiali and others. Are some suggestions in PRC circles of a different trade-off, Aksai Chin to India and Arunachal Pradesh to China, serious? Did China's acceptance in 2003 of Nathu La as an official border trade post between India and China represent full and definitive acceptance by China of Sikkim's incorporation into India; and what is the significance of rising "incursion" incidents into Sikkim during 2008 by Chinese troops; uncertainties that undermine Wen Jiabao's assertions in 2005 that "Sikkim is no longer the problem between China and India?" Is talk in the PRC that "China won't make any compromises in its border disputes with India" a tactical ploy by China to get India to make compromises? If it is, then a trade-off deal is likely at some point. If it is not, then indefinite deadline/stand off is likely, unless one or the other disputant state attempts to decide it on the military battlefield.

One emerging line from the PRC, with implications for India, is PRC emphasis and definition of a "core interests" diplomacy, reflecting the rise of China; "as the country becomes stronger, China is now on the trajectory to develop its own doctrine of diplomacy". This has been a development in the last couple of years, overlapping with rising friction along the disputed Himalayan reaches; generally what the PRC calls "the recalibration of its strategic focus in diplomacy to 'core interests'", over which it is taking a more obstructive/assertive line. This sense of "core interest" can be primarily seen at stake for the PRC in Taiwan and also Xinjiang. It can also be seen with PRC statements with regard to Tibet, whereby "Tibet related issues remain a core interest of China that refers to state sovereignty and territorial integrity. This is neither a religious issue nor a human right issue". The question is how far China's "core interest" framework may be "expanding". If such a "core interest" linkage is also invoked for Arunachal Pradesh (or in PRC eyes *Zang Nan* "Southern Tibet") as "Tibet-related issues", then one would have less expectations of territorial agreements being reached between India and China, and more likelihood of armed resolution in the future. Such trends were the spur for Barat Verma at the *India Defence Review* to warn that for the PRC "the most attractive option is to attack a soft target like India and forcibly occupy its territory in the Northeast...Beijing's cleverly raising the hackles on its fabricated dispute in Arunachal Pradesh to an alarming level, is the preparatory groundwork for imposing such a conflict on India"; a scenario dismissed in China as a "provocative and inflammatory illusion". Nevertheless, IR security dilemma dynamics may indeed lead to increasing military tension as both sides reinforce their military positions, and "war talk" about the disputed territories increases.

Concerned voices are easy to find as "tensions over a boundary dispute between the two sides are escalating". One reason for Indian concerns is the increasing number of "incursion" incidents along the border, though denied by China. The official India leadership downplays such trends, India's Foreign Secretary Niripuma Rao thus asserting in September 2009 that "there has been no significant increase in intrusions across all Sectors of the Line of Actual Control (LAC)", but that such India-perceived incursions were "because there is no mutually agreed or delineated border". This ignores the earlier increase the previous year, whereby the number of India-perceived "incursions" by the PRC has increased from 140 in 2007 to 280 in 2008, with a similar number in 2009. Such incursion incidents involved not just the *Eastern Sector* around Arunachal Pradesh but now also the *Western Sector* around Aksai Chin/Ladakh; a particular widening development that Indian commentators like Bhaskar Roy have found "sinister" and which Kanwal sees as "aggressive tactical posturing" on the part of China. Admittedly, such border incursions, reflecting different perceptions of where the LAC actually is, have often been trivial in themselves; for example Chinese troops painting rocks in red paint or cross-LAC sheep grazing. Chinese troop movements near and around the narrow Siliguri corridor "chicken's neck" linking north-east India to the rest of India do though cause immediate geopolitical concerns to India.

Certainly, a substantive military build up along the Aksai Chin and Arunachal Pradesh borderlines has also been evident. Partly this has been an infrastructure race, in which India has been belatedly trying to catch up and match China's better established road, and now railway, infrastructure in these disputed borderlands. It has also involved increasing military deployment, again by India to match China's already established forces in places like Linzi airbase. This is reflected in India increasing its ground forces in the border regions facing China. In the *Eastern Sector*, this has also involved the Indian Air Force (IAF) deploying advanced long range Sukhoi Su-30 warplanes to Tezpur for potential cross-LAC operation; complemented by six surface-to-air Akash missile squadrons. In the *Western Sector*, this has also involved the Indian Air Force reactivating disused high altitude airstrips like Daulat Beg Oldi and Fukche. Such reinforcements have been picked up in the PRC, and denounced as "unwise military moves".

Meanwhile, Brahma Chellaney asked the question in 2006 "will India—China border talks ever end"? He argued that "after a quarter century of unrewarding negotiations with Beijing, India ought to face up to the reality that it is being taken round and round the mulberry bush by an adversarial state that has little stake in an early border resolution"; in which "the more the talks have dragged on, the less Beijing has appeared interested in resolving the border disputes other than on its terms". His prognosis was simple, "it is time for it to draw the line, at least in the negotiations" and "to re-evaluate the very utility of staying absorbed in a never-ending process". Three years later, in the wake of the 2009 talks, his sense was the same, "the latest round of the unending and fruitless India—China talks on territorial disputes was a fresh reminder of the eroding utility of this process". The PRC may indeed wish to keep the issue open as a way of distracting and threatening India; but other dynamics may be leading the PRC to postpone decisive border negotiations. The PRC may well consider tightening its hold on Tibet itself as a greater priority, shaken during the disturbances that swept across Tibet and Tibetan areas in the spring of 2008? The PRC may also want to delay decisive border territorial resolution with India until it has resolved the Taiwan issue first? Garver also has wondered how far Beijing's apparent slowdown and readiness to avoid territorial resolution with India, is because of "understanding between Pakistan and China that neither will settle their territorial disputes with India independently of the other". Such a consideration point to the wider Pakistan—China—India triangle interplay around the disputed territories that stretch along the Himalayas from Arunachal Pradesh in the east to Aksai Chin and Kashmir in the west, which overlap with basic power balancing by the China—Pakistan "nexus" against India. The overlaps between the varied territorial disputes was shown in 2009 when China gave visas for the entry of Kashmiri separatists to visit China, in the wake of India giving permission to the Dalai Lama to visit Arunachal Pradesh.

What is certain is that any quick decisive territorial resolution between India and China is unlikely. Following rising border frictions, the PRC media reported "China—India border dispute turns sour", with hard hitting nationalist blogs being noticeable in the Chinese official and state controlled media in the autumn of 2009. Admittedly, the Indian and Chinese leadership did again reaffirm dialogue in autumn 2009. However, this reaffirmation was in cautious terms "to gradually narrow differences on border issues between the two countries ... to continue talks, with the aim of incrementally removing the barriers to a solution that was fair and acceptable to both sides". Despite the euphemistic headline from the official Chinese media that the two countries had reached "concensus on narrowing border differences"; in reality this merely indicated the existence of a gap without showing how and when it would be resolved. Talk of "gradually" and "incrementally removing" barriers to a solution flags up the slowness of any likely process, whilst offering nothing on what solutions could then emerge once such barriers have been, incrementally, removed.

What of solutions? Could outside arbitration be one way forward? Nehru himself had offered such a route in the immediate aftermath of war in the shape of the International Court of Justice (ICJ) at The Hague. However this was badly received in Parliament and Nehru then backed away immediately from this. In reality the ICJ seems ill equipped to deal with direct large scale territorial disputes between major powers, whilst China's reluctance to have outside bodies disposing of sovereignty issues is higher even than India's.

One bilateral solution which we can return to, involves a *logic of geography,* the "watershed/crestline" line along the Himalayas/ Karakoram. It has a degree of clearness, "the advantage of having a border on such a prominent line as the high watershed of the Himalaya is that it is easily identifiable, historically traditional and politically neutral". It may also be sellable to both parties. Thus, "as far as the Indian public is concerned, they have been brought up to believe that the Himalaya is the traditional boundary and they will be willing to concede any territory that lies beyond it without demur"; whilst "such a boundary should also be acceptable to China as it is based on the same watershed principle which they have accepted in defining their boundaries with Myanmar, Sikkim and Nepal. This watershed principle was an angle suggested by Zhou Enlai in the abortive 1960 discussions. In effect, applying the watershed principle would leave Aksai Chin to China and almost all Arunachal Pradesh with India.

Admittedly, Tawang remains problematic. The Tawang District's 2,085 square kilometres is around 2.5% of Arunachal Pradesh's entire 82,743 area, and its population of 38,924 is around 3.6% of Arunachal Pradesh's 1,091,120 inhabitants (2001 figures), relatively small shares on paper. Neutralization of the entire Tawang subdivision pocket might be an option. Within the Tawang District, given that the Tawang Subdistrict and the District capital Tawang (27°34′47"N) itself lies north of the Se la Pass and the Ka crest line

(27°32'26"N), whereas the Lumla and Jang Subdistricts lie on the southerly India-facing slopes of that crest line; could a division of Tawang District be carried out, with the Tawang Subdistrict allocated to China and the Lumla and Jang Subdistricts allocated to India? However, local opinion at the District capital Tawang, population c. 20,000, would probably vote in favour of staying in 'India' rather than going into the 'PRC', though an independent 'Tibet' option would provide an interesting third option. Having Tawang subdivision inhabitants relocate further south if they wished might be another solution, though ugly in political and human terms. Meanwhile, if the Dalai Lama's death was followed by any proclaimed rebirth at Tawang, a not impossible scenario, the situation would be still more complicated with the PRC.

Failing dramatic regime change scenarios of regime collapse/ democratization in the PRC, and re-establishment of a genuinely autonomous or independent Tibet, and Tawang notwithstanding; some sort of trade off involving Aksai Chin and Arunachal Pradesh seems the most likely way forward. In using relatively clear cut neutral geographic principles, the deadlocked politics and unclear history could perhaps be sidelined? Such a trade off would give neither side too much geopolitical advantage, but also ensure a degree of security for each? A *logic of geography* for the future for the national leaderships that would enable these two neighbours to get past the inconclusive divisive *logic of history* between them, and would provide a mutually satisfactory *logic of power* in terms of geopolitical equilibrium outcomes. Failing resolution of their territorial issues, the grinding tectonic plates along the Himalayas will continue to have their geopolitical counterpart as the two Asian giants look at each other across these disputed areas.

EVENTS LEADING UP TO WAR

Tibet and the border dispute

The 1940s saw huge change in South Asia with the Partition of India in 1947 (resulting in the establishment of the two new states of India and Pakistan), and the establishment of the People's Republic of China (PRC) in 1949. One of the most basic policies for the new Indian government was that of maintaining cordial relations with China, reviving its ancient friendly ties. India was among the first nations to grant diplomatic recognition to the newly created PRC.

At the time, Chinese officials issued no condemnation of Nehru's claims or made any opposition to Nehru's open declarations of control over Aksai Chin. In 1956, Chinese Premier Zhou Enlai stated that he had no claims over Indian controlled territory. He later argued that Aksai Chin was already under Chinese jurisdiction and that the McCartney MacDonald Line was the line China could accept. Zhou later argued that as the boundary was undemarcated and had never been defined by treaty between any Chinese or Indian government, the Indian government could not unilaterally define Aksai Chin's borders.

In 1950, the Chinese People's Liberation Army annexed Tibet and later the Chinese extended their influence by building a road in 1956–67 and placing border posts in Aksai Chin. India found out after the road was completed, protested against these moves and decided to look for a diplomatic solution to ensure a stable Sino-Indian border. To resolve any doubts about the Indian position, Prime Minister Jawaharlal Nehru declared in parliament that India regarded the McMahon Line as its official border. The Chinese expressed no concern at this statement, and in 1951 and 1952, the government of China asserted that there were no frontier issues to be taken up with India.

In 1954, Prime Minister Nehru wrote a memo calling for India's borders to be clearly defined and demarcated; in line with previous Indian philosophy, Indian maps showed a border that, in some places, lay north of the McMahon Line. Chinese Premier Zhou Enlai, in November 1956, again repeated Chinese assurances that the People's Republic had no claims on Indian territory, although official Chinese maps showed 120,000 square kilometres (46,000 sq mi) of territory claimed by India as Chinese. CIA documents created at the time revealed that Nehru had ignored Burmese premier Ba Swe when he warned Nehru to be cautious when dealing with Zhou. They also allege that Zhou purposefully told Nehru that there were no border issues with India.

In 1954, China and India negotiated the Five Principles of Peaceful Coexistence, by which the two nations agreed to abide in settling their disputes. India presented a frontier map which was accepted by China, and the slogan *Hindi-Chini bhai-bhai* (Indians and Chinese are brothers) was popular then. However, Nehru in 1958, had privately told G. Parthasarathi, the Indian envoy to China not to trust the Chinese at all and send all communications directly to him, bypassing the Defence Minister VK Krishna Menon since his communist background clouded his thinking about China. According to Georgia Tech political analyst John W Garver, Nehru's policy on Tibet was to create a strong Sino-Indian partnership which would be catalysed through agreement and compromise on Tibet. Garver believes that Nehru's previous actions had given him confidence that China would be ready to form an "Asian Axis" with India.

This apparent progress in relations suffered a major setback when, in 1959, Nehru accommodated the Tibetan religious leader at the time, the 14th Dalai Lama, who fled Lhasa after a failed Tibetan uprising against Chinese rule. The Chairman of the Chinese Communist Party, Mao Zedong, was enraged and asked the Xinhua News Agency to produce reports on Indian expansionists operating in Tibet.

Border incidents continued through this period. In August 1959, the People's Liberation Army took an Indian prisoner at Longju, which had an ambiguous position in the McMahon Line, and two months later in Aksai Chin, a clash led to the death of nine Indian frontier policemen.

On 2 October, Soviet Premier Nikita Khrushchev defended Nehru in a meeting with Mao. This action reinforced China's impression that the Soviet Union, the United States and India all had expansionist designs on China. The People's Liberation Army went so far as to prepare a self-defence counterattack plan. Negotiations were restarted between the nations, but no progress was made.

As a consequence of their non-recognition of the McMahon Line, China's maps showed both the North East Frontier Area (NEFA) and Aksai Chin to be Chinese territory. In 1960, Zhou

Enlai unofficially suggested that India drop its claims to Aksai Chin in return for a Chinese withdrawal of claims over NEFA. Adhering to his stated position, Nehru believed that China did not have a legitimate claim over either of these territories, and thus was not ready to concede them. This adamant stance was perceived in China as Indian opposition to Chinese rule in Tibet. Nehru declined to conduct any negotiations on the boundary until Chinese troops withdrew from Aksai Chin, a position supported by the international community. India produced numerous reports on the negotiations, and translated Chinese reports into English to help inform the international debate. China believed that India was simply securing its claim lines in order to continue its "grand plans in Tibet". India's stance that China withdraw from Aksai Chin caused continual deterioration of the diplomatic situation to the point that internal forces were pressuring Nehru to take a military stance against China.

The Forward Policy

At the beginning of 1961, Nehru appointed General B. M. Kaul as army Chief of General Staff, but he refused to increase military spending and prepare for a possible war. According to James Barnard Calvin of the U.S. Navy, in 1959, India started sending Indian troops and border patrols into disputed areas. This programme created both skirmishes and deteriorating relations between India and China.

The aim of this policy was to create outposts behind advancing Chinese troops to interdict their supplies, forcing them north of the disputed line. There were eventually 60 such outposts, including 43 north of the McMahon Line, to which India claimed sovereignty. China viewed this as further confirmation of Indian expansionist plans directed towards Tibet.

According to the Indian official history, implementation of the Forward Policy was intended to provide evidence of Indian occupation in the previously unoccupied region through which Chinese troops had been advancing. Kaul was confident, through contact with Indian Intelligence and CIA information, that China would not react with force. Indeed, at first the PLA simply withdrew, but eventually Chinese forces began to counter-encircle the Indian positions which clearly encroached into the north of McMahon Line.

This led to a tit-for-tat Indian reaction, with each force attempting to outmanoeuver the other. However, despite the escalating nature of the dispute, the two forces withheld from engaging each other directly.

Chinese attention was diverted for a time by the military activity of the Nationalists on Taiwan, but on 23 June the U.S. assured China that a Nationalist invasion would not be permitted. China's heavy artillery facing Taiwan could then be moved to Tibet. It took China six to eight months to gather the resources needed for the war, according to Anil Athale, author of the official Indian history. The Chinese sent a large quantity of non-military supplies to Tibet through the Indian port of Calcutta.

Early incidents

Various border conflicts and "military incidents" between India and China flared up throughout the summer and autumn of 1962. In May, the Indian Air Force was told not to plan for close air support, although it was assessed as being a feasible way to counter the unfavourable ratio of Chinese to Indian troops. In June, a skirmish caused the deaths of dozens of Chinese troops. The Indian Intelligence Bureau received information about a Chinese buildup along the border which could be a precursor to war.

During June–July 1962, Indian military planners began advocating "probing actions" against the Chinese, and accordingly, moved mountain troops forward to cut off Chinese supply lines.

According to Patterson, the Indian motives were threefold:

- Test Chinese resolve and intentions regarding India.
- Test whether India would enjoy Soviet backing in the event of a Sino-Indian war.
- Create sympathy for India within the U.S., with whom relations had deteriorated after the Indian annexation of Goa.

On 10 July 1962, 350 Chinese troops surrounded an Indian occupied post in Chushul (north of the McMahon Line) but withdrew after a heated argument via loudspeaker. On 22 July, the Forward Policy was extended to allow Indian troops to push back Chinese troops already established in disputed territory. Whereas Indian troops were previously ordered to fire only in self-defence, all post commanders were now given discretion to open fire upon Chinese forces if threatened. In August, the Chinese military improved its combat readiness along the McMahon Line and began stockpiling ammunition, weapons and gasoline.

Given his foreknowledge of the coming Cuban Missile Crisis, Mao Zedong was able to persuade Nikita Khrushchev to reverse the Russian policy of backing India, at least temporarily. In mid-October, the Communist organ *Pravda* encouraged peace between India and China. When the Cuban Missile Crisis ended and Mao's rhetoric changed, however, Russia reversed course.

CONFRONTATION AT THAG LA

In June 1962, Indian forces established an outpost at Dhola, on the southern slopes of the Thag La Ridge. Dhola lay north of the McMahon Line but south of the ridges along which India interpreted the McMahon Line to run. In August, China issued diplomatic protests and began occupying positions at the top of Thag La. On 8 September, a 60-strong PLA unit descended to the south side of the ridge and occupied positions that dominated one of the Indian posts at Dhola. Fire was not exchanged, but Nehru said to the media that the Indian Army had instructions to "free our territory" and the troops had been given discretion to use force. On 11 September, it was decided that "all forward posts and patrols were given permission to fire on any armed Chinese who entered Indian territory".

However, the operation to occupy Thag La was flawed in that Nehru's directives were unclear and it got underway very slowly because of this. In addition to this, each man had to carry 35 kilograms (77 lb) over the long trek and this severely slowed down the reaction. By the time the Indian battalion reached the point of conflict, Chinese units controlled both banks of the Namka Chu

River. On 20 September, Chinese troops threw grenades at Indian troops and a firefight developed, triggering a long series of skirmishes for the rest of September.

Some Indian troops, including Brigadier Dalvi who commanded the forces at Thag La, were also concerned that the territory they were fighting for was not strictly territory that "we should have been convinced was ours". According to Neville Maxwell, even members of the Indian defence ministry were categorically concerned with the validity of the fighting in Thag La.

On 3 October, a week before the start of the war, Zhou Enlai visited Nehru in New Delhi promising there would be no war. On 4 October, Kaul assigned some troops to secure regions south of the Thag La Ridge. Kaul decided to first secure Yumtso La, a strategically important position, before re-entering the lost Dhola post. Kaul had then realised that the attack would be desperate and the Indian government tried to stop an escalation into all-out war. Indian troops marching to Thag La had suffered in the previously unexperienced conditions; two Gurkha soldiers died of pulmonary edema.

On 10 October, an Indian Punjabi patrol of 50 troops to Yumtso La were met by an emplaced Chinese position of some 1,000 soldiers. Indian troops were in no position for battle, as Yumtso La was 16,000 feet (4,900 m) above sea level and Kaul did not plan on having artillery support for the troops. The Chinese troops opened fire on the Indians under their belief that they were north of the McMahon Line. The Indians were surrounded by Chinese positions which used mortar fire. However, they managed to hold off the first Chinese assault, inflicting heavy casualties.

At this point, the Indian troops were in a position to push the Chinese back with mortar and machine gun fire. However, Brigadier Dalvi opted not to fire, as it would mean decimating the Rajput who were still in the area of the Chinese regrouping. They helplessly watched the Chinese ready themselves for a second assault. In the second Chinese assault, the Indians began their retreat, realising the situation was hopeless. The Indian patrol suffered 25 casualties, and the Chinese 33. The Chinese troops held their fire as the Indians retreated, and then buried the Indian dead with military honours, as witnessed by the retreating soldiers. This was the first occurrence of heavy fighting in the war. This attack had grave implications for India and Nehru tried to solve the issue, but by 18 October, it was clear that the Chinese were preparing for an attack on India, with massive troop buildups on the border. A long line of mules and porters had also been observed supporting the buildup and reinforcement of positions south of the Thag La Ridge.

DISPUTED TERRITORY BETWEEN CHINA AND INDIA

Arunachal Pradesh

Both countries retain their strong claims to the disputed territory, however, fueled by national pride and national security interests. China's "Go West" development policy and July 2006 opening of the Qinghai-Tibet railway have received mixed responses from Indian policymakers; those who favour expanded trade and people-to-people contacts have regarded the developments as positive, but some within the national security establishment have raised concerns that they will allow Beijing to extend its military power projection into Tibet and beyond into South and Central Asia.

Three rivers running through India—the Indus/Sengge Chu, Sutlej/Langqen Tsangbo, and Brahmaputra/Sang Po—originate in Tibet, a fact that has spurred Indian fears that China could use upstream dams and barrages to control the flow of water into India. India, for instance, has blamed a series of flash floods along the Sutlej River in its state of Himachal Pradesh to China's reluctance to supply hydrological data to India in a timely manner or allow Indian scientists to conduct surveys of melting glaciers on Chinese soil. The absence of any water-sharing treaty between both states as a result of the disputed status of their borders contributes to these water tensions.

Regional Affairs

Regionally, Sino-Indian cooperation has been the exception rather than the rule. Beijing watches closely New Delhi's increasing engagement of East Asia, including relations with nations that have historically had particularly difficult interactions with Beijing, such as Japan, Vietnam, and Indonesia. At the same time, Indian strategists have expressed quiet concern over China's growing influence in the subcontinent, not only its maintenance of a robust political and military relationship with India's rival Pakistan, but also its extensive political, economic, and security relationship with Burma, growing relations with Bangladesh and Nepal, and increasing naval presence in the Indian Ocean. China's admission as an observer to the South Asian Association for Regional Cooperation (SAARC) in November 2005, with New Delhi's reluctant acquiescence, has been cited as further evidence of China's emergence as a player in India's backyard and the desire of India's smaller neighbours to draw China into the region as leverage.

India has viewed growing Chinese influence in Burma, which is strategically located along the eastern end of the Indian Ocean, with great suspicion. In the mid-1990s, India had been one of the most vocal and ardent supporters of Burma's democracy movement, led by Aung San Suu Kyi. However, the combination of India's aim to forge closer links with Southeast Asia as part of its "Look East" policy, its need for Burma's support in countering insurgent groups in India's northeast, its desire for access to Burma's natural resources, including energy (often in competition with China), and its alarm over China's growing military ties to the Burmese junta led India to adopt a more conciliatory engagement policy with the Burmese leadership by the late 1990s to counterbalance Chinese influence. Most notably, the presence of Chinese radar technicians in Burma's Coco Islands, which border India's Andaman and Nicobar

Islands, has fueled concern in New Delhi (and Washington) that Beijing is monitoring naval activities in the region.

Furthermore, China's efforts to develop alternative overland routes to transport oil and gas imports through port facilities at Gwadar in Pakistan's Baluchistan province, which is at the entrance of the Strait of Hormuz, as well as through Bangladesh and Burma, have been viewed by India as part of a Chinese "string of pearls" strategy of economic and military encroachment into South and

Central Asia. Indeed, China's senior-most leaders have openly declared Beijing's attention to placing priority focus on naval modernization, including greater power-projection capability. Indian policymakers fear that China's moves could undermine India's regional preeminence.

At the same time, India's joint naval exercises in the South China Sea—with Vietnam in 2000 and Singapore in 2005, joint patrols with Indonesia in the Andaman Sea beginning in 2002, and exercises off the Japanese coast with the U.S. and Japanese navies in April 2007, have sparked concerns in Beijing. The Indian Navy, the world's fifth-largest, has also set up a Far Eastern Naval Command (FENC) off Port Blair on the Andaman Islands to increase its presence in the Strait of Malacca and potentially monitor Chinese naval activities in the region. Such mutual suspicions could result in China-Indian naval rivalry in and around the Indian Ocean over time.

For their part, East Asian nations have increasingly looked to India as a potential partner in economic and regional security affairs, with some, such as Japan, apparently considering India as a potential element in a hedging strategy against China. South Asian countries have likewise begun to play the "China card" in order to counterbalance India's influence in their affairs or gain policy concessions from India and the West.

For instance, as relations have soured between New Delhi and Dhaka in recent years, China has become Bangladesh's largest supplier of military hardware and has replaced India as Bangladesh's overall largest trading partner. In Nepal, China defied international suspension of military aid and other support to King

Gyanendra's regime after the monarch suspended democracy from February 2005 to April 2006, calling the situation Nepal's "internal affair." King Gyanendra reciprocated by shutting down the office of the Dalai Lama's representative in Nepal as well as the Tibetan Refugee Welfare Office.

In the end, China and India each recognize the inexorable reality of the other's increasing involvement in its neighborhood. In response, the two nations are quietly balancing the prospects for cooperation and competition in their relationship without letting any residual suspicions, tensions, or mistrust derail their mutual desire to test the possibilities of political rapprochement, economic engagement, and confidence-building in the years ahead.

People-to-People Contacts

People-to-people contacts between China and India have increased in recent years, albeit from a low base. Regular direct flights were established in 2002, when China's tourism authorities designated India as an "authorized destination." More than 5,000 Indian students are currently studying in Chinese universities. In India, enthusiasm for Chinese popular culture is growing, and Indians tend to respect, if not envy, China's economic and political rise, which they would like to have their own country mirror. India dubbed 2006 the "Year of Friendship with China," and China declared 2007 the "Year of China-India Friendship through Tourism."

Nonetheless, while official interaction is on the rise and public opinion polls suggest that a majority of citizens and businessmen in both states hold favorable views of each other overall, popular interaction remains relatively minimal, restricted by the language barrier, cultural differences, and other factors. Chinese and Indian observers alike will note that the Chinese have more natural affinity with countries in East and Southeast Asia, while Indians are more comfortable in dealing with English-speaking countries and other South Asian states.

Mutual mistrust persists, particularly within India's older generation, whose memories of the Sino-Indian border conflict lead it to view China with suspicion. India's media and educational system have also nurtured the notion that China "stabbed India in the back" in 1962 and is sitting on Indian land. India's visa policy, in fact, is very restrictive and suspicious of the entry of citizens from China (among other nations, including the United States), further constraining popular contact.

For their part, the Chinese have expressed difficulty in understanding India's cultural and interpersonal style and have tended to be snobbish in their view of India and its state of development relative to China. While Indians may be focusing increasingly on China, relatively little Chinese popular attention is directed toward India. Few Chinese students study in India, for instance. Even at the official level, a similar lack of symmetry in the level of attention paid by China and India toward each other appears to prevail.

CHINA AND INDIA'S RELATIONSHIPS

Pakistan

China's continued support for Pakistan has long been a source of friction in China-India relations. The China-Pakistan relationship has been described as an "all-weather relationship" by both states, with President Hu Jintao reaching hyperbolic heights when he described it as "higher than the Himalayas, deeper than the Indian Ocean, and sweeter than honey" during his November 2006 visit to Islamabad.

The China-Pakistan relationship grew out of their mutual desire beginning in the 1960s to counterbalance India, which had closely aligned with the Soviet Union against China, following the 1962 border war. Pakistan's nascent relationship with China can in fact be traced as far back as 1954, when Pakistan reassured Beijing that the Southeast Asia Treaty Organization (SEATO) was not directed against China, and 1961 when it supported a draft resolution to restore China's membership in the United Nations. In 1963, Pakistan ceded to China the Trans-Karakoram Tract, also known as Shaksam Valley, in the disputed territory of Kashmir. The area subsequently became part of the land bridge linking Pakistan to China's Xinjiang along the Karakoram Highway.

China sided with Pakistan during the 1965 and 1971 wars with India, during which China put its own forces along the Indian border on full alert. In April 2005, China and Pakistan signed the "Treaty of Friendship, Cooperation, and Good Neighborly Relations," which binds both signatories to desist from joining "any alliance or bloc which infringes upon the sovereignty, security, and territorial integrity of the other side."

In recent years, China's engagement with Pakistan has been further motivated by Beijing's desire to extend its influence into

South and Central Asia in order to maintain a stable periphery; gain access to markets, natural resources, and raw materials; and maintain amicable relations with the Islamic world to mitigate support for the Islamic insurgency in Xinjiang province. Pakistan is the leading recipient of China's arms exports and has received substantial support from China for its civilian and military nuclear program.

In recent years, however, China has adopted a more balanced approach toward its relationship with Pakistan and India, fueled by Beijing's desire to maintain amicable relations with all states along its periphery, its recognition of India's growing economic and strategic potential, especially in the wake of improving U.S.-India relations, rising concern over Pakistan's future viability, and China's shared concerns with India over Islamic extremism and separatism. China has also noted the rapprochement in U.S.-Pakistan relations following September 11, which has encouraged Beijing to diversify its relations on the subcontinent in turn. To display its credentials as a responsible international actor, China has lessened its material support for Pakistan's ballistic missile and nuclear weapons programs and its automatic political, moral, and rhetorical support to Pakistan in its relations with India.

The shift in China's policy toward the India-Pakistan relationship has been most visible over the issue of Kashmir. Although China supported Pakistan's position during the India-Pakistan conflicts of 1965 and 1971, Beijing announced in January 1994 that it not only favored a negotiated solution on Kashmir but also opposed any form of independence for the region. During the Kargil conflict in 1999, when Pakistani and Kashmiri forces advanced provocatively into the Indian side of the Line of Control, China for the first time adopted a neutral position rather than siding with Pakistan.

China adopted a similar position when both states were on the verge of war in December 2001 following a terrorist attack on the Indian parliament. Indeed, unless India is the clear aggressor, China is unlikely to support Pakistan automatically in any future India-Pakistan conflict, as China's focus on internal development and maintaining a stable periphery will lead Beijing to place its primary emphasis on stopping any hostilities or unrest along its border.

Nonetheless, Beijing continues to employ the "Pakistan card" in voicing its displeasure over Indian behaviour. Beijing's reluctance to admit India to the Shanghai Cooperation Organization (SCO) while supporting Pakistan's bid, and its offer to support Pakistan's civilian nuclear program following the conclusion of the U.S.-India nuclear deal, suggests that China has not completely abandoned its traditional loyalty to Pakistan. Indeed, China benefits today from the reduction of tensions between India and Pakistan, which allows Beijing to continue its two-track approach. China's relationship with Pakistan however continues to rile New

International Security [Oxford: Oxford University Press, 2005, 420–1]). According to one source, as much as 80 percent of Pakistan's military hardware, including 60 percent of its military aircraft, has come from China. Ramtanu Maitra, "China and India Aim to Extend Cooperation," *Executive Intelligence Review*, February 18, 2005. Delhi, which remains resentful and suspicious over continued arms sales and other elements of the historical partnership over the past 45 years.

United States

Many Chinese have viewed the Bush administration's attention to developing strategic relations with India since 2001 as an attempt to contain or at least counterbalance China in South and East Asia. President George W. Bush has stated that the United States is committed to helping India become a world power, and in June 2005, India and the United States signed the New Framework for the U.S.-India Defense Relationship, a 10-year agreement paving the way for joint weapons production, cooperation on missile defense, and a possible lifting of U.S. export controls on sensitive military technologies.

Growing U.S.-India military-to-military cooperation, most notably in the Indian Ocean, has emerged as a particular source of concern in Beijing, given China's growing dependence on oil imports transiting the Indian Ocean. China expressed principled discomfort over the March 2006 U.S.-India civil nuclear agreement, which in essence recognized India as a nuclear weapons state and granted India assistance for its civilian nuclear program in exchange for India's promise to open its civil nuclear facilities to international inspection and safeguards. China initially criticized the deal as creating a "nuclear exception" and undermining the nonproliferation regime, although its opposition has cooled due to concern about its potential impact on relations with New Delhi.

Nonetheless, while the United States does seek to draw India into a values-based strategic and operational partnership to handle common international challenges, U.S. officials have denied that the relationship is meant to contain or otherwise oppose China.

Regardless, absent extraordinary provocation from Beijing, New Delhi will have no interest in allying with Washington in any active strategy to contain or oppose China. As a legacy of its "nonaligned" foreign policy, Indian policymakers maintain an aversion to alliances, especially those that are perceived as counterbalancing or containing other countries. This has prompted India to keep its distance thus far from both China-centered forums such as the Shanghai Cooperation Organization, and U.S.-centered organizations such as the Proliferation Security Initiative and the U.S.-Japan-Australia Trilateral Strategic Dialogue.

The legacy of nonalignment has made India particularly resistant to becoming anything resembling a junior partner of the United States (or China) and allergic to anything that constrains its flexibility and policy options. Indeed, India's position toward the United States has not emerged from its Cold War shadow, and New Delhi is taking the bilateral partnership slowly. In the end, India will maintain its strategic independence to pursue a multilayered approach combining both cooperation and competition with China in a way that serves its own unique political, economic, and security interests.

Taiwan

India recognized the People's Republic of China over the exiled Republic of China on the island of Taiwan in 1950 and has never wavered in its perspective on formal relations with the two sides. Nevertheless, Taiwan's leadership has reached out actively to New

Delhi in recent years. Taiwan's government has spoken openly about how India could serve as an alternative investment destination and a democratic comrade-in-arms with which the island might work to raise its international profile and perhaps constrain mainland action across the strait. Indian leaders and close advisers within the nongovernmental community have increased their interaction with Taiwanese delegations in recent years, but New Delhi has been very reluctant to accept Taiwan's overtures for more official ties and closer relations. There remains little overt interaction between the political communities, and even that has largely been focused on economic issues. In 1995, India and Taiwan founded the India-Taipei Association, India's trade mission in Taiwan. The organization had been led by retired government officials, but in 2003 India raised the level of its representation by assigning leadership to a serving official.

In February 2006, the two sides established the Taiwan-India Cooperation Council, which was intended to promote and facilitate Taiwanese business investment in India. Taiwanese leaders like to note that Taiwan's hardware expertise and India's strong software industry are an excellent complement to each other. Presently, about 70 percent of hardware and IT components manufactured on the Chinese mainland are based on Taiwanese investments, and this has prompted Taiwanese businesses to seek to diversify their IT market. Nonetheless, Taiwan-India bilateral trade reached about $2 billion in 2005. India makes up only 0.67 percent of Taiwan's total trade, although the figure has grown by 33 percent between 1995 and 2002. Investment also lags considerably, with Taiwanese businesses investing a total of $116 million in India as opposed to well over $100 billion in China.

Taiwan has made quiet overtures to India to establish military cooperation, but so far military interaction remains very limited. Nonetheless, New Delhi has benefited from the insights of Taipei's intelligence establishment that assist India in understanding developments on the mainland.

In the end, however, India views Taiwan as an economic partner more than as a potential political partner. India is quite aware of the sensitivity of the Taiwan issue to China and the potential for it to affect China-India relations. India's desire for stable relations with China, and in particular its aim of encouraging Beijing to pursue more balanced relations between India and Pakistan in South Asia, make India's leaders extremely cautious to not inflame tensions over the issue about which Beijing is most sensitive.

Indian decisionmakers reject any notion of using the Taiwan issue as a way to distract or exercise leverage against China. They do note, however, that peaceful resolution of the Taiwan issue will be an important indicator of China's future direction as a peaceful and responsible international actor and have linked the way China deals with Taiwan with the way it will handle Tibet, an issue of more direct salience for India.

Russia

The legacy of India's close relations with the Soviet Union during the Cold War lingers in its attitudes toward Russia. India signed the "Treaty of Peace, Friendship, and Cooperation" with the Soviet Union in 1971 at the height of the Sino-Soviet split, which led Beijing to denounce India as "tool of Soviet expansionism."

As far back as 1959, as the split emerged, the Soviet Union supplied India with transport planes for use during border clashes with China. Russia remains the main source of India's advanced weaponry today; Moscow, in fact, provides technologies even further advanced than those it sells to China.

In the post–Cold War period, China-Russia rapprochement has brought about a convergence in Chinese, Russian, and Indian interests. The three countries have a shared an interest in combating Islamic extremism within their borders. They each are committed to promoting a multipolar world and preserving strict adherence to the principles of state sovereignty and noninterference in states' internal affairs. China and India share an interest in importing Russian energy resources and intersect in their interest in confidence-building in Central Asia.

As a result, some U.S. analysts have worried about an emerging strategic triangle between China, India, and Russia that could seek to counterbalance the United States, especially after India acquired observer status in the Shanghai Cooperation Organization in 2005 and trilateral foreign-minister talks began the same year. There is little possibility of such a strategic triangle, however. Not only do India and China continue to mistrust one another, but India at least shows no desire to collaborate with China and Russia at the expense of its ongoing political rapprochement with the world's only superpower. India has distanced itself from the Shanghai Cooperation Organization, for example; India was the only country not to send its head of state to the June 2006 SCO summit in Shanghai. The trilateral meetings themselves are in a nascent phase in which nonmilitary, nonstrategic issues, such as energy, agriculture, industrial restructuring, and environmental protection, are discussed.

CHINA AND INDIA : THE 'EMERGING GIANTS' AND GROWTH

The economic performance of China and India is critical. This holds the key to global progress. China and India have been relatively 'closed' economies with limited dependence on trade. But they have been opening up. This is particularly so in the case of China.

Trade as a % of GDP has been 32% in China compared to 25% in India. This should be seen against a backdrop of relatively open East and South Asian economies: Malaysia (206%), Korea (Republic) (72%), Thailand (82 %), Pakistan (36%) and Bangladesh (35%). India's import duties as a % of imports, a key measure of openness, have also been declining in China and India. But it is lower in China compared to India: 3% in the former and 24% in the latter.

Foreign Direct Investment (FDI) can enable access to resources and increase productivity. There are two types: one by the transnationals from industrialized countries and the other by overseas Chinese and Non Resident Indians. In China overseas Chinese have been primarily responsible for Chinese FDI while India's FDI has been channeled through the Transnationals. Net flows of FDI as a % of GDP in China have been 12% in contrast to India's 0.61%.

Both countries have been growing fast over the last 25 years: China by 21 fold and India by 8 fold. The growth rate in China has been over 9% per annum making it possibly the fastest growing world economy while India's, too, has been impressive with over 8% per annum. The % living below the poverty line (1 $ a day) has also been appreciably reduced in both though it is more impressive in China compared to India: 12% in the former and 26% in the latter.

The major effect of China's and India's economic advance is evidenced by their contribution to global output: China's and India's share being 20% and 7% respectively in 2004. Both, moreover, have rising demand for energy, raw materials and commodities. This has a positive impact on increasing the exports of developing countries, improving their terms of trade, and initiating shifts in their pattern of trade and investment.

Liberalisation policies have enhanced the economic prowess of both nations. China, moreover, as a recent member of the World Trade Organization (2001), could firmly influence global trade negotiations, possibly joining forces with India, and champion the rights of poor nations. They could establish a 'level playing field' in world trade. Indeed the combined efforts of China and India could ensure that the Uruguay Round (1986-93) to accelerate trade liberalization can be successful. They could pressurize the developed nations to fulfil their promise of opening up their markets to developing country agricultural and non agricultural exports.

Liberalisation emerged much earlier in China, in 1978, while it was initiated in India in 1991 though initial steps were taken in the 1980's. Pre-reform or pre-liberalisation forces laid the basis on which such measures were evolved. China's policies unfolded in the context of bold economic policies in the East Asia region between 1960-1990 emphasizing agricultural development, primary education, macroeconomic stability, firm public policies to support markets, and regional dynamism. China's liberalization has been embodied in market based thrusts in agriculture, industry and services, state owned enterprises, and deregulation of product prices. These have been backed by measures to induce labour mobility, and formation of Special Economic Zones. On the domestic front, in the pre reform era in China, the savings level was high with significant capital formation (30%) and investment in infrastructure, irrigation and land development. Literacy and primary health care, too, have been impressive with virtual elimination of landlessness. It has also shed surplus labour-a move which has been inhibited in India possibly due to strong trade unions to safeguard the interest of workers. On the external front China's integration with the world economy, as mentioned earlier, has been advanced through its trade and FDI policies. This has made a significant contribution to China's growth and productivity.

India's growth rates have been relatively low in the pre-liberalisation period-4%-5% per annum compared to East Asia's 7%-8% per annum. The level of savings, too, has been lower than in China and East Asia; the levels of literacy and health care, too, have been lower, coupled with the presence of significant landlessness, and marked poverty and inequality between and within regions, sectors and socio-economic groups.

Liberalisation was initiated in India in the 1980's with a shift in attitude towards the private sector. Its momentum was increased from 1991 onwards. The high growth rate (8% per annum) in the post liberalization period and the future targets (9%-10%) are necessary but not sufficient. The structure of the economy has to be transformed. In this respect, though the % contribution of agriculture to GDP has been reduced to about 25% it still absorbs over 60% of the employed, while manufacturing and services contribute 28% and 55 % respectively to GDP. Over 62% of India's growth over 1990-2003 has been in services but it has been employment inelastic. Hence, the pace of industrialization has to be reinforced.

Though poverty in India has been reduced to about 26% it is critical to widen participation by the poor in development programmes. This can ensure that high growth rates are sustained. This calls for the use of labour intensive techniques, investment in human and physical capital, and infrastructure, enhanced flexibility in labour laws, and supporting institutions to meet socio-economic goals. The state has to play an active role to fulfil such goals though market forces may guide policies. This could enable the poor to be lifted from poverty.

No doubt China has grown faster and sharply reduced the % of people below the poverty line compared to India. However, inter regional and inter group inequalities in China have increased. China and India need to persist with their integration with the international economy to sustain growth. This should encompass incorporating the poor in the process, particularly in India, and reducing regional and inter-group disparities in China. Such goals are intertwined with maintaining peace within the respective regions. This is exemplified in India by efforts to minimize conflicts with neighbouring Pakistan, curbing terrorism from within and outside the state, resolving historical border disputes between India and China, and meeting the needs of dissatisfied groups within the state. In China it is essential to respect human rights.

China-India co-operation

Enhanced economic cooperation between India and China could bolster their economic power in spite of differing positions on politics and international affairs. Thus, it emerges that the economic relationship between China and India has taken place against a backdrop of tensions.

This is exemplified by China's past political, military and economic support for Pakistan, and China's claim to Arunachal Pradesh which has been vehemently challenged by India. Leaving aside such differences China and India are seen as contributors rather than competitors to each other's development. This is welcomed by India which has adopted a 'Look East' policy to expand trade and investment links with East Asia and forge strong ties with regional institutions (eg. Association of South East Asian Nations, Asia Pacific Economic Cooperation).

The recent visit of the Chinese President Hu Jintao to Delhi is a significant move in initiating a platform on development, peace and stability in Asia and the world. This was underscored by the Chinese President. He perceived the relationship between China and India as being between 'old and close brothers' citing the vision of Rabindranath Tagore the Nobel Indian poet. The

President's visit culminated in a pledge to double trade between the two nations to $ 40 billion by 2010. This contrasts with $ 250 million in the 1990's.

China and India have been competing for resources in Asia and Africa. China has been the winner in virtually all the sectors excepting technology. However, the two nations could devise policies to complement each other's need. Thus, India could meet China's growing appetite for raw materials (iron ore, steel and plastics) fuelling its massive manufacturing sector. China in turn could furnish manufacturing expertise and investment for Indian infrastructure. Indian critics of Chinese policies have expressed concern over the lack of transparency exemplified by their high level of subsidies. They are also anxious over the sharply increasing Indian imports from China of clothes, electronic goods and even fireworks. The Chinese have responded by highlighting India's blocking of their investments in ports and telecommunications. This has been justified by India on grounds of security. Overall, though, as the Chinese President reaffirmed, the relationship between China and India was "an opportunity and not a threat." This could pave the way for cooperation between China and India and enhance the nature and pace of globalization.

5

Chinese and Indian Preparations

MOTIVES

Two of the major factors leading up to China's eventual conflicts with Indian troops were India's stance on the disputed borders and perceived Indian subversion in Tibet.

There was "a perceived need to punish and end perceived Indian efforts to undermine Chinese control of Tibet, Indian efforts which were perceived as having the objective of restoring the pre-1949 status quo ante of Tibet". The other was "a perceived need to punish and end perceived Indian aggression against Chinese territory along the border". John W. Garver argues that the first perception was incorrect based on the state of the Indian military and polity in the 1960s. It was, nevertheless a major reason for China's going to war. However, he argues the Chinese perception of Indian aggression to be "substantially accurate".

The CIA's recently declassified POLO documents reveal contemporary American analysis of Chinese motives during the war. According to this document, "Chinese apparently were motivated to attack by one primary consideration — their determination to retain the ground on which PLA forces stood in 1962 and to punish the Indians for trying to take that ground". In general terms, they tried to show the Indians once and for all that China would not acquiesce in a military "reoccupation" policy.

The secondary reasons for the attack, which had made it desirable but not necessary, included a desire:

- To damage Nehru's prestige by exposing Indian weakness.
- To expose as traitorous Khrushchev's policy of supporting Nehru against a Communist country.

Another factor which might have affected China's decision for war with India was a perceived need to stop a Soviet-U.S.-India encirclement and isolation of China. India's relations with the Soviet Union and United States were both strong at this time, but the Soviets (and Americans) were preoccupied by the Cuban Missile Crisis and would not interfere with the Sino-Indian War. P. B. Sinha suggests that China waited until October to attack because the timing of the war was exactly in parallel with American actions so as to avoid any chance of American or Soviet involvement. Although American buildup of forces around Cuba occurred on the same day as the first major clash at Dhola, and China's buildup between 10 and 20 October appeared to coincide exactly with the United States establishment of a blockade against Cuba which began 20 October, the Chinese probably prepared for this before they could anticipate what would happen in Cuba. Another explanation is that the confrontation in the Taiwan Strait had eased by then.

Garver argues that the Chinese correctly assessed Indian border policies, particularly the Forward Policy, as attempts for incremental seizure of Chinese-controlled territory. On Tibet, Garver argues that one of the major factors leading to China's decision for war with India was a common tendency of humans "to attribute others behaviour to interior motivations, while attributing their own behaviour to situational factors". Studies from China published in the 1990s confirmed that the root cause for China going to war with India was the perceived Indian aggression in Tibet, with the forward policy simply catalysing the Chinese reaction.

Neville Maxwell and Allen Whiting argue that the Chinese leadership believed they were defending territory that was legitimately Chinese, and which was already under de facto Chinese occupation prior to Indian advances, and regarded the Forward

Policy as an Indian attempt at creeping annexation. Mao Zedong himself compared the Forward Policy to a strategic advance in Chinese chess:

- Their [India's] continually pushing forward is like crossing the Chu Han boundary. What should we do? We can also set out a few pawns, on our side of the river. If they don't then cross over, that's great. If they do cross, we'll eat them up [chess metaphor meaning to take the opponent's pieces]. Of course, we cannot blindly eat them. Lack of forbearance in small matters upsets great plans. We must pay attention to the situation.

India claims that the motive for the Forward Policy was to cut off the supply routes for Chinese troops posted in NEFA and Aksai Chin. According to the official Indian history, the forward policy was continued because of its initial success, as it claimed that Chinese troops withdrew when they encountered areas already occupied by Indian troops. It also claimed that the Forward Policy was having success in cutting out supply lines of Chinese troops who had advanced South of the McMahon Line, though there was no evidence of such advance before the 1962 war. However, the Forward Policy rested on the assumption that Chinese forces "were not likely to use force against any of our posts, even if they were in a position to do so". No serious re-appraisal of this policy took place even when Chinese forces ceased withdrawing. Nehru's confidence was probably justified given the difficulty for China to supply the area over the high altitude terrain over 5000 km from the more populated areas of China.

The Chinese leadership initially held a sympathetic view towards India as the latter had been ruled by British colonial masters for centuries. However, Nehru's forward policy convinced PRC leadership that the independent Indian leadership was a reincarnation of British imperialism. Mao Zedong stated: "Rather than being constantly accused of aggression, it's better to show the world what really happens when China indeed moves its muscles."

Chinese policy towards India, therefore, operated on two contradictory assumptions in the first half of 1961. On the one hand, the Chinese leaders continued to entertain a hope, although a shrinking one, that some opening for talks.would appear. On, the other hand, they read Indian statements and actions as clear signs that Nehru wanted to talk only about a Chinese withdrawal. Regarding the hope, they were willing to negotiate and tried to prod Nehru into a similar attitude. Regarding Indian intentions, they began to act politically and to build a rationale based on the assumption that Nehru already had become a lackey of imperialism; for this reason he opposed border talks.

Krishna Menon is reported to have said that when he arrived in Geneva on 6 June 1961 for an international conference in Laos, Chinese officials in Chen Yi's delegation indicated that Chen might be interested in discussing the border dispute with him. At several private meetings with Menon, Chen avoided any discussion of the dispute and Menon surmised that the Chinese wanted him to broach the matter first. He did not, as he was under instructions from Nehru to avoid taking the initiative, leaving the Chinese with the impression that Nehru was unwilling to show any flexibility.

In September, the Chinese took a step towards criticizing Nehru openly in their commentary. After citing Indonesian and Burmese press criticism of Nehru by name, the Chinese critiqued his moderate remarks on colonialism (People's Daily Editorial, 9 September) - Somebody at the Non-Aligned Nations Conference advanced the argument that the era of classical colonialism is gone and dead...contrary to facts." This was a distortion of Nehru's remarks but appeared close enough to be credible. On the same day, Chen Yi referred to Nehru by implication at the Bulgarian embassy reception: 'Those who attempted to' deny history, ignore reality, and distort the truth and who attempted to divert the Conference from its important object have failed to gain support and were isolated." On 10 September, they dropped all circumlocutions and criticized him by name in a China Youth article and NCNA report—the first time in almost two years that they had commented extensively on the Prime Minister.

By early 1962, the Chinese leadership began to believe that India's intentions were to launch a massive attack against Chinese troops, and that the Indian leadership wanted a war. In 1961, the Indian army had been sent into Goa, a small region without any other international borders apart from the Indian one, after Portugal refused to surrender the exclave colony to the Indian Union. Although this action met little to no international protest or opposition, China saw it as an example of India's expansionist nature, especially in light of heated rhetoric from Indian politicians. India's Home Minister declared, "If the Chinese will not vacate the areas occupied by it, India will have to repeat what it did in Goa. India will certainly drive out the Chinese forces", while another member of the Indian Congress Party pronounced, "India will take steps to end [Chinese] aggression on Indian soil just as it ended Portuguese aggression in Goa".

By mid-1962, it was apparent to the Chinese leadership that negotiations had failed to make any progress, and the Forward Policy was increasingly perceived as a grave threat as Delhi increasingly sent probes deeper into border areas and cut off Chinese supply lines. Foreign Minister Marshal Chen Yi commented at one high-level meeting, "Nehru's forward policy is a knife. He wants to put it in our heart. We cannot close our eyes and await death." The Chinese leadership believed that their restraint on the issue was being perceived by India as weakness, leading to continued provocations, and that a major counterblow was needed to stop perceived Indian aggression.

Xu Yan, prominent Chinese military historian and professor at the PLA's National Defence University, gives an account of the Chinese leadership's decision to go to war. By late September 1962, the Chinese leadership had begun to reconsider their policy of "armed coexistence", which had failed to address their concerns with the forward policy and Tibet, and consider a large, decisive strike. On 22 September 1962, the *People's Daily* published an article which claimed that "the Chinese people were burning with 'great indignation' over the Indian actions on the border and that New Delhi could not 'now say that warning was not served in advance'."

Military planning

The Indian side was confident war would not be triggered and made little preparations. India had only two divisions of troops in the region of the conflict. In August 1962, Brigadier D. K. Palit claimed that a war with China in the near future could be ruled out. Even in September 1962, when Indian troops were ordered to "expel the Chinese" from Thag La, Maj. General J. S. Dhillon expressed the opinion that "experience in Ladakh had shown that a few rounds fired at the Chinese would cause them to run away." Because of this, the Indian army was completely unprepared when the attack at Yumtso La occurred. Recently declassified CIA documents which were compiled at the time reveal that India's estimates of Chinese capabilities made them neglect their military in favour of economic growth. It is claimed that if a more military-minded man had been in place instead of Nehru, India would have been more likely to have been ready for the threat of a counter-attack from China.

On 6 October 1962, the Chinese leadership convened. Lin Biao reported that PLA intelligence units had determined that Indian units might assault Chinese positions at Thag La on 10 October (Operation Leghorn). The Chinese leadership and the Central Military Council decided upon war to launch a large-scale attack to punish perceived military aggression from India. In Beijing, a larger meeting of Chinese military was convened in order to plan for the coming conflict.

Mao and the Chinese leadership issued a directive laying out the objectives for the war. A main assault would be launched in the eastern sector, which would be coordinated with a smaller assault in the western sector. All Indian troops within China's claimed territories in the eastern sector would be expelled, and the war would be ended with a unilateral Chinese ceasefire and withdrawal to prewar positions, followed by a return to the negotiating table. India led the Non-Aligned Movement, Nehru enjoyed international prestige, and China, with a larger military, would be portrayed as an aggressor. However, he said that a well-fought war "will guarantee at least thirty years of peace" with India, and determined the benefits to offset the costs.

China also reportedly bought significant amount of Indian Rupee currency notes from Hong Kong, supposedly to distribute amongst its soldiers in preparation for the war.

On 8 October, additional veteran and elite divisions were ordered to prepare to move into Tibet from the Chengdu and Lanzhou military regions.

On 12 October, Nehru declared that he had ordered the Indian army to "clear Indian territory in the NEFA of Chinese invaders" and personally met with Kaul, issuing instructions to him.

On 14 October, an editorial on *People's Daily* issued China's final warning to India: "So it seems that Mr. Nehru has made up his mind to attack the Chinese frontier guards on an even bigger scale....It is high time to shout to Mr. Nehru that the heroic Chinese troops, with the glorious tradition of resisting foreign aggression, can never be cleared by anyone from their own territory... If there are still some maniacs who are reckless enough to ignore our well-intentioned advice and insist on having another try, well, let them do so. History will pronounce its inexorable verdict... At this critical moment...we still want to appeal once more to Mr. Nehru: better rein in at the edge of the precipice and do not use the lives of Indian troops as stakes in your gamble."

Marshal Liu Bocheng headed a group to determine the strategy for the war. He concluded that the opposing Indian troops were among India's best, and to achieve victory would require deploying crack troops and relying on force concentration to achieve decisive victory. On 16 October, this war plan was approved, and on the 18th, the final approval was given by the Politburo for a "self-defensive counter-attack", scheduled for 20 October.

CHINESE OFFENSIVE

On 20 October 1962, the Chinese People's Liberation Army launched two attacks, 1000 kilometres apart. In the western theatre, the PLA sought to expel Indian forces from the Chip Chap valley in Aksai Chin while in the eastern theatre, the PLA sought to capture both banks of the Namka Chu river. Some skirmishes also took place at the Nathula Pass, which is in the Indian state of Sikkim (an Indian protectorate at that time). Gurkha rifles travelling north were targeted by Chinese artillery fire. After four days of fierce fighting, the three regiments of Chinese troops succeeded in securing a substantial portion of the disputed territory.

Eastern theatre

Chinese troops launched an attack on the southern banks of the Namka Chu River on 20 October. The Indian forces were undermanned, with only an understrength battalion to support them, while the Chinese troops had three regiments positioned on the north side of the river. The Indians expected Chinese forces to cross via one of five bridges over the river and defended those crossings. However, the PLA bypassed the defenders by crossing the shallow October river instead. They formed up into battalions on the Indian-held south side of the river under cover of darkness, with each battalion assigned against a separate group of Rajputs.

At 5:14 am, Chinese mortar fire began attacking the Indian positions. Simultaneously, the Chinese cut the Indian telephone lines, preventing the defenders from making contact with their headquarters. At about 6:30 am, the Chinese infantry launched a surprise attack from the rear and forced the Indians to leave their trenches.

The Chinese troops overwhelmed the Indians in a series of flanking manoeuvres south of the McMahon Line and prompted their withdrawal from Namka Chu. Fearful of continued losses, Indian troops escaped into Bhutan. Chinese forces respected the border and did not pursue. Chinese forces now held all of the territory that was under dispute at the time of the Thag La confrontation, but they continued to advance into the rest of NEFA.

On 22 October, at 12:15 am, PLA mortars fired on Walong, on the McMahon line. Flares launched by Indian troops the next day revealed numerous Chinese milling around the valley. The Indians tried to use their mortars against the Chinese but the PLA responded by lighting a bushfire, causing confusion amongst the Indians. Some 400 Chinese troops attacked the Indian position. The initial Chinese assault was halted by accurate Indian mortar fire. The Chinese were then reinforced and launched a second assault. The Indians managed to hold them back for four hours, but the Chinese used sheer weight of numbers to break through. Most Indian forces to withdraw to established positions in Walong, while a company supported by mortars and medium machine guns remained to cover the retreat. On the morning 23 October, the Indians discovered a Chinese force gathered in a cramped pass and opened fire with mortars and machine guns, leading to heavy fighting. About 200 Chinese soldiers were killed and wounded in this action. Nine Indian soldiers were also killed. The fighting continued well into the afternoon, until the company was ordered to withdraw. Meanwhile, the 4th Sikhs made contact with the Chinese and subjected them to withering mortar and machine gun fire as the Chinese set off a brushfire and attempted to sneak forward. Sepoy Piara Singh tried to douse the fire while fighting the enemy, but died after he was wounded and refused to be evacuated.

Elsewhere, Chinese troops were launched a three-pronged attack on Tawang, which the Indians evacuated without any resistance. Over the following days, there were clashes between Indian and Chinese patrols at Walong as the Chinese rushed in reinforcements. On 25 October, the Chinese made a probe, which was met with resistance from the 4th Sikhs. As some Chinese soldiers began to close in, Sepoy Kewal Singh charged them with his bayonet and killed a few of them in hand-to-hand combat, but he himself was killed. The following day, a patrol from the 4th Sikhs was encircled, and after being unable to break the encirclement, an Indian unit sneaked in and attacked the Chinese flank, allowing the Sikhs to break free.

Western theatre

On the Aksai Chin front, China already controlled most of the disputed territory. Chinese forces quickly swept the region of any remaining Indian troops. Late on 19 October, Chinese troops launched a number of attacks throughout the western theatre. By 22 October, all posts north of Chushul had been cleared.

On 20 October, the Chinese easily took the Chip Chap Valley, Galwan Valley, and Pangong Lake. Many outposts and garrisons along the Western front were unable to defend against the surrounding Chinese troops. Most Indian troops positioned in these posts offered resistance but were either killed or taken prisoner. Indian support for these outposts was not forthcoming, as evidenced by the Galwan post, which had been surrounded by enemy forces in August, but no attempt made to relieve the besieged garrison. Following the 20 October attack, nothing was heard from Galwan.

On 24 October, Indian forces fought hard hold the Rezang La Ridge, in order to prevent a nearby airstrip from falling to the Chinese. After realising the magnitude of the attack, the Indian Western Command withdrew many of the isolated outposts to the south-east. Daulet Beg Oldi was also evacuated, but it was south of the Chinese claim line and was not approached by Chinese forces. Indian troops were withdrawn in order to consolidate and regroup in the event that China probed south of their claim line.

LULL IN THE FIGHTING

By 24 October, the PLA had entered territory previously administered by India to give the PRC a diplomatically strong position over India. The majority of Chinese forces had advanced sixteen kilometres south of the control line prior to the conflict. Four days of fighting were followed by a three-week lull. Zhou ordered the troops to stop advancing as he attempted to negotiate with Nehru. The Indian forces had retreated into more heavily fortified positions around Se La and Bombdi La which would be difficult to assault.

Zhou sent Nehru a letter, proposing

- A negotiated settlement of the boundary
- That both sides disengage and withdraw twenty kilometres from present lines of actual control
- A Chinese withdrawal north in NEFA
- That China and India not cross lines of present control in Aksai Chin.

Nehru's 27 October reply expressed interest in the restoration of peace and friendly relations and suggested a return to the "boundary prior to 8 September 1962". He was categorically concerned about a mutual twenty kilometre withdrawal after "40 or 60 kilometres of blatant military aggression". He wanted the creation of a larger immediate buffer zone and thus resist the possibility of a repeat offensive. Zhou's 4 November reply repeated his 1959 offer to return to the McMahon Line in NEFA and the Chinese traditionally claimed MacDonald Line in Aksai Chin. Facing Chinese forces maintaining themselves on Indian soil and trying to avoid political pressure, the Indian parliament announced a national emergency and passed a resolution which stated their intent to "drive out the aggressors from the sacred soil of India". The United States and the United Kingdom supported India's response. However, the Soviet Union was preoccupied with the Cuban Missile Crisis and did not offer the support it had provided in previous years. With the backing of other great powers, a 14 November letter by Nehru to Zhou once again rejected his proposal.

Neither side declared war, used their air force, or fully broke off diplomatic relations; however, the conflict is commonly referred to as a war. This war coincided with the Cuban Missile Crisis and was viewed by the western nations at the time as another act of aggression by the Communist bloc. According to Calvin, the Chinese side evidently wanted a diplomatic resolution and discontinuation of the conflict.

CONTINUATION OF WAR

After Zhou received Nehru's letter (rejecting Zhou's proposal), the fighting resumed on the eastern theatre on 14 November (Nehru's birthday), with an Indian attack on Walong, claimed by China, launched from the defensive position of Se La and inflicting heavy casualties on the Chinese. The Chinese resumed military activity on Aksai Chin and NEFA hours after the Walong battle.

Eastern theatre

On the eastern theatre, the PLA attacked Indian forces near Se La and Bomdi La on 17 November. These positions were defended by the Indian 4th Infantry Division. Instead of attacking by road as expected, PLA forces approached via a mountain trail, and their attack cut off a main road and isolated 10,000 Indian troops. Se La occupied high ground, and rather than assault this commanding position, the Chinese captured Thembang, which was a supply route to Se La.

Western theatre

On the western theatre, PLA forces launched a heavy infantry attack on 18 November near Chushul. Their attack started at 4:35 am, despite a mist surrounding most of the areas in the region. At 5:45 the Chinese troops advanced to attack 2 platoons of Indian troops at Gurung Hill.

The Indians did not know what was happening, as communications were dead. As a patrol was sent, China attacked with greater numbers. Indian artillery could not hold off against superior Chinese forces. By 9:00 am, Chinese forces attacked Gurung Hill directly and Indian commanders withdrew from the area and also from the connecting Spangur Gap.

The Chinese had been simultaneously attacking Rezang La which was held by 123 Indian troops. At 5:05 am, Chinese troops launched their attack audaciously. Chinese medium machine gun fire pierced through the Indian tactical defences.

At 6:55 am the sun rose and the Chinese attack on the 8th platoon began in waves. Fighting continued for the next hour, until the Chinese signaled that they had destroyed the 7th platoon. Indians tried to use light machine guns on the medium machine guns from the Chinese but after 10 minutes the battle was over. Logistical inadequacy once again hurt the Indian troops. The Chinese gave the Indian troops a respectful military funeral. The battles also saw the death of Major Shaitan Singh of the Kumaon Regiment, who had been instrumental in the first battle of Rezang La. The Indian troops were forced to withdraw to high mountain positions. Indian sources believed that their troops were just coming to grips with the mountain combat and finally called for more troops. However, the Chinese declared a ceasefire, ending the bloodshed.

Indians suffered heavy casualties, with dead Indian troops' bodies being found in the ice, frozen with weapons in hand. Chinese forces also suffered heavy casualties, especially at Rezang La. This signalled the end of the war in Aksai Chin as China had reached their claim line – many Indian troops were ordered to withdraw from the area. China claimed that the Indian troops wanted to fight on until the bitter end. However, the war ended with their withdrawal, so as to limit the amount of casualties.

The PLA penetrated close to the outskirts of Tezpur, Assam, a major frontier town nearly fifty kilometres from the Assam-North-East Frontier Agency border. The local government ordered the evacuation of the civilians in Tezpur to the south of the Brahmaputra River, all prisons were thrown open, and government officials who stayed behind destroyed Tezpur's currency reserves in anticipation of a Chinese advance.

CEASEFIRE

China had reached its claim lines so the PLA did not advance farther, and on 19 November, it declared a unilateral cease-fire. Zhou Enlai declared a unilateral ceasefire to start on midnight, 21 November. Zhou's ceasefire declaration stated,

- Beginning from 21 November 1962, the Chinese frontier guards will cease fire along the entire Sino-Indian border. Beginning from 1 December 1962, the Chinese frontier guards will withdraw to positions 20 kilometres behind the line of actual control which existed between China and India on 7 November 1959. In the eastern sector, although the Chinese frontier guards have so far been fighting on Chinese territory north of the traditional customary line, they are prepared to withdraw from their present positions to the north of the illegal McMahon Line, and to withdraw twenty kilometres back from that line. In the middle and western sectors, the Chinese frontier guards will withdraw twenty kilometres from the line of actual control.

Zhou had first given the ceasefire announcement to Indian chargé d'affaires on 19 November (before India's request for United States air support), but New Delhi did not receive it until 24 hours later. The aircraft carrier was ordered back after the ceasefire, and thus, American intervention on India's side in the war was avoided. Retreating Indian troops, who hadn't come into contact with anyone knowing of the ceasefire, and Chinese troops in NEFA and Aksai Chin, were involved in some minor battles, but for the most part, the ceasefire signalled an end to the fighting. The United States

Air Force flew in supplies to India in November 1962, but neither side wished to continue hostilities.

Towards the end of the war India increased its support for Tibetan refugees and revolutionaries, some of them having settled in India, as they were fighting the same common enemy in the region. The Nehru administration ordered the raising of an elite Indian-trained "Tibetan Armed Force" composed of Tibetan refugees. The CIA had already begun operations in bringing about change in Tibet.

WORLD OPINION

The Chinese military action has been viewed by the United States as part of the PRC's policy of making use of aggressive wars to settle its border disputes and to distract from its internal issues. According to James Calvin from the United States Marine Corps, western nations at the time viewed China as an aggressor during the China–India border war, and the war was part of a monolithic communist objective for a world dictatorship of the proletariat. This was further triggered by Mao Zedong's views that: "The way to world conquest lies through Havana, Accra, and Calcutta".

Calvin believes that Chinese actions show a "pattern of conservative aims and limited objectives, rather than expansionism" and blames this particular conflict on India's provocations towards China. However, Calvin also expresses that China, in the past, has been adamant to gain control over regions to which it has a "traditional claim", which triggered the dispute over NEFA and Aksai Chin and indeed Tibet. Calvin's assumption, based on the history of the Cold War and the Domino Effect, assumed that China might ultimately try to regain control of everything that it considers as "traditionally Chinese" which in its view includes the entirety of South East Asia.

The Kennedy administration was disturbed by what they considered "blatant Chinese communist aggression against India". In a May 1963 National Security Council meeting, contingency planning on the part of the United States in the event of another Chinese attack on India was discussed. Defence Secretary Robert McNamara and General Maxwell Taylor advised the president to use nuclear weapons should the Americans intervene in such a situation. McNamara stated "Before any substantial commitment to defend India against China is given, we should recognize that in order to carry out that commitment against any substantial Chinese attack, we would have to use nuclear weapons. Any large Chinese Communist attack on any part of that area would require the use of nuclear weapons by the U.S., and this is to be preferred over the introduction of large numbers of U.S. soldiers."

After hearing this and listening to two other advisers, Kennedy stated "We should defend India, and therefore we will defend India." It remains unclear if his aides were trying to dissuade the President of considering any measure with regard to India by immediately raising the stakes to an unacceptable level, nor is it clear if Kennedy was thinking of conventional or nuclear means when he gave his reply. By 1964 China had developed its own nuclear weapon which would have likely caused any American nuclear policy in defence of India to be reviewed. The Johnson Administration considered and then rejected giving nuclear weapons technology to the Indians. However India developed its own nuclear weapon by 1974, within 10 years of the Chinese.

The non-aligned nations remained mostly uninvolved, and only the United Arab Republic openly supported India. Of the non-aligned nations, six, Egypt, Burma, Cambodia, Sri Lanka, Ghana and Indonesia, met in Colombo on 10 December 1962. The proposals stipulated a Chinese withdrawal of 20 km from the customary lines without any reciprocal withdrawal on India's behalf. The failure of these six nations to unequivocally condemn China deeply disappointed India.

In 1972, Chinese Premier Zhou explained the Chinese point of view to President Nixon of the US. As for the causes of the war, Zhou asserted that China did not try to expel Indian troops from south of the McMahon line and that three open warning telegrams were sent to Nehru before the war. However, Indian patrols south of the McMahon line were expelled and suffered casualties in the Chinese attack. Zhou also told Nixon that Chairman Mao ordered the troops to return to show good faith. The Indian government maintains that the Chinese military could not advance further south due to logistical problems and the cut-off of resource supplies. While Western nations did not view Chinese actions favourably because of fear of the Chinese and competitiveness, Pakistan, which had had a turbulent relationship with India ever since the Indian partition, improved its relations with China after the war. Prior to the war, Pakistan also shared a disputed boundary with China, and had proposed to India that the two countries adopt a common defence against "northern" enemies (*i.e.* China), which was rejected by India. However, China and Pakistan took steps to peacefully negotiate their shared boundaries, beginning on 13 October 1962, and concluding in December of that year.

Pakistan also expressed fear that the huge amounts of western military aid directed to India would allow it to threaten Pakistan's security in future conflicts. Mohammed Ali, External Affairs Minister of Pakistan, declared that massive Western aid to India in the Sino-Indian dispute would be considered an unfriendly act towards Pakistan. As a result Pakistan made efforts to improve its relations with China. The following year, China and Pakistan peacefully settled disputes on their shared border, and negotiated the China-Pakistan Border Treaty in 1963, as well as trade, commercial, and barter treaties. On 2 March 1963, Pakistan conceded its northern claim line in Pakistani-controlled Kashmir to China in favour of a more southerly boundary along the Karakoram Range.

The border treaty largely set the border along the MacCartney-Macdonald Line. India's military failure against China would embolden Pakistan to initiate the Second Kashmir War with India. However, it effectively ended in a stalemate as Calvin states that the Sino-Indian War had caused the previously passive government to take a stand on actively modernising India's military.

China offered diplomatic support to Pakistan in this war but did not offer military support. In January 1966, China condemned the Tashkent Agreement between India and Pakistan as a Soviet-US plot in the region. In the Indo-Pakistani War of 1971, Pakistan expected China to provide military support, but it was left alone as India successfully helped the rebels in East Pakistan to found the new nation-state of Bangladesh.

INVOLVEMENT OF OTHER NATIONS

During the conflict, Nehru wrote two desperate letters to U.S. President John F. Kennedy, requesting 12 squadrons of fighter jets and a modern radar system. These jets were seen as necessary to beef up Indian air strength so that air to air combat could be initiated safely from the Indian perspective (bombing troops was seen as unwise for fear of Chinese retaliatory action).

Nehru also asked that these aircraft be manned by American pilots until Indian airmen were trained to replace them. These requests were rejected by the Kennedy Administration (which was involved in the Cuban Missile Crisis during most of the Sino-Indian War). According to former Indian diplomat G Parthasarathy, "only after we got nothing from the US did arms supplies from the Soviet Union to India commence." In 1962, President of Pakistan Ayub Khan made clear to India that Indian troops could safely be transferred from the Pakistan frontier to the Himalayas.

AFTERMATH

China

According to the China's official military history, the war achieved China's policy objectives of securing borders in its western sector, as China retained de facto control of the Aksai Chin. After the war, India abandoned the Forward Policy, and the de facto borders stabilised along the Line of Actual Control.

According to James Calvin of Marine Corps Command and Staff College, even though China won a military victory it lost in terms of its international image. China's first nuclear weapon test in October 1964 and it support of Pakistan in the 1965 India Pakistan War tended to confirm the American view of communist world objectives, including Chinese influence over Pakistan.

Lora Saalman opined in a study of Chinese military publications, that while the war led to much blame, debates and ultimately acted as causation of military modernization of India but the war is now treated as basic reportage of facts with relatively diminished interest by Chinese analysts.

India

The aftermath of the war saw sweeping changes in the Indian military to prepare it for similar conflicts in the future, and placed pressure on Indian prime minister Jawaharlal Nehru, who was seen as responsible for failing to anticipate the Chinese attack on India. Indians reacted with a surge in patriotism and memorials were erected for many of the Indian troops who died in the war.

Arguably, the main lesson India learned from the war was the need to strengthen its own defences and a shift from Nehru's foreign policy with China based on his stated concept of "brotherhood". Because of India's inability to anticipate Chinese aggression, Prime Minister Nehru faced harsh criticism from government officials, for having promoted pacifist relations with China. Indian President Radhakrishnan said that Nehru's government was naive and negligent about preparations, and Nehru admitted his failings. According to Inder Malhotra, a former editor of *The Times of India* and a commentator for *The Indian Express*, Indian politicians invested more effort in removing Defence Minister Krishna Menon than in actually waging war. Krishna Menon's favouritism weakened the Indian Army, and national morale dimmed.

The public saw the war as political and military debacle. Under American advice (by American envoy John Kenneth Galbraith who made and ran American policy on the war as all other top policy makers in USA were absorbed in coincident Cuban Missile Crisis) Indians refrained, not according to the best choices available, from using the Indian air force to beat back the Chinese advances.

The CIA later revealed that at that time the Chinese had neither the fuel nor runways long enough for using their air force effectively in Tibet. Indians in general became highly sceptical of China and its military. Many Indians view the war as a betrayal of India's attempts at establishing a long-standing peace with China and started to question the once popular "Hindi-Chini bhai-bhai" (meaning "Indians and Chinese are brothers"). The war also put an end to Nehru's earlier hopes that India and China would form a strong Asian Axis to counteract the increasing influence of the Cold War bloc superpowers.

The unpreparedness of the army was blamed on Defence Minister Menon, who resigned his government post to allow for someone who might modernise India's military further. India's policy of weaponisation via indigenous sources and self-sufficiency was thus cemented. Sensing a weakened army, Pakistan, a close ally of China, began a policy of provocation against India by infiltrating Jammu and Kashmir and ultimately triggering the Second Kashmir War with India in 1965 and Indo-Pakistani war of 1971. The Attack of 1965 was successfully stopped and ceasefire was negotiated under international pressure. In the Indo-Pakistani war of 1971 India won a clear victory, resulting in liberation of Bangladesh (formerly East-Pakistan).

As a result of the war, the Indian government commissioned an investigation, resulting in the classified Henderson-Brooks-Bhagat Report on the causes of the war and the reasons for failure. India's performance in high-altitude combat in 1962 led to an overhaul of the Indian Army in terms of doctrine, training, organisation and equipment. Neville Maxwell claimed that the Indian role in international affairs after the border war was also greatly reduced after the war and India's standing in the non-aligned movement suffered.

According to James Calvin, an analyst from the U.S. Navy, India gained many benefits from the 1962 conflict. This war united the country as never before. India got 32,000 square miles (8.3 million hectares, 83,000 km) of disputed territory even if it felt that NEFA was hers all along. The new Indian republic had avoided international alignments; by asking for help during the war, India demonstrated its willingness to accept military aid from several sectors. And, finally, India recognised the serious weaknesses in its army. It would more than double its military manpower in the next two years and it would work hard to resolve the military's training and logistic problems to later become the third-largest army in the world. India's efforts to improve its military posture significantly enhanced its army's capabilities and preparedness. This played a role in subsequent wars against Pakistan.

Internment and Deportation of Chinese Indians

Soon after the end of the war, the Indian government passed the Defence of India Act in December 1962, permitting the "apprehension and detention in custody of any person [suspected] of being of hostile origin." The broad language of the act allowed for the arrest of any person simply for having a Chinese surname, a drop of Chinese blood, or a Chinese spouse. The Indian government incarcerated thousands of Chinese-Indians in an internment camp in Deoli, Rajasthan, where they were held for years without trial. The last internees were not released until 1967. Thousands more Chinese-Indians were forcibly deported or coerced to leave India. Nearly all internees had their properties sold off or looted. Even after their release, the Chinese Indians faced many restrictions in their freedom. They could not travel freely until the mid-1990s.

LATER CONFLICTS

India also reported a series of military conflicts after the 1962 war. One report provided by India shows that in late 1967, there were two incidents in which both countries exchanged fire in Sikkim. The first one was dubbed the "Nathu La incident", and the other being "Chola incident".

DIPLOMATIC PROCESS

In 1993 and 1996, the two sides signed the Sino-Indian Bilateral Peace and Tranquility Accords, agreements to maintain peace and tranquility along the Line of Actual Control (LoAC). Ten meetings of a Sino-Indian Joint Working Group (SIJWG) and five of an expert group have taken place to determine where the LoAC lies, but little progress has occurred.

On 20 November 2006 Indian politicians from Arunachal Pradesh expressed their concern over Chinese military modernization and appealed to parliament to take a harder stance on the PRC following a military buildup on the border similar to that in 1962. Additionally, China's military aid to Pakistan as well is a matter of concern to the Indian public, as the two sides have engaged in various wars.

On 6 July 2006, the historic Silk Road passing through this territory via the Nathu La pass was reopened. Both sides have agreed to resolve the issues by peaceful means.

In Oct 2011, it was stated that India and China will formulate a border mechanism to handle different perceptions as to the LAC and resume the bilateral army exercises between Indian and Chinese army from early 2012.

SINO-INDIAN TIES: NEED FOR BOLD INITIATIVES

According to most available estimates, the normalisation of Sino-Indian ties to their pre-Pokhran II process of rapprochement seems to be taking far too much time. This is primarily because, putting these tests in the backdrop of India's nuclear explosion of May 1974, most Indians had visualised this second series of India's nuclear tests as having only declared and demonstrated the capabilities that India was known to have had all these years. Accordingly, China was not only expected to be well aware of India's nuclear capabilities but was also believed to be fully prepared to deal with such an eventuality, as and whenever it arose. Besides, there were other reasons to doubt the credibility (as also the longevity) of China's harsh reactions against India's nuclear tests. First of all, China, in fact, had been an ardent defender of India's sovereign right to keep its nuclear option open. Therefore, the very motives of China becoming the torch-bearer for the nuclear weapon powers' anti-India campaign—that ironically still revolves around their old and ineffective prescription of "cap, reduce and eliminate" India's nuclear programme—were not only highly confusing and but even suspect right from the beginning. But the same seems to be the case with most Chinese officials and experts, many of whom have also continued to grapple with the actual impact of India's nuclear explosions of May 1998.

Most experts had brushed aside Beijing's initial reactions to India's nuclear tests as either a mere exercise in public relations or borne out of a knee-jerk panic reaction which was expected to subside with the passage of time. Even the Indian Prime Minister's letter to President Clinton was either completely ignored or defended or simply underplayed. The significance of this letter—

which cited China's nuclear weapons and their proliferation to India's western neighbour as the reason for India going nuclear—was sought to be brushed aside by saying that the Chinese would have reacted this harshly with or without this letter. All, it was said, this letter had done was to provide the Chinese side with a perfect excuse to raise their anti-India clamour at various global and regional meets. In retrospect, this had not only pushed important issues to the margins but also caused further delay in both sides coming to terms with each other's misperceptions and apprehensions. Also, contrary to all expectations, this very letter was to gradually emerge to form the very core of China's critique of India's post-Pokhran II nuclear policy postures. The two sides have, of course, moved much further since then and this letter has gradually been allowed to move to the periphery as more substantive Sino-Indian contentions have come to the forefront. Nevertheless, it is the contention of this article that, apart from the confusion that was generated by the heat and dust of the nuclear explosion of May 1998 as also by the explanations that followed, it is either the faulty understanding of each other's security sensibilities or lack of willingness to appreciate each other's security needs that has been responsible for this lack of any major success in limiting the fallout of these nuclear tests on the future of Sino-Indian ties. And nothing reflects it better than their attempts at interpreting this post-Pokhran II new reality that has so far been painted simply as seen from either side.

INTERPRETING NEW REALITIES

No doubt, there was definitely an element of rhetoric and public relations in China's initial reactions to India's nuclear tests. However, with the passage of time, what has gradually come to the fore is the fact that the advent of two nuclear weapon states on its southern borders has perturbed China's leaders far more deeply than what has been either highlighted in China's official reactions or appreciated in most Indian commentaries. At the least, this new reality has completely upset Beijing's security paradigms for the 21st century world. Thanks partly to the assessments and analysis of China's India experts, the challenge to China's uncontested rise had been least expected from its southern frontiers where the most powerful country—India—was being dealt with their time-tested double-edged policy of slow-moving confidence building measures (CBMs) while simultaneously China also continued aiding and abetting Pakistan's nuclear and missile capabilities. But this constantly increasing proximity with both India and Pakistan was a contradiction in terms. And the nuclear tests in Pokhran and Chagai were perhaps the natural outcome of such contradiction. And now, with two of these South Asian powers going overtly nuclear, the new reality, unlike the past, does not seem to conform to Beijing's policy framework. This is simply because, despite its increasing engagements in the Near and Far East, greater resources and attention may have now be devoted for dealing with these new challenges from its southern frontiers.

Accordingly, with the passage of time, as China's leaders revalue their expert analysis on these post-Pokhran II realities of Sino-Indian ties, this weakening of rhetoric has been gradually replaced by relatively hardened attitudes as also by far too well thought out expressions of their India policy. To give one example, while China has lately toned down its international campaign on seeking reversal of India's nuclear policies, it has simply shifted the pressure on bilateral policies.1 At the core of the current bilateral stalemate, as of now, the "hurt" caused by India's nuclear tests and their explanations remains at the core of the Chinese critique. They have since continued to stress that it is India which has to "untie these knots" in Sino-Indian ties. According to various official and non-official statements from China, Beijing perhaps expects India to demonstrate its sincerity in building rapprochement by taking what it calls some "concrete steps" in that direction. These "concrete steps", however, remain undefined, which has further complicated India's policy choices. Most interpretations, however, broadly hint that China perhaps wishes New Delhi to retreat from it position whereby it explained its decision to conduct nuclear tests in terms of China's nuclear weapons and their proliferation and described China as its potential threat number one. As a result, there are far too many important questions that have today come to the table. The problem, however, is that both sides have not yet been able to agree to sit across this table and take these issues one by one.

There is no doubt that India understands its responsibilities. Partly this is borne out of various initiatives that the Indian side has been taking at all possible levels and forums. However, all this does not seem to as yet assuage China's feelings. But, for some, that perhaps has been the normal, well-known refrain in Sino-Indian ties since the early 1950s. Notwithstanding all this, one thing remains very clear that, even today, New Delhi is not likely to be found wanting in taking positive initiatives provided there is an appropriate place and time for this as also a more or less positive response from the Chinese side. This is because by doing so, India will only be carrying further its time-tested tradition of taking bold political initiatives for improving Sino-Indian ties. However, such a policy may have its own limitations in the entirely new context of Sino-Indian nuclear stalemate following India's decision to exercise its nuclear weapon option. This proposition has also to be qualified by the following two conditions. One, that India does not need any certification for its nuclear weapon status but sees its efforts at reviving Sino-Indian rapprochement as part of its efforts at further strengthening India's image as a peace-loving country and to demonstate its commitment towards its long-standing disarmament policies. Secondly, any such decision to make the first move towards rapprochement will not mean any deviation from India's past record and, in fact, it fully conforms to the ethos of India's China policy over the last five decades.

Also, considering that historically Indian leaders have always sought security-in-peace and not peace-in-security, it falls in line with India's ethos, the current strategic thinking and future security needs. Therefore, to provide them appropriate atmospherics and meaning, India's policy initiatives vis-à-vis China would have to be viewed as very much part of India's larger policy objectives for international peace. However, compared with India's fire-fighting approach in responding to China's initial critical statements, dealing with China may now need a far more planned, integrated and piecemeal approach that should stress on areas of agreement while, at the same time, provide this long-term process a kick-start in the form of bold political initiatives from the highest level. While the results of such initiatives, as also the time-frame for achieving such results, may be difficult to predict, such a bold policy decision to be the first is not likely to have any adverse impact in terms of India's domestic politics. In fact, if anything, the impact of such bold political initiatives in the past has only been positive.

India's Track Record

In fact, going by the track record of the last 50 years, or even earlier, India's leaders have never been found wanting in taking bold political initiatives regardless of the fact as to who had tied the so-called knots and for what purpose. In fact, Prime Minister Atal Bihari Vajpayee, himself had been the first Indian Foreign Minister ever to visit Beijing in 1979. To recall a few of the major examples, India was not only amongst the first to recognise the new Communist regime but also at the forefront of defending China's membership of the UN Security Council while the Americans were sending feelers to New Delhi that India could well replace China as the permanent member at the UN Security Council. Even the 1962 war did not change New Delhi's policy stance on this issue and China was finally inducted into the United Nations in 1971. Later, during the second phase of Sino-Indian rapprochement as well, India was the first to announce as well as exchange Ambassadors (July 1975), and again the first to send its Foreign Minister (February 1979), Prime Minister (December 1988) and President (May 1992) to Beijing. This, of course, is not to say that China did not make any contribution to the process of Sino-Indian friendship. Nevertheless, China's reactions had often been long-drawn, reluctant and from the periphery of China's leadership, though the tenor in the end was invariably positive.

Especially seen in the backdrop of Prime Minister Jawaharlal Nehru's decision to surrender India's historic "presence" in Tibet followed by the Dalai Lama's arrival in India in 1959 and the Sino-Indian border war of 1962, the visit by Prime Minister Rajiv Gandhi in December 1988, had marked the most critical historic initiative by New Delhi that was aimed at building Sino-Indian rapprochement. During this visit, New Delhi virtually took a U-turn and agreed to the Chinese position that asked both sides to concentrate on areas of agreement and put aside difficult issues until the two sides had generated the required level of mutual confidence to resolve those disputes. The strength of such bold political initiatives has also to be seen in the face of the fact that there was a historic November 1962 resolution of India's Parliament that bound successive ruling regimes in India to open relations with China only after taking back "every inch" of India's sacred territory that was either claimed by, or under the occupation of, the Chinese. Accordingly, this was perhaps the most important instance when India's leaders so clearly demonstrated its commitment to making all possible efforts towards improving ties with China.

To appreciate the fact that this strategic U-turn by India was not an aberration, one has to see this historic visit as the culmination of the log-term initiatives that were started during Mrs. Indira Gandhi's regime. This piecemeal approach that had already begun to improve Sino-Indian ties since the early 1970s, raised diplomatic ties to Ambassador level in 1975, and carried out border talks from 1981. It is in this backdrop that the November 1988 resolution of the All India Congress Committee was seen as technically enabling Rajiv Gandhi's government to open formal negotiations with China. This resolution briefly urged the Rajiv Gandhi government to seek a settlement with China through "peaceful negotiations" based on "mutual interests" and "acceptable to the people of both countries", even if it took time. Even the Chinese scholars have recognised the importance of India's initiatives in building Sino-Indian rapprochement. For example, when, following the Tiananmen Square incidents of June 1989, most Western powers had imposed sanctions and isolated China, the period between the second half of 1989 and 1990 witnessed 10 high-level visits exchanged between India and China. These included visits by Vice Premier Wu Xueguian in October 1989 and by Foreign Minister Qian Qichen in March 1990.4 Moreover, barely five weeks following the historic incidents at the Tiananmen Square, the annual meeting of the Sino-Indian Joint Working Group on the Boundary Question was held as scheduled for July 1, 1989. What more could have demonstrated India's sincerity in improving Sino-Indian ties?

China's Policy Options

While India has always been at the forefront of making initiatives, China, on the other hand, has been generally slow and reluctant, though its belated response was nevertheless always positive and made India's initiatives workable. However, this has not been necessarily the result of some ill will on the part of Beijing. Instead, it is partly the outcome of policy perceptions from both sides which, of course, continue to be varied. Due to their respective historical legacies, compulsions and priorities, while China has perhaps been relatively higher in India's list of foreign policy priorities, the same has not been true of India's place in the case of China's list of priorities. In line with China's so-called "Middle Kingdom" syndrome, China's leaders have always sought to compare themselves with big powers like the United States and the former Soviet Union (now Russia).

Accordingly, while China viewed itself in the larger global context, it has historically tried to deal with India in a smaller regional framework of either Asia or, lately, in the still smaller context of the South Asian subcontinent. And, in this case, Beijing's policy towards India simply aimed at the following two objectives: (i) propping up India's smaller neighbours to keep New Delhi tied down to the South Asian region; and (ii) continuing the rapprochement efforts by accepting an extremely slow-moving process of CBMs. But China's ever expanding indulgence, aimed at enabling Pakistan to be a counter-balance against New Delhi, was to gradually lead New Delhi to lose patience with China's slow pace in the process of CBMs. These contradictory policies were finally to result in India breaking out of China's traditional low-cost India policy by finally exercising its nuclear weapon option, and India's capabilities today can no longer be dealt with by China in that old framework of the Indian subcontinent.

China, as a result, is in a difficult position today to continue to pay lip service to its desire to solve problems with India, as it is now required to respond to the new hard realities of a nuclear India. Beijing is accordingly required to move from its traditional approach of abetting Pakistan towards a more substantive nuclear policy towards South Asia in general and India in particular. No doubt, China's best interests will be served by making sure that India gives up its resolve to develop the nuclear deterrent vis-à-vis China and that Pakistan remains subservient to Beijing's piecemeal transfers in these sensitive technologies. But since that status quo has already been challenged by the nuclear explosions by India and Pakistan, the second best option available to China is to make sure that India's nuclear weapons remain focused or even equated with those of Pakistan and, therefore, never visualised or actually deployed for dealing with China's nuclear capabilities. And here, assessing the inevitability of the new realities, China has already moved away from seeking their roll-back or total elimination to stressing more and more on containing their negative fallout for Beijing. What makes China's policy options all the more limited is that, even after its decision to go nuclear, India continued to swear by its commitment to general and comprehensive nuclear disarmament. New Delhi believes that it is in a non-nuclear environment that its national interests will be best served. Also, even after demonstrating the capability to design and develop fairly sophisticated nuclear weapons, New Delhi has already announced its commitment to the doctrine of no-first-use and minimum deterrence that has further weakened China's credentials in raising anti-India campaigns at various global and regional forums.

But this should, in no way, obtain India any more leeway, for continued failure to open a dialogue with the Chinese can only further increase New Delhi's difficulties in sustaining such pacific postures. This is because leaders in New Delhi have to constantly seek approval for their policy postures from the masses who, thanks to the television era, have become much more aware and vigilant. Accordingly, New Delhi may come under domestic pressures for persisting with the olive branch for far too long, especially if the attitude in Beijing remains one of apathy or negation. It is not understandable to most Indians as to why China has been so averse to holding talks at established forums like the Sino-Indian Joint Working Group on the Boundary Question. The very ideal behind creating such a forum was to sort out all such differences under difficult circumstances. Sitting across the table, the two sides are sure to be in a much better position to explain their policy postures. This will any day better be than holding negotiations through the media or through third country forums where India is not even present. This confidence that talks will do only better is borne out of the good working relationship that the two sides have so assiduously evolved during the last three decades of Sino-Indian rapprochement.

Enhancing Areas of Agreement

To recall their cooperation before India's nuclear explosions last year, both India and China had evolved, over the years, a fairly good working relationship at various bilateral, regional and international forums. So much so that their cooperation at forums like the UN Human Rights Commission annual session at Geneva had come to be a major irritant in the Western powers' campaign to censure China (and India) on the question of human rights. While there is no dearth of examples on India's initiatives and many of these have already been listed under the aforesaid section on "India's Track Record", the important fact is that the 1990s had witnessed even the reluctant Chinese making an eloquent contribution to the Sino-Indian rapprochement. To give some examples of China's major conciliatory initiatives, Kashmir perhaps forms one good example where China had become increasingly objective in its assessment even at the cost of its closest ally, Pakistan. Though it was from the early 1980s that China had gradually evolved a more neutral tone in its statements on the Kashmir question, it was the Narasimha Rao-Li Peng Joint Statement of 1991 that provided the most favoured expression from the highest level of China's leadership. The statement clearly described Kashmir as a bilateral dispute between India and Pakistan and urged both sides to resolve it under the framework of the Shimla Agreement. By doing this, China in fact had nearly endorsed India's own position with relation to Jammu & Kashmir province.

Later, in December 1996, President Jiang Zemin, in fact, went a step further and suggested in his address to Pakistan's Senate that both sides should set aside their pending problematic issues left over by history and build a stronger network of ties in areas of mutual agreement. Also, it was the persuasion by China (and

Iran) that resulted in Pakistan withdrawing its resolution on Kashmir at the UN Human Rights Commission's annual session at Geneva in March 1996. Similarly, in January 1995, when the Western powers had withdrawn the promise of supplying fissile fuel for India's Tarapore nuclear power plant, it was China that had come forward and supplied one instalment of enriched uranium. Similarly, the two countries had evolved a strong working relationship at various regional forums, be it in the Indian Ocean or East Asia. Most scholars have seen this goodwill as a result of expanding interactions between these two countries. India, for example, hosted the the China Fair in 1991 and later China hosted the India Fair in 1993. The two sides in 1995 became Asia's first two countries to actually implement disarmament as both of them agreed to pull out four military posts in the Wangdong region in the Eastern Sector where troops had been deployed at alarming proximity to each other. But the most important factor expanding their mutual stakes had been perhaps their bilateral trade since the early 1990s. By 1994, India had actually become China's largest trading partner from South Asia, thus, crossing Beijing's closest ally, Pakistan. This boosted their mutual confidence in such a way that the Joint Sino-Indian Business Council, in fact, declared in the 1997 meeting at Beijing that their bilateral trade would increase by at least five times during the 1990s decade, thus, crossing the $ 4 billion figure by the year 2000. And especially the fact that the post-Pokhran II confusion in Sino-Indian ties has not really affected their bilateral trade all that much makes it the strongest as also the most reliable (and most agreeable) pillar of Sino-Indian rapprochement during the 1990s. And this is perhaps one area that promises to bear dividends for the future as well.

Bilateral Trade: Positive Trends

Going by the experience of the last two decades, Sino-Indian trade has been one aspect of their bilateral ties that has shown constant improvement. According to recently released statistics by the China State Statistical Bureau for the last 20 years—1978-1997—while China's total international trade has gone up by 14 times, the Sino-Indian trade has gone up by 16 times during the same period. Also, despite the apparent reluctance in India's business community to invest in China, both China and India have already established over 50 big and small joint ventures in various areas. Over two dozen Indian companies are today doing business with their Chinese counterparts with most of them being success stories. But the importance of Sino-Indian trade cannot be gauged from statistics alone. In fact, the value of Sino-Indian trade does not really lie in terms of its total volume, which, however remains limited. Instead, its value has to be seen in terms of its intangible benefits in resolving Sino-Indian ties and these have made an important contribution. Viewed as a CBM, Sino-Indian trade has led to greater (a) mutual confidence; (b) mutual commitment; and (c) greater transparency (i) in the interactions of their border communities and (ii) in the willingness to collaborate on the part of their national elite from both sides.

Their border trade may have remained extremely low as a percentage of their total bilateral trade volume, yet, considering the freedom and interaction that it has brought for the border communities from both sides, it has greatly improved mutual trust on both sides. The two sides have, for example, free trade in 15 local items which include yak-tail, salt, borax, China clay, China silk, etc. Obviously, transactions in these items are not capital intensive and are not going to be correctly reflected when seen in terms of their monetary value. Nevertheless, increased border trade during the 1990s has resulted in the revival of various related cottage industries. In Pithoragarh district of India, for example, this has resulted in the revival of the carpet-weaving industry which had been completely shut down as it depended entirely on Tibetan wool. And finally, this border trade has also to be seen in the backdrop of the poor road and communication infrastructure and generally backward conditions of these border communities. And, in that context, this increased activity has resulted in generating momentum leading to improvement in these remote regions which ensures peace and stability in these otherwise disputed borders between China and India. Apart from improving the interactions and living standards of the border communities, their border trade has also facilitated the border management activities by both countries' personnel deployed for maintaining peace and tranquillity in the Sino-Indian border regions.

What perhaps most clearly brings out the strength of positive trends in Sino-Indian trade is that nothing of the recent temporary political problems following the nuclear tests of May 1998 seems to have affected the normal pace of improvement throughout last year. For example, even in the post-Pokhran II context of nuclear stalemate between India and China, scholars from China have continued to advocate for concepts like sub-regional cooperation between China's south-western and India's north-eastern regions which have remained relatively neglected in terms of building infrastructure for development.

Though the symbolic cancellation of the China Commodity Fair in Mumbai and China's low-profile presence during last year's India International Trade Fair in New Delhi did create a flutter amongst businessmen on both sides, the projections for 1998—based on half yearly trade statistics compiled by the Confederation of Indian Industry (CII)—clearly project how Sino-Indian trade does not even seem to notice India's nuclear tests at all. Especially, compared to China's recent trade statistics vis-a-vis East Asian countries this, in fact, shows encouraging signs for the future of Sino-Indian ties. In the long term, therefore, making efforts towards expanding mutual trade and investments can be one sure way of enhancing mutual stakes for building peace and security between India and China. But, looking at the continued stalemate in Sino-Indian ties, this would perhaps require some sort of a kick-start by bold political initiatives.

Atmospherics for Political Initiatives

Apart from these positive trends in Sino-Indian trade and commerce in the post-Pokhran II period, the first indicator of positive atmospherics in terms of bilateral relations was witnessed in the month of October (1998) when the first delegation of Indian academics visiting Beijing at the invitation of the China Institute for Contemporary International Relations (CICIR) which organised a seminar on the future of Sino-Indian ties. In response, a 16-member Chinese delegation (academics from the provinces of

Yunnan, Sichuan, and Beijing) travelled to the Indian cities of Calcutta, New Delhi, Mumbai, Bangalore and Chennai where it participated in seminars and meetings on Sino-Indian ties during November-December 1998. Besides, various other Sino-Indian businessmen and experts, continued to exchange visits at their normal, earlier pace. All this portends more positive interactions at the formal level as well, and indications are that Sino-Indian ties may gather greater momentum during 1999.

Equally important initiatives have also been taken at the highest level of India's leadership. Jaswant Singh (then as the Prime Minister's special emissary) held a meeting in September 1998 with China's Foreign Minister, Tang Jiaxuan, during the Asean Regional Forum's (ARF) annual meet at Manila. This had generated speculations that Jaswant Singh may be leading another high-level dialogue with China, just like the one he has been holding with Strobe Talbott of the United States. Such ideas have been further strengthened by the Prime Minister's statements in Parliament as also by repeated statements by the Prime Minister's Principal Secretary, Brijesh Mishra, echoing sentiments in favour of improving Sino-Indian ties. In fact, following Jaswant Singh's taking over as Foreign Minister during December 1998, the possibilities for an early Sino-Indian dialogue are understood to have increased manifold.

This is partly because, according to Press reports, in his letter of congratulations to Jaswant Singh, China's Foreign Minister Tang Jiaxuan, expressed the hope that under his stewardship of India's Ministry of External Affairs, China and India should be able to further "consolidate and develop" the friendly and good neighbourly relations between their two nations. An equally positive response was reportedly provided by Jaswant Singh's reply to Tang Jiaxuan's letter. Also, addressing his first formal Press conference after taking over as Foreign Minister, Jaswant Singh reiterated India's commitment to "further improving" ties with China and he urged China's leaders to help India "untie the knots" through frequent consultations and dialogue. And going by the current whispers-in-the-wind, the official Sino-Indian dialogue is now expected to begin some time early next year.

To conclude, therefore, it is only a matter of time for the Sino-India rapprochement to come back to its normal equilibrium. Looking at China's own example, India can perhaps afford to wait or even ignore China's criticism. In the face of China's own nuclear explosion in October 1964, the Kennedy Administration had even thought of physically eliminating China's nuclear facilities.

In such adversity, Beijing had, however, continued to denounce American reactions to its nuclear weapons and Washington had to finally give up its policies and build détente with the Chinese. And going by their interactions during 1990, the two sides have since evolved into strategic partners. So much so that, in the case of the Indian tests, China seems to be speaking the language of the United States, and President Clinton seems to have given China a free hand in leading the anti-Indian campaign on behalf the Five Nuclear Weapon Powers. However, it is not the outcome but the time involved that is important. And here, New Delhi may not feel the need for a Chinese certification of India's nuclear weapon power status and also it may be in position to wait and watch until China decides to come around and recognise the new reality of India's nuclear weapons; yet, there are reasons why the two sides should hasten to open their official dialogue.

However, these comparisons from history have their own limitations. First of all, the non-proliferation lobby seems today far better organised and far more coercive in nature. Its leader, the United States, is also no longer either deterred by a parallel superpower (like the Soviet Union) or embroiled in any Vietnam War type protracted quagmire. China, on the other hand, happens to be the most adversely affected party from India's decision to exercise its nuclear option, and its disaffection is clearly being used by the non-proliferation lobbies to wedge further distrust between India and China. But, at the same time, India's nuclear tests happen to be a reality which cannot be "dis-invented", and all parties involved have to come to terms with this basic fact. In such as a scenario, any hardened attitude by China (and other nuclear weapon powers) will only make India stick to its guns and become far more defensive and perhaps inflexible in any unduly delayed negotiations. The only way to evolve mutual understanding, therefore, is dialogue and deliberation at an early date.

Considering the fact that it is the evolution of Sino-Indian good neighbourly relations and not browbeating that happens to be India's objective, any indefinite delay will only further weaken the prospects for peace between India and China. This will also further reduce their options in opening talks and make matters far more difficult for both sides. All this makes it imperative for both Beijing and New Delhi to put a premium on time and try to resolve their ties as early as possible. However, opening a serious official dialogue may, once again, require, some bold political initiatives. As regards India, this should not deter New Delhi from taking initiatives like proposing a Foreign Minister's visit to Beijing for this would well conform to India's China policy of the last 50 years. But the Chinese side will also have to, once again make a contribution by positively responding to India's initiatives for opening a high-level official dialogue.

6

Scenario of Resolving India-China Boundary Argument

Today, some security experts such as Mr. Bharat Verma, the editor of *Indian Defence Review*, in this world are still talking about China's military attacks on India before 2012, or even within 6 months.

However, such noises cannot halt the historic wheels of Chindia partnership from rolling forward. As the two new emerging powers, their leaders know clearly that each is not a threat to the other. China has been called the world workshop whileIndia the world office. In the course of their rise, the challenges they will face are the same or similar. They need more policy coordination and more functional cooperation in the world dominated by the developed nations in the global platforms such as G20, BRIC, BASIC, and China-Russia- India Trilateral Dialogue. Chinaand India joined hands last year during the United Nations Climate Change Conference in Copenhagen, effectively presenting the stance of emerging economies and developing countries on climate change.

For the past 10 years, the two governments have made joint efforts to cement and strengthen their bilateral relations. In 2003, Indian Prime Minister Atal Vajpayee visited China and signed Declaration on Principles for Relations and Comprehensive Cooperation between China and India. Both sides reaffirmed that they would promote a long-term constructive and cooperative partnership.

They emphasized that their common interests outweigh their differences. The two countries are not a threat to each other. Neither side shall use or threaten to use force against the other.

They are committed to qualitatively enhance the bilateral relationship at all levels and in all areas while addressing differences through peaceful means in a fair, reasonable and mutually acceptable manner. They emphasized that the differences should not be allowed to affect the overall development of bilateral relations.

On the border question, they reiterate their determination to seek a fair, reasonable, and mutually acceptable solution through consultations on an equal footing. They agreed that pending an ultimate solution, they should work together to maintain peace and tranquility in the border areas, continue implementation of h agreements signed for this purpose, including the clarification of the line of actual control. The two governments decided to appoint special representatives to promote the process of the border negotiations.

As one of the sensitive issues in the China-India relations, India recognizes that the Tibet Autonomous Region is part of the territory of the People's Republic of China and India does not allow Tibetans to engage in anti-China political activities in India.

In recent years, the trade relationship between the two countries has been seen in both countries as a crucial driver of overall bilateral relations, amid persisting political strains over the long-running border dispute.

China became India's largest trading partner in 2008, with bilateral trade reaching $52 billion. Trade fell to $43 billion on account of the financial crisis, but has rebounded in the first two months of this year with Indian exports, mainly driven by iron ore, rising 75 per cent. It is predictable that rapid development of trade relations will certainly affect bilateral political relations in a positive manner.

Fast growing trade relations have come under increasing strain with India's trade deficit continuing to widen.India filed a record number of anti-dumping investigations against China at the World

Trade Organization in 2009. India's recent restrictions on the import of Chinese telecom equipment, in light of security concerns, have added to the list of strains. The telecom issue, however, was not raised by China during the President's ongoing visit. With the bilateral trade rapidly growing, these differences or disputes are normal. We believe that all these problems can be resolved by bilateral consultations. Describing trade and economic cooperation as a pillar of bilateral ties, Indian president Patil said India and China should work together to realize trade target of US$ 60 billion in 2010 that had been set.

In 2006 Presiden Hu Jintao visited India and the two sides agreed on a 10-pronged strategy to expand and intensify bilaterlal strategic and cooperative partnership.

In 2008, during the Indian Prime Minister Manmohan Singh visit to China, the two countries concluded a " Shared Vision for the 21st century", which forms the basis for bilateral cooperation on global issues.

China and India have agreed to enhance political, economic ties and bolster people-to-people contact during a meeting between Indian President Pratibha Patil and Chinese Premier Wen Jiabao here on May 27, 2010. President Hu Jintao held talks with her. President Patil said India-China relations were of global and strategic significance, and all political parties in India were supportive of further advancing such relations. President Hu said that China and India should work more closely to address global issues such as economic downturn, climate change, energy security and food security. The two countries should maintain close communication and coordination within multilateral mechanisms such as China-Russia-India, BRIC, BASIC, and G20, in a bid to increase the voice of developing countries.

China and India do not pose as threat to each other and their common interests far outweigh their differences. The two countries should understand and respect each other's core national interests and major concerns, properly handle their differences, and seek common development and a win-win situation. A good China-India relationship makes both winners while a confrontational one makes both losers.

1962: THE VIEW FROM BEIJING

In 1985, the Chinese side formally reinterpreted the package proposal saying that we had misunderstood Deng's words. The fresh Chinese position was that since the area of largest dispute was in the eastern sector, India had to make meaningful concessions in that sector and the Chinese side would then make appropriate and corresponding concessions in the western sector. Additionally, an explicit demand was now advanced for ceding Tawang, which the Indian side was accused of occupying at a much later date after its independence. It was pointed out to us that since the fifth Dalai Lama had been born in Tawang, the place was of special significance for the Chinese people, in particular for China's Tibetan nationality. This remains the current Chinese position on the border dispute and the Indian side, of course, rejects it.

In 1992, an informal suggestion was made to the Chinese side that India gives free access to Chinese pilgrims to Tawang, while China reciprocally gives similar access to Indian pilgrims to Kailash Mansarovar. The Chinese never responded. One reason for the insistence on Tawang being conceded may be the fear that if the next Dalai Lama were to be "discovered" in Tawang , a Chinese rival may not enjoy the same legitimacy. As will be apparent, the issue of Tibet continues to be embedded in any consideration of the border.

In 2005, during Chinese Premier Wen Jiabao's visit, India and China announced a set of Guiding Principles and Political Parameters for resolving the border issue. From India's standpoint, these principles and parameters are welcome as they include those that are extremely relevant, such as the need to consider the interests of "settled populations". This would have a direct bearing on the status of Tawang. However, in typical Chinese fashion, there is a continuous attempt to reinterpret these principles to suit Chinese positions. In the series of talks between the Special Representatives of the two prime ministers, now in their 11th year, little progress has been recorded on settling the border issue, though the talks have been useful in managing the border and in advancing confidence-building measures.

Given this chequered history, what are the prospects of an India-China border settlement and what are its likely contours? One cannot see a solution that diverges significantly from the existing alignment of the Line of Actual Control (LAC), and the longer the status quo continues the more likely is the LAC to eventually morph into a settled boundary. At a recent track-II interaction, a senior Chinese army official remarked that India was unlikely to go to war to recover Aksai Chin just as China was unlikely to go to war to recover southern Tibet, or what India refers to as Arunachal Pradesh. In the meantime, he went on to add, the LAC needed to be clarified so that incidents such as the recent one at Depsang could be avoided.

Given the experience of 1962, however, one should never base one's actions on the basis of perceptions of the other side's intentions. It was the entrenched belief that China would never attack that caught Indian forces totally unprepared and virtually defenceless. Our border defences including logistics, must take into account the rapidly growing capabilities on the Chinese side. Although the size of our forces deployed at the border and its vicinity is substantial, our transport infrastructure and logistical capabilities have fallen steadily behind that of China. These shortcomings are being addressed but we need to consider ways in which we can cope with the growing asymmetry. The use of air capabilities may be one answer. There is also an urgent need to improve and extend our reconnaissance capabilities, so that there is sufficient warning time in case of an attack. Intelligence failure was one of the major causes of our failure to anticipate and respond to the 1962 crisis. The point one is making is that any prospect of sustaining the status quo at the border is dependent upon our ability to make any attempt to change it costly and risky to the other side.

It is also clear that the evolution of the Tibet issue will have a significant influence on both the prospects of an eventual border settlement with China and, in the meantime, maintaining peace and tranquility along the LAC. A successful reconciliation process between the Dalai Lama and the Chinese side would be to India's advantage. There were some signs earlier last year that the new

Chinese leadership was reaching out to the Dalai Lama but these seem to have lost momentum. If there are ways in which India could encourage this, it would help in managing India-China relations. A worsening of the situation inside Tibet or greater militancy among Tibetan youth in India could make the job of keeping India-China relations on an even keel more difficult.

China is likely to show restraint in dealing with India, including on the border issue, the more diversified and stronger India's relations are with other countries. China was more amenable and sensitive to India's interests in 2005 because of India's growing relationship with the US, Japan and the countries of South East Asia. The fewer options India is seen to have in its external relations, the more likely Chinese pressures on it will increase. This will be particularly relevant if the capability gap between the two countries continues to widen. Alternatively, if the forthcoming elections throw up a political leadership that enables India to resume accelerated economic growth and pursue a more coherent foreign policy, the prospects for India-China relations will improve. One should watch carefully the changing dynamics among major powers as a result of the Ukraine crisis and the worsening of relations between Russia and the West. On balance, China appears to be a net gainer with both Russia and the West seeking its neutrality, if not support. For India, the choices are more difficult.

Much will be determined by what the Indian electorate delivers in terms of a new political dispensation later this year. In 2005, India was riding high. New Delhi was the indispensable destination for leaders from across the world and the Indian growth story was putting India in the same league as China. Permanent membership of the UN Security Council seemed to be within reach. One could feel that one had more cards to play with in dealing with the world. That is no longer the case. The impending political renewal nevertheless gives one hope that India will get another chance to get back into reckoning.

COPING WITH ASYMMETRY

A reading of the document, now widely available on the internet, does not reveal any fresh, earth-shaking revelations or insights. Much of the report has been leaked in bits and pieces over the years and supplemented by considerable details supplied by other actors involved in this unfortunate saga. The main conclusions of earlier analyses remain valid:

* Right up to the point when China launched a major offensive, both the political *and* the Indian Army top brass were convinced that military engagement at the contested border would never go beyond small-scale skirmishes and limited operations. There was no expectation and hence preparation for dealing with a large-scale assault, despite mounting evidence to the contrary

* The so-called Forward Policy was a political initiative and not a military operation, designed to strengthen Indian territorial claims and forestall further Chinese ingress. China had been putting in place its own version of a forward policy through the relentless advance into the unoccupied border zones separating the two countries. This had intensified after the Tibet revolt and the Dalai Lama's escape to India in 1959. That same year, the first serious incidents of Chinese aggression took place, one in Longju in the eastern sector and the other at Galwan in the western sector. Chinese territorial assertiveness continued thereafter, accompanied by a significant build-up of both logistics and forces. It was only in November 1961 that the Forward Policy was adopted in response but without corresponding means in men and material to respond to a serious military attack, the capabilities for which were being steadily built up on the Chinese side. The ill-considered probing missions and the setting up of additional and mostly isolated and indefensible posts were, therefore, more in the nature of "showing the flag" operations rather than military manoeuvres.

The revelations in the Henderson Brooks Report should be examined in the light of considerable archival material that is now available on Chinese perceptions and decision-making on India-China relations leading up to the breakout of hostilities on October 20, 1962.

The first important point to note is that the India-China border dispute took on an altogether different dimension in Chinese perceptions as a result of the Tibet revolt of 1959 and the subsequent grant of refuge by India to the Dalai Lama and a large number of Tibetans, who were escaping a violent Chinese crackdown. Indian statements and actions on the border were increasingly interpreted as aimed at undermining Chinese control over Tibet. Even contemporary Chinese studies of the 1962 conflict, such as those by Xu Yan and Wang Hongwei, make this point repeatedly, accusing Nehru of trying to "convert Tibet into a buffer zone" and to "instigate Tibet to leave China". In 1964, while speaking to a visiting Nepali delegation, Mao Zedong said the major problem between India and China was not the McMahon Line but Tibet, which Indians considered to be theirs.

A second conclusion to emerge from the archives is the key role played by Mao himself in the events leading up to the war. The failure of the Great Leap Forward and three years of economic distress and famine between 1959 and 1961 had forced Mao to retreat to the "second line of leadership", yielding place to pragmatists such as Liu Shaoqi, Deng Xiaoping and Peng Zhen. By the summer of 1962, however, Mao was already in the process of regaining his control over the levers of power, using the People's Liberation Army under a new commander, Marshal Lin Piao, as his ally. From the summer of 1962, it was Mao who was personally issuing directives on the evolving military situation on the India-China border. It was his decision in August 1962, to launch a full-scale military assault on Indian forces and to "liquidate the invading Indian army".

Interestingly, it now transpires that this decision was a contested one. A Chinese TV feature on the 1962 war, broadcast in January 2005, reveals that there were differences of opinion among the leadership with some arguing that it would be unwise to make an enemy out of India just when China was confronting both domestic and external challenges. However, according to the broadcast, these elements were denounced as "right opportunists" and the military offensive went ahead.

It is also clear now that China made a careful assessment of the regional and international situation before undertaking these military operations. There were fears in China that the US may help the Chiang Kai-shek regime in Taiwan launch attacks on China across the Taiwan Straits. These were laid to rest when

China's ambassador to Warsaw, Wang Bingnan, was able to get a categorical assurance from his American counterpart that the US had no intention of supporting any Taiwanese offensive against China by taking advantage of Sino-Indian tensions. In his memoirs, Wang claims that this assurance played an important part in enabling the decision to attack India later in the year.

Similarly, fears that the Soviet Union would play a negative role on the Sino-India dispute were laid to rest as Moscow sought to obtain Chinese support in the looming Cuban missile crisis, which would burst into the open around the same time as the India-China war. This also distracted the major powers from taking full cognisance of what was happening on a remote border somewhere in Asia.

Just as the Chinese military offensive came as a rude surprise, so did the subsequent Chinese decision to withdraw from the territories it occupied as a result of the 1962 operations with some exceptions particularly in the Western sector. The Indian leadership fully believed that the withdrawal was probably due to approaching winter and extended supply lines and that a renewed offensive was likely during the summer the following year. This explains the sense of panic that prevailed in those days evident in Jawaharlal Nehru's desperate letter to US President John F Kennedy, which surfaced recently. Chinese archives, however, suggest that it was always Mao's plan that Chinese forces should withdraw after delivering a knockout blow on the Indians. The objective was not territorial. It was to forestall any threat to Chinese consolidation in Tibet, while bringing a chastened India to the negotiating table to acquiesce in a Chinese package proposal for settling the border. Neither objective was achieved in any real sense.

In 1980, the two countries resumed a bilateral dialogue on the border after a gap of two decades. In the initial phase the Chinese terms for settlement were the same as in 1960, i.e. that China would retain Aksai Chin in the West but would generally settle along the alignment corresponding to the McMahon Line, though it would never accept the legitimacy of that line. In his interview to the editor of *Vikrant* in 1982, Deng Xiaoping explicitly put forward the "package proposal" as the basis for a border settlement, arguing that in keeping the area currently in its occupation in the east, India was getting a very good deal. After all, he suggested, Nehru himself had described Aksai Chin as a desert where "not a blade of grass grows".

INDIA-CHINA BORDER DISPUTE

The continuing (since April 15,2013) Chinese troop intrusion (about 20 troops) 10 kms into Indian territory near Burthe in the Daulat Beg Oldi (DBO) area of Eastern Ladakh in the western sector of the Sino-Indian border should be a matter for careful analysis and concern, but not alarm.

A spokesman of the Chinese Foreign Office has denied any Chinese intrusion into Indian territory in this area. The Government of India, for the present, has been treating it as one of those intrusions which take place sometimes due to differing perceptions of the Line of Actual Control (LAC) in this area and trying to deal with it through the normal mechanism for handling such issues without disturbing peace and tranquillity across the border.

There is no evidence to show that this could be a prelude to a major Chinese assertion of territorial sovereignty in this area. The Chinese aim seems to be to re-assert their claim of sovereignty over this area without disturbing peace and tranquillity. The Chinese troops are presently camping in the area in a tent. We will have reasons to be more than concerned only if they stay put there and construct permanent defences as they often do in the uninhabited islands of the South China Sea.

Since last year, the Chinese have been a little more assertive of their sovereignty claims over the islands of the South and East China Seas.

They have reportedly constructed permanent defensive and administrative structures on some of the islands over which they have disputes with Vietnam and the Philippines. In the East China Sea, where they have sovereignty disputes with Japan, they have avoided any such construction, but stepped up seemingly aggressive air and naval patrols of the areas in the vicinity of these islands. The Chinese Navy has also stepped up its visits to the islands in the South China Sea claimed by Beijing.

Till now we have seen greater Chinese activism in the enforcement of their sovereignty claims only in the South and East China seas, but not across the Sino-Indian border. If the Chinese troops stay put in the Burthe area and construct defensive structures in the area, that will be an indicator of their deciding to follow a similar policy of activism across the Sino-Indian border too. That should add to our border concerns. We may have to revisit our peace and tranquillity strategy and think of a more activist policy to face the Chinese activism.

In the Western sector of the border, which is largely unpopulated, the status quo favours the Chinese. Since 1962, they are already in occupation of whatever territory they have claimed. We have very few options to re-assert our sovereignty in any area of this sector which is under Chinese control. In the Eastern sector (Arunachal Pradesh, which the Chinese call Southern Tibet), the area is populated and the status quo favours India. Even though our defensive and administrative infrastructure in the Arunachal Pradesh area is not comparable with the Chinese infrastructure in the Tibet Autonomous Region (TAR), we are in a much stronger position in the Eastern sector than in the Western.

While the Chinese continue to repeat from time to time their claims to the Arunachal Pradesh area, they have avoided in the Eastern sector the kind of ground activism that one comes across in the Western sector. There is a noticeable keenness on the part of both China and India to avoid any provocative incident either in the Eastern or Western sector. The Chinese are unlikely to relent in their claims to Indian territory in the Eastern sector till after they have succeeded in imposing on the Tibetans a Dalai Lama chosen by the Communist Party of China (CPC) with the help of the Panchen Lama chosen by the CPC.

The wave of self-immolations (115 incidents so far) in the Tibetan areas of China since March 2009 has created concerns in Chinese mind of possible political instability in the Tibetan areas after His Holiness the Dalai Lama when the CPC imposes its nominee on the Tibetans.

The older generation of Tibetans continues to abide by His Holiness' exhortations for peaceful means of protest. The Chinese are worried that the GenNext of Tibetans represented by organisations such as the Tibetan Youth Congress (TYC) may take to violent means to resist the imposition of a Dalai Lama chosen by the CPC. In their calculation, this may necessitate action by the PLA in the populated areas of Arunachal Pradesh. Till Tibet is pacified without fears of any further trouble and the Chinese have forced the Tibetans to accept their nominee as the Dalai Lama, Beijing would like to maintain its claim to Arunachal Pradesh to justify action by the PLA in that area to contain trouble, if need be.

If they now make a deal with India recognising Arunachal Pradesh as an integral part of India, they will not be able to act in that area. By recognising Tibet as an integral part of China we have given up our options for action in Tibet. The Chinese would not want to commit the same mistake by recognising Arunachal Pradesh as an integral part of India. They will, therefore, keep the Arunachal Pradesh issue alive till they have forced the Tibetans to accept their decision regarding succession of His Holiness. We should factor this into our border strategies relating to China.

THE SINO/INDIAN DISPUTE

Ever since its establishment in 1949, the attitude of the Communist Chinese Government towards India has been bound up with the Tibetan issue. India had, on gaining independence in 1947, inherited the British "special position" in Tibet, along with the Mission in Lhasa and trade agencies in larger towns. It had retained the services of British officials stationed in Tibet. When, in 1949, Tibetan leaders made their bid to contact foreign Governments, they first contacted these officials, and it was only a short step for the suspicious minded Chinese to regard this as evidence of Indian collusion with the British.

The Communist Chinese also had ideological reasons for believing that such collusion existed. At the time of their coming to power, Moscow was propagating the line of a world divided into two camps, with the Indian Government depicted as a tool of British imperialism and firmly situated in the opposing camp. The Communist Chinese leaders, who previously had had little contact with the outside world, faithfully repeated these accusations against Nehru and his Government.

Following the Chinese occupation of Tibet in late 1950, Peking's suspicions of the Indians were further aroused when Nehru, in notes to the Chinese Government, expressed the "surprise and regret" of his Government at the Chinese action. He described as "deplorable" the Chinese use of force in Tibet.

Standard diplomatic practice stipulates that a state does not criticise the behaviour of another state acting within its own territorial boundaries unless there are special reasons for so doing. The Indians justified their criticism of the Chinese on the ground of their special interest in Tibet, from which the Chinese inferred that the Indians were implying some restriction on Chinese sovereignty. A sharp reply was received from the Chinese accusing the Indians of unwarranted interference and claiming that the policy of the Indian Government was "affected by foreign influences hostile to China in Tibet".

Nevertheless, whatever suspicions the Chinese may have felt about the Indians in 1949-50 must to some extent have been allayed by subsequent developments. India opposed the 1950 Tibetan appeal to the United Nations; it was one of the few non-communist countries not to condemn China's intervention in the Korean War; it sought to have China seated an the United Nations. The culmination of these moves to improve relations with China was the signing, in April 1954, of an agreement by which India recognised without qualification China's sovereignty over Tibet and conceded many of India's former rights there. A few months later the Chinese Premier, Chou En-lai, paid a successful visit to India, and in October of the same year Nehru visited Peking.

The very considerable improvement in Sino/Indian relations from 1950 to 1954 was on the Indian side almost entirely the result of efforts by Nehru, who saw friendship between China and India as the starting point of a new order in world affairs. It must have been obvious to the Chinese that considerable opposition to Nehru's pro-China policies, at least as far as Tibet was concerned, existed both within and outside the Indian Government. It should also have been clear that problems were going to arise over wide discrepancies in the claimed Sino/Indian border, as shown in maps published by both sides.

However, as long as Nehru's China policy appeared to produce results, his opposition in India remained silent. It was important for both Nehru and the Chinese that this policy continued to appear to give results, and hence the efforts made by both sides to keep intact the edifice of good relations. The Chinese, under the 1954 agreement, allowed India to maintain certain trade and pilgrimage rights in Tibet. They sought to play down the significance of border differences, stating that they had simply inherited their claimed Sino/Indian frontier from the pre-1949 Nationalist Government and that it would be "revised" in due course. Nehru, for his part, avoided public mention of the reality and extent of border differences, and it seemed that both sides were moving towards a compromise settlement of the question.

What were these differences, and what evidence was there that both sides were in fact prepared to compromise?

The Sino/Indian border can be divided into three sectors:

(i)an eastern sector where 99,000 square kilometres of territory described by the Indians as the Northeast Frontier Agency, or N.E.F.A is in dispute: (ii) a middle sector where some 2.000 square kilometres of territory on either side of the main Himalayan passes is disputed: and (iii) a western sector where the Indian province of Ladakh borders on Tibet and Sinkiang and where both the Indian/Tibet and Indian/Sinkiang borders are disputed, in particular the ownership of some 30,000 square kilometres of high plateau country known as the Aksai Chin.

To an outside observer looking at the frontier as it stands, an apparent basis for a compromise settlement would be for China to drop its claim to the N.E.F.A. in exchange for India dropping its claim to the Aksai Chin, with both sides making concessions over the middle sector and the Ladakh/Tibetan border. Such a settlement accords with the realities of both geography and administrative control two important criteria in the settlement of border disputes. The N.E.F.A. lies to the south of the Himalayan watershed and is controlled by India. The Aksai Chin, for the most part, lies to the north of the main range, and the Chinese claim to have controlled the area since 1950. In 1956-7, they built a strategic road across the Aksai Chin, linking Sinkiang with Tibet. That the Indians learnt about the road only from a map published by the Chinese in 1958 is substantial evidence that India was not in control of the area.

The historical basis of the border is more confused. The Indian claim to the N.E.F.A. rests almost entirely on acceptance of the McMahon Line, a line agreed to by the Tibetans and British in 1914 as the border in this area. In the Aksai Chin area no agreement has ever been reached on the alignment of the border. Nevertheless, if both sides were to take a generous view of the historical data, a basis for a N.E.F.A./Aksai Chin exchange could be found.

During the post-1954 honeymoon period of Sino/Indian relations, both sides did in fact seem prepared to take a generous view of the situation and to move towards a compromise settlement. In 1956, Chou En-lai admitted privately to Nehru that, although lie thought the McMahon line "was not fair", nevertheless China would accept the line as the border with India after they had "consulted with the Tibetan authorities". Chinese recognition of the McMahon Line was also implied when its eastern extension was accepted as a basis for border negotiations with Burma, and by Chinese de facto acceptance of the line as the dividing line between Chinese and Indian forces in the area.

Nehru, for his part, appeared willing to play down the Indian claims to the Aksai Chin. He tried to delay disclosure if the news that the Chinese had built a road in the area. After the news had been revealed, he sought to play down the economic significance of the area, describing it as a "barren tundra". He even went so far as to cast doubt on the validity of the Indian claim to the area. In statements to the Indian Parliament during early 1959, Nehru pointed out that "during British rule, this area was neither inhabited: nor were there any outposts", adding that "this place, Aksai Chin area, is distinguish completely from other areas. It is a matter for argument which part belongs to us and which part belongs to somebody else. It is not clear".

Nehru's efforts to take the heat out of the Aksai Chin question were not entirely successful. (One of his critics even suggested building an atomic reactor in the area to promote its economic development.) News of the Chinese road in the area appeared to trigger off long-suppressed Indian sensitivity over the border issue, and, in August 1958, the Indian Government made a formal claim to the disputed territory in all three sectors. In a letter to Nehru of January 1959, Chou En-lai claimed that the Aksai Chin was Chinese territory and added that the McMahon Line was a "product of British aggression", illegal, and had "never been recognised by the Chinese Central Government". He proposed that the existing status quo he maintained, however, pending a negotiated settlement of the dispute, and added that China would take a "realistic attitude" over the McMahon Line.*

The Tibetan uprising of March 1959 upset the delicate balance of Sino/Indian relations. Reports of Chinese military action to suppress the uprising, together with the sight of thousands of Tibetan refugees crossing into Indian territory, quickly aroused feelings of alarm and anger in India, particularly among those who believed their country had an historic interest in Tibet. Nehru's Right-Wing critics charged that India should never have allowed the Chinese into Tibet in the first place. Nehru, influenced possibly both by Indian public opinion and his own feelings on the question, came out in open condemnation of Chinese behaviour in Tibet.

The Chinese reacted even more strongly than they had in 1950. Nehru, in addition to condemning the Chinese, had spoken of his sympathy with "the aspirations of the Tibetans for autonomy". He had given asylum to the Dalai Lama, who was also allowed facilities to make his 1959 appeal for U. N. action over Tibet. And finally, the Chinese had reason to believe that the Tibetan guerrillas were receiving arms from across the Indian border.

In May 1959 the Chinese published a long article urging, almost begging, Nehru not to be swayed by his reactionary Right-Wing critics and to return to the path of Sino/Indian friendship. With a frankness and detail probably unmatched by any other Chinese statement on foreign policy, the article set out the Chinese case over Tibet, and accused the Indians of unjustified interference. Indian trade with Tibet was greatly restricted. Clashes involving casualties occurred at several points along the disputed border as the Chinese Army extended its control over border areas in an effort to restrict the move- court of Tibetans across the frontier.

These border clashes, following in the wake of the Tibetan uprising, appeared to put an end to Nehru's willingness to compromise over the border dispute. Having earlier in 1959 cast doubt on the Indian claim to the Aksai Chin, in September he stated before the Indian Parliament that the Chinese claims were "absurd" and would mean "handing over the Himalayas to them as a gift". A Chinese call in November 1959 for negotiations and a twenty-kilometre military withdrawal from the McMahon Line in the east and the "line of actual control" in the west to prevent a recurrence of border clashes was met with an Indian demand for a prior Chinese withdrawal from the Aksai Chin. A Chinese reply pointing out that this should also be paralleled by an Indian withdrawal from the NE.F.A. was ignored. In the end the Chinese appeared to settle for a freezing of the existing status quo - without negotiations or a twenty-kilometre withdrawal.

However, if the Chinese were happy to keep things as they were (keeping also their road across the Aksai Chin), Nehru and his Government were not. Throughout 1960-61 Indian opinion progressively hardened, and demands for the Government to do something about Tibet and the disputed border increased. The army was given full control over the frontier districts and it proceeded to build up its strength in these areas.

During the summer (northern) of 1962, Indian military patrols repeatedly crossed the Chinese-claimed line of actual control in the western sector of the frontier. Posts were established well behind the Chinese forward positions in territory claimed and occupied by the Chinese. Frequent and insistent Chinese protests were met with the bald statement that the Indians were merely operating in Indian territory. By August 14, Nehru was able to announce that India had three times as many posts in the western sector as the Chinese. He asked for a free hand to continue the build-up of Indian strength in the area.

The Chinese had repeatedly warned that a continuation of such activity would end in hostilities. On July 9, they had warned the Indians "to rein in on the brink of the precipice". On August 4, they called for immediate negotiations on the border. The Indians replied that negotiations could not be held until the Chinese had ceased their occupation of "every square inch of sacred Indian territory", and that the Chinese must first "vacate their aggression" in the Aksai Chin. The Chinese replied on September 13 proposing talks to begin on October 15 "without preconditions", that is, without a Chinese withdrawal from the Aksai Chin. The Indians refused the offer.

While Indian military pressure was building up along the Chinese-claimed border in the western sector, a curious situation was developing along the McMahon Line in the eastern sector. The Indians claim that at its western end the McMahon Line was not accurately drawn: that it was meant to have followed the crest of a line of hills known as the Thag La ridge. The Chinese claim, and have produced the original McMahon Line from the Tibetan archives to prove their point, that the line as originally drawn lies approximately twelve miles south of this ridge along the southern side of a small river valley. (Western maps show the McMahon Line in conformity with the Chinese claim.) The area between the Indian and Chinese versions of the McMahon Line is described by the Indians as the Dho La strip.

This was not the only unilateral revision of the McMahon Line carried out by the Indians. In his letter to Chou En-lai of September 29, 1959, Nehru admitted that in the Migyitun area (to the east of the Dho La strip) the border shown on Indian maps "differs slightly from the boundary shown in the Treaty map". He claimed that when the McMahon line was drawn, "the exact topographical features in this area were not known". The Indians have also now come to admit that "blind adherence" to the original McMahon Line would leave the Dho La strip on the Chinese side at the border.

It is not clear who first occupied the Dho La strip. The Chinese claim that the area had always been under their control and that Indian troops moved in during 1962. The Indians claim they had long occupied the area and that the Chinese began a to establish posts in the area after September 8, 1962. What is clear is that on October 12, 1962, Nehru announced in the Indian Parliament that he had given the order to drive the Chinese out of the Dho La strip.

Eight days later, on October 20, the Chinese attacked in force across the Thagla La ridge and into the disputed strip, while advancing their troops into the Chinese-claimed territory in the western sector where the Indians had earlier established posts. Four days later, the Chinese called for a ceasefire to be followed by a withdrawal of both sides from the line that separated them at that moment (the so-called October 24 line of actual control). Failing to get a satisfactory response from the Indians, they advanced troops south of the Dho La strip into the N.E.F.A., defeating Indian military forces in the area. Two weeks later, they withdrew to the positions occupied on October 24. The main point of contention between the Chinese and Indians ever since has been whether the Chinese should maintain their October 24 positions or withdraw further to the positions they occupied before fighting broke out.

The Chinese attack of October 1962 has led to an almost complete breakdown in relations between China and India. The level of each country's diplomatic representation in the other has been greatly reduced. Many thousands of Chinese nationals have been expelled from India. The few Indian nationals living in China have, in one way or another, been forced to leave. Border incidents have continued. Both sides have launched extreme propaganda campaigns against each other, the Chinese denouncing Nehru as a representative of the "big bourgeoisie" and a tool for U. S. aggressive designs against Tibet, while the Indians denounce the Chinese for having aggressive, imperialist designs against Indian territory. Both sides have gone to great lengths to discredit each other inter- nationally. Both sides have increased their military preparedness along the Himalayan frontier, particularly India, which has doubled its military budget to a level it cannot afford.

The question thus arises: Who is primarily to blame for the hostility in Sino/Indian relations? From the account already given, the primary cause of the hostility was the post-1959 dispute over the Sino/Indian border leading to the Chinese attack of October 20. But why the sudden emergence of such a dispute between two countries previously enjoying good relations?

Reverting to the terminology of our previous discussion on hostility between states, both sides see the breakdown in relations as being caused by the active hostility of the other side. This hostility, they claim, is both ideologically and national- interest based. The Chinese are accused of having acted in a hostile manner out of a desire to acquire territory and out of strong ideological dislike for the Indian Government. The Chinese claim the Indians have designs against Chinese territory and that their Government is under the influence of anti-Chinese and pro-U. S. reactionary elements.

Both sides realise that they have somehow or other to explain why the other side suddenly, in 1959, decided that its interests were no longer served by the maintenance of normal relations. The Indian explanation is that Chinese pre-1959 policy was designed to lull India into a false sense of security and so facilitate Chinese ambitions. The Chinese explanation was that reactionary elements began to gain the upper hand in the Indian Government in 1959, and point to the post-1959 increase in U. S. aid to India as evidence.

In fact there is good reason to believe that the hostility shown by each side towards the other was reactive rather than active: that each side was reacting to the believed hostility of the other. To take the Chinese side of things first.

In terms of the account already given, it seems likely that the Chinese attack of October 20, 1962, was primarily a reaction to Indian military pressure along the disputed frontier during preceding months. It could be argued, however. that the behaviour of the Chinese before October 20, and in particular their propaganda attacks against the Indians from 1960 onwards, cannot be explained simply as a reaction to previous events: that overall Chinese behaviour must therefore include some aggressive component.

The Chinese had in fact made their first hostile move against the Indians back in 1959 when they restricted Indian trading and other rights in Tibet. The Chinese had also, according to the Indians, extended somewhat the area they claimed in the western sector. And they had, according to the Indians, been responsible for the 1959 border clashes already mentioned. The Indian charge is based on alleged differences between the frontier claimed by the Chinese to 1956 and that shown on a map of the claimed Sino/Indian frontier handed to the Indians by the Chinese in 1960. The Chinese deny any difference between the two lines.

Unless these apparently hostile acts of the Chinese can be explained in reactive terms., in terms of their reacting to previous Indian actions, then it would seem that the Chinese had taken the initiative in hostility towards India and were largely responsible for the eventual breakdown in relations.

The hardening of the Chinese attitude towards India in 1959 was clearly related to Tibetan developments in that year. In judging the behaviour of the Chinese, we need, in effect, to ask whether their sensitivity over Tibet was sufficient to explain this hardening of attitude.

To accept that the Communist Chinese are, in fact extremely sensitive toward Tibet does not necessarily imply a simple acceptance of Chinese propaganda. What we know of Chinese thinking and behaviour, strongly suggests that this sensitivity does exist. If all non-communist Chinese believe that China has the right to consider Tibet as an integral part of her territory, we should accept that Communist Chinese are equally convinced. If many non-communist Chinese believe (as they do) that Britain had designs against Tibet, we should accept that Communist Chinese, educated to believe in the evils of US Western imperialism, will be at least equally fearful. We do not need accept that these views are correct; we may even consider they are absurd. But if we are going to get anywhere in trying to understand China's behaviour, we should start from the assumption that these views may be sincerely hold in Peking.

Nor may it be so absurd for the Communist Chinese to think along these lines. The Chinese legal claim to Tibet, it has been argued, appears difficult to refute. As for fears of foreign designs, if the British had earlier convinced themselves that the activities of one Russian agent in Lhasa could lead the politically unstable Tibetans to ally themselves with Tsarist Russia, the Chinese could be excused for thinking that the presence of a British Mission in Lhasa dealing directly with the independent-minded Tibetans and arranging on occasion for the supply of arms from India was evidence of British ambitions eventually to detach Tibet from China, and that India may have inherited these ambitions.

Similarly, it would not be entirely surprising if the Chinese viewed the supply of foreign arms to Tibetan guerrillas from northern India in 1959 as confirmation that such ambitions existed. Finally, the Chinese were hound to be impressed by the demands of the Indian Right Wing for action against the Chinese in Tibet.

For example: some weight could be attached to the fact that the then Chief of the Indian Army Staff wrote a not unenthusiastic foreword for a book published in 1961 entitled The Chinese Aggression. The author of the hook, a Dr. Satyanarayan Sinha, predicted that the "clash of the Indochinese weapons for the possession of the Himalayas will lead to making Tibet an independent country again", and suggested ways in which this could be done.

These, then, are the reasons for believing the Chinese may he sensitive about Tibet. Chinese behaviour provides further confirmation. British officials captured in Tibet in 1950 were subjected to long imprisonment and continual interrogation - treatment far more severe than that meted out to British nationals who fell into communist hands elsewhere in China. And there was Nehru's sad admission to the Indian Parliament in 1959 after talks with Chou En-Iai, of the Chinese having "some sort of kink in their minds... of foreign countries, United Kingdom or America, somehow making incursions into Tibet".

In sum, therefore, it does not seem unreasonable to conclude that the Communist Chinese sincerely believed they had a right to Tibet and that their position in the area was threatened from the direction of India. In which case they would have interpreted Indian behaviour in 1959 as an indication of hostility to which they felt compelled, or entitled, to react.

However, if Chinese behaviour in 1959 can be explained in reactive terms, can the same be said about the Chinese attack of October 1962? Even if the Indian claim to the Dho La strip was doubtful, does not the violence and intensity of the 1962 attack suggest that China was doing more than retaliate for any wrongs she may have believed the Indians to base committed?

By 1962, the Chinese were confronted not only by Indian agitation over Tibet, but also by two further aspects of Indian behaviour which would even more easily have been misunderstood. They were: (i) the Indian military build-up along the Sino/Indian border in 1961-2 and (ii) rigid Indian insistence that, as a precondition to border negotiations, the Chinese must first evacuate the whole of the Aksai Chin.

At the time, the Indians justified their position on negotiations and their military build up in terms of the correctness of their border claims. Indeed, the official Indian position was that the line claimed by India as a border had already been defined historically, and that the only purpose of negotiations was to demarcate on the ground the exact alignment of this border. From this it followed that they were justified (a) in regarding rival Chinese claims, and the occupation of the Aksai Chin, as evidence of Chinese hostility, and (b) in insisting that occupied territory had to be vacated before there could be negotiations. In the meantime the Indians had no alternative but to use military means to counter the Chinese "aggression".

If India was in fact the injured party in the territorial dispute, the Indian attitude over the disputed border would have been explicable at least to an impartial observer, and possibly even to the less impartial Chinese. There would be less justification for the Chinese reacting in the way they did. But was this the case? To answer this question we need to take a closer look at the historical background to the Sino /Indian frontier, and shall begin with the eastern sector, or N.E.F.A.

Until the 1920's, the region now known as the N.E.F.A. was largely unexplored. It was, and still is, inhabited by tribes of Tibeto-Burmese origin, some of which enjoyed trade and tributary relations with Tibet. Certain areas in the north of the region, the

Tawang district for example, were inhabited by Tibetans and were under administrative control from Tibet.

The McMahon Line was negotiated with the Tibetans in 1914 at the time of the Simla Conference. It was drawn as far to the north as possible, since the British at the time sought to forestall a feared Chinese expansion into the foothills bordering the Assam plains. The McMahon Line as part of a bargain whereby the British would press the Chinese to concede territory elsewhere to Tibet.

Even so, the Tibetans were not entirely happy about losing territory south of the McMahon Line, the Tawang district in particular. Their acceptance of the line was conditional on possible future adjustments in their favour. No such adjustments, were ever made. The British also failed to extract the promised concessions from the Chinese, since the latter refused to accept the Convention produced at the Simla Conference. Thus, even as a Tibetan/British frontier, the McMahon Line does not have full validity, particularly as the Tibetans subsequently, in 1936, made a formal request to the British for revision of the line in their favour a request which the British ignored. As late as 1946, the Tibetans were still collecting taxes in the Tawang area. And, in 1947, the Tibetans approached the newly established Indian Government, seeking the "return" of "Tibetan territories" from Assam to Ladakh.

The Indian reply to this approach may be of interest in the light of complaints to be voiced later by the Indians over the manner in which the Chinese spoke of their border claims being inherited from previous Chinese Governments "The Government of India should be glad to have an assurance that it is the intention of the Tibetan Government to continue relations an the existing basis until new Agreements are any reached... This is the procedure adopted by all other countries with which India has inherited Treaty relations from His Majesty's Government".

The validity of the McMahon Line as a Chinese/Indian frontier is considerably more doubtful. True, in rejecting the draft Simla Contention, the Chinese did not specifically object to the McMahon Line as drawn on the map of Tibet attached to the Convention. But, as the Chinese point out, the then Chinese Government had no way of knowing what this line was supposed to represent, since the terms of the McMahon Line agreement were for some reason kept secret by the British and Tibetans until 1929. It could, in theory, have been a border between Tibet and a Chinese-owned N.E.F.A. Moreover, Chiang Kaishek's Government was later to make it clear to the British (and the Indians after 1947) that it did not accept the McMahon Line. The Chinese have also pointed out that, since neither the British nor the Chinese regarded Tibet as a sovereign entity, the Tibetans were obliged to obtain Chinese approval for any frontier negotiated with a foreign power. * Failure to obtain this approval, both at the Simla Conference and later, meant that the McMahon Line never at any stage enjoyed international legality. And finally, as the Chinese never tire of pointing out, many Western and Indian maps, including one reproduced in a book by Nehru himself, Discovery of India, have, even in recent years., shown the Sino/Indian border as running along the edge of the Assam plain in conformity with the traditional Chinese claim.

The 1906 Convention between Britain and China (see page 95) had required China to accept responsibility for Tibet's foreign relations. "The 1907 Anglo/Russian Convention required Britain 'not to enter into negotiations with Tibet except through the intermediary of the Chinese Government". Negotiations with the Tibetans over the McMahon Line were thus a breach of both conventions - a possible reason why the terms of the McMahon Line agreement were kept secret.

For the Communist Chinese to appear to be willing to drop their N.E.F.A. claim is no small concession in view of the very considerable doubts as to the validity of the McMahon Line. Indeed, the Nationalist Government in Taiwan feels so strongly shout the justice of the Chinese clams that its official newspapers have accused Peking of being willing to abandon "sacred" Chinese territory. They have predicted that the present Communist Chinese leaders will be condemned by future generations of Chinese for their betrayal of China's interests.

Nevertheless, the Indian position was that the Chinese should not only drop their claim to the N.E.F.A. but to the Aksai Chin also. How strong is the Indian claim in the western sector of the disputed frontier?

The province of Ladakh, which lies on the Indian side of the disputed western sector, was originally a semi-independent state with a complex tributary relationship with Tibet. It was far from being clearly defined Indian territory. These links with Tibet were severed as a result of the 1841 invasion of Tibet from Kashmir, and Ladakh was incorporated into India. In the agreement which followed the invasion, the Ladakh/Tibet border was defined simply as following "the old established frontier", and it was only subsequently that British cartographers decided where this frontier should lie. A small area lying between the Chinese-claimed and Indian-claimed frontiers is in dispute.

By far the larger area in dispute, the Aksai Chin, lies for the most part north of the Ladakh/Tibet frontier, and its ownership depends on a definition of the Ladakh/Sinkiang border. At the end of the nineteenth century, the British decided an effort should be made to define this border, and in 1899 a note was delivered to the Chinese suggesting a possible alignment. This alignment is shown on the map above, and it will be seen that it leaves with China much of the territory at present in dispute. The Chinese never replied to the note. Shortly afterwards, the British attitude changed. Alarmed by growing Chinese weakness in Central Asia, and fearing Russian expansion into the area (fears similar to those being entertained in connection with Tibet), the British felt they should establish the border as far north as possible to forestall any southward advance by the Russians. British maps began to show the border as lying far to the north along the Kun Lun mountains. Chinese agreement was never sought for this claimed border (despite the fact that the British recognised Chinese sovereignty in Sinkiang) ; presumably it was only being put forward as an emergency measure in case the Russians attempted to seize Sinkiang. By the 1920's the Russian threat had disappeared, and it was deemed safe to drop this particular claim.

In subsequent years, British and Indian maps showed a variety of claim lines some coinciding with the present Chinese claim line, some the claim line along the Kun Lun mountains, and some an in-between claim line which ran south of the Kun Lun mountains but which included the Aksai Chin as Indian territory. Maps showing this last claim line were in general use at the time of the 1947 transfer of power, and appear to constitute the basis of the present Indian claim to the Aksai Chin. However, the only border to have ever been officially proposed to the Chinese by the British in this area was that of 1899, and, as already mentioned, this border left most of the Aksai Chin with China.

Whatever the merits of rival Chinese and Indian claims to the Aksai Chin area, it does seem clear that the Indians can hardly speak of the frontier they claim in this area as being already defined by history and therefore subject only to demarcation. In this connection a rather curious aspect of the Indian position should be mentioned - an aspect which has been overlooked by most students of the Sino/Indian dispute. Numerous Indian authorities, including Nehru himself, have claimed historical validity for their version of the Indian! Sinkiang frontier on the ground that the line proposed by the British in 1899 "ran along the Kun Lun range to a point east of 80° longitude, where it met the eastern boundary of Ladakh". In fact, the 1899 line ran well to the south of the Kun Lun mountains, and the text of the proposal speaks only of the tine meeting "the spur running south from the Kun Lun range, which [the spur] has hitherto been shown on our maps as the eastern boundary of Ladakh. This is a little east of 80° east longitude".* A misquotation of these dimensions is rather serious, particularly when it is used to justify an official claim to some 30,000 square kilometres of territory, and when, on the basis of this claim, negotiations are refused in favour of a military solution of a complex border dispute.

The only observer who appears to have noted this misquotation is Alastair Lamb. In his book, *The China-India Border,* he gives the full text of the British note of 1899 and lists some of the Indian authorities who have misquoted the 1899 proposal. Distribution of his book within India has been banned.

It would seem, therefore, that an impartial observer who takes into account not only the historical background of the border dispute, but also the equally relevant criteria of geography and administrative control, would agree that the Chinese are not being unreasonable when they call for border negotiations on the basis of the present status quo. If, as seems to be the case, the Chinese are prepared to do a N.E.F.A./Aksai Chin exchange leaving India in control of far the largest and most valuable of the territories in dispute, he may even feel that the Chinese are being quite generous.

And if our impartial observer were to reach such a conclusion, it seems highly likely that the Chinese would be convinced of the reasonableness of their position and the unreasonableness of the Indian demand for a unilateral Chinese withdrawal from the Aksai Chin.

If the Chinese were in fact convinced that they were in the right over the border dispute, they would in all probability have interpreted the Indian military build-up along the disputed border in 1961-2 as evidence of active hostility. Striking confirmation that this was the case is contained in the "Tibetan Documents" - official Chinese documents which were captured by Tibetan rebels in 1961 and which subsequently found their way to the U.S., where they have been translated and published. These documents were intended as background briefing to senior Chinese military commanders stationed along the Sino/ Indian border. As such, their contents cannot be dismissed simply as propaganda. The documents warned of U.S./Indian collusion to build up pressure along the Tibetan frontier as a prelude to a joint attack against Tibet. Military commanders were instructed to observe strictly the twenty-kilometre troop withdrawal from the line of actual control and to avoid clashes with advancing Indian patrols since this would provide the "imperialists" with the pretext they needed to justify their planned attack.*

INDIA-CHINA BORDER AGREEMENT: MUCH ADO ABOUT NOTHING

Beijing successfully engineered signing a border defense cooperation agreement (BDCA) with India on October 23, 2013, in what seems to be a Chinese plot to subvert the debate surrounding its recent strategic offensive behavior. While the agreement seems to have set a positive tone to future talks between

New Delhi and Beijing, it does not translate into any substantial shift in the Chinese policy. The latest mechanism is a mere token agreement that has not resulted in tangible progress on the ground.

India and China display a peculiar case of "constrained cooperation," in which the convergence of their economic interests tends to mask their prevailing strategic differences. Yet these divergences, of which the territorial and boundary dispute is foremost, still hold the potential of upstaging ties at any point.

This was demonstrated in April 2013, when a platoon-strength contingent of the Chinese People's Liberation Army (PLA) intruded deep inside the Depsang Plateau in eastern Ladakh, a region of Jammu and Kashmir that shares a border with China. The troops pitched tents in Indian-claimed territory, violating earlier confidence-building measures and pushing India into a diplomatic and military tizzy.

What perhaps is most distressing is that China's Depsang offensive happened despite numerous meetings of the India-China Joint Working Group and four confidence-building agreements, signed in 1993, 1996, 2005, and 2012. In addition to the Depsang occurrence, border guards of the PLA have repeatedly intruded into the eastern sector of Arunachal Pradesh, a state in northeast India, and the northern Ladakh sector.

The writing on the wall following the Depsang incident was clear. China holds the political and military will and capability to covertly notch up tensions in the Himalayas with India, at any time and place of its choosing.

Given that China and India have not mutually agreed upon a Line of Actual Control (LAC), sporadic incidents of border transgressions increasingly appear to be becoming a covert Chinese strategy of asserting its claims in India's western sector, especially in northeastern Ladakh and in Arunachal Pradesh in the eastern sector. The LAC is not physically demarcated on the ground or in military maps, and there is continuing reluctance and official refusals by China to show its version of the LAC to India-thus pointing towards a larger ploy of progressively building up a case for its claims in eastern Ladakh and Arunachal Pradesh.

China and India reiterated in the latest BDCA that neither side would use its military capability against the other. But in the event of China launching another underhanded operation in Arunachal Pradesh or the Ladakh sector, what picture would emerge?

Following the Depsang incident, India announced that both sides would pull back troops to their earlier positions along the LAC. But China haggled with India, agreeing to withdraw its troops from Indian territory provided that New Delhi tear down a line of defensive fortification in an area called Chumar. China also managed to get India to restrict its forward patrols in the area and unflinchingly negotiated for a BDCA. At this stage, India cannot afford to give in to further Chinese demands, such as suspending infrastructure development in its own territory near the LAC. Has China ever offered an explanation for the blizzard ininfrastructure construction it is carrying out in the Tibet Autonomous Region adjoining India?

China's cross-frontier incursions undermine the spirit of every confidence-building measure relating to the border areas New Delhi and Beijing have undertaken. The Depsang incident of 2013 casts an ominous shadow on Chinese intentions with respect to the border issue and sweeps away the spirit of the prior border-peace arrangements. In terms of making tangible progress toward a breakthrough on the larger question of border resolution, India and China have failed abjectly.

A Toothless Agreement

It appears that China has successfully managed to call the shots in the drafting of the BDCA by skirting the primary issue of resolving the boundary dispute. There are no lucid answers as to how exactly the BDCA stands apart from the other confidence-building measures that India already shares with China vis-à-vis the border question. And in many respects, the BDCA is loaded in China's favor.

For example, the BDCA's Article II stipulates that the two countries should share strategic information, but it does not elaborate on what specifically constitutes "information about military exercises, aircraft, demolition operations and unmarked mines." It is doubtful that China will be transparent enough to provide information about its military and cargo flights to forward landing strips near the borders. Article II also appears to be drafted so as to provide a cover for the Chinese Air Force in "locating aerial vehicles that may have crossed or are possibly in the process of crossing the line of actual control" in the border areas - suggesting China may be upping the ante and securing the possibility of launching an air offensive in these areas.

Overall, the BDCA remains a commitment-deficient agreement. It contains no binding assurance that the Indian and Chinese military headquarters will set up a hotline, stating that the two sides "may consider" the move. Article VI states that there would be "no tailing" of each other's patrols in disputed forward areas. However, Indian border guards placed to check and prevent such incursions have been met with an antagonistic Chinese PLA.

Article III elaborates the process through which the BDCA shall be implemented through meetings between border personnel, military officers, and other departments and groups. There is nothing novel in these announcements; they have been in place for many years.

A Problem "Left over from History"

The banality of the text of the latest border defense cooperation agreement is proof that India is losing to China in terms of strategic leverage. With recent confidence-building measures only seeking to "consult" and "coordinate" border affairs, the ability of these mechanisms to achieve any sort of breakthrough to the interminable territorial and boundary dispute between China and India appears increasingly doubtful.

Instead, China has chosen to use the BDCA as a platform which provides it official cover to bide its time and strike when the Chinese political and military leadership see a window of vulnerability. Chinese politico-military history contains many references to dealing with obdurate problems "left over from history" by patiently waiting to resolve them "once conditions are ripe," in the words of the China's first premier, Zhou Enlai. Sun Tzu, the ancient Chinese military strategist, famously stated,

"Engage people with what they expect... It settles them into predictable patterns of response, while you wait for the extraordinary moment — that which they cannot anticipate."

Demonstrating politico-military belligerence and stealth on various fronts appears to have become a defining feature of Chinese strategy, be it the protracted standoffs with India over the border, with Japan over the Senkaku Islands, or with the Philippines over the Scarborough Shoal. China's creation of the East China Sea Air Defense Identification Zone byon November 23 is testament to Chinese attempts at force projection that provides a stage for the long-term Chinese strategy of chipping away at contested claims with India.

Beijing appears intent at keeping the border dispute alive as a tactical pressure point against India. China seems to be awaiting an opportune moment in which the existing military asymmetry with India will widen and Beijing will be positioned to bring the dispute to a close on its own terms.

DALAI LAMA VISIT IGNITES SINO-INDIAN BORDER DISPUTE

In early November, the Dalai Lama is going to visit the majestic Tawang Monastery, perched atop a ridge in the Indian province of Arunachal Pradesh. Surrounded by thick clouds and perennial mist, the monastery sometimes seems almost to be suspended from heaven. It is also at the very centre of thousands of square kilometres of terrain claimed by both China and India, although India currently possesses it. It now risks becoming a proxy battleground on which both India and China seek to proclaim their sovereignty. The religious leader's visit can be seen as a card played by both India and the Tibetan exile community to keep pressure on China.

Home to one of the most sacred Buddhist monasteries, Tawang is the birthplace of the sixth Dalai Lama, Tsayang Gyatso, in the 17th century. The current Dalai Lama passed through this region when he fled into exile in 1959. Chhime Chhoekyapa, the exiled Tibetan spiritual leader's aide, told the media that the Dalai Lama is "going there for teaching. This has nothing to do with politics, there is nothing political about it." In Chinese eyes, however, and perhaps Indian eyes as well, everything the Dalai Lama does has something to do with politics. And this is a region that Beijing calls "Southern Tibet."

When asked about the Dalai Lama's upcoming visit, Beijing officials have fumed. "China expresses strong concern about this information," said Jiang Yu, the spokeswoman for China's Foreign Ministry. "The visit further reveals the Dalai clique's anti-China and separatist essence. China's stance on the so-called Arunachal Pradesh is consistent. We firmly oppose Dalai visiting the so-called Arunachal Pradesh." Tension has slowly been ratcheting up between the two Asian giants, with media commentators fanning the flames. "Is China itching to wage war on India?" asked Professor Brahma Chellaney in the September issue of the Far Eastern Economic Review. Reports have appeared in Chinese state media alleging that India was moving troops and fighter aircraft to the northeast, specifically into Sikkim and Arunachal Pradesh.

India, however, is acutely aware of its shortcomings in the territory it controls. The Chinese, with their extensive roads and railways, can actually come up to the Line of Actual Control, take a stroll and walk back. Two years ago, Chinese soldiers demolished a Buddhist statue that Indians had erected at Bumla, the main border pass above Tawang, according to a member of the Indian Parliament, Nabam Rebia. It takes several days for India's troops to get to the border. But slowly India is finding its voice as it struggles to speed up its own preparedness.

China claims around 90,000 square kilometres of territory, roughly the size of Arunachal Pradesh, regarding the area as "disputed." China lays claim to Tawang on behalf of the Tibetans. But in the exile community in Dharamsala, where the Dalai Lama and thousands of Tibetan refugees live, the community is not impressed. They do not claim Tawang as Tibetan, let alone Chinese territory. The Dalai Lama's travel plans were announced a week after his recent visit to Taiwan to visit victims of tropical storm Morakot. China denounced the Taiwan trip, although its complaints were remarkably muted. The visit to Arunachal Pradesh has now drawn further attention to China's treatment of Tibetan activists and the Dalai Lama's calls for cultural and religious freedom and autonomy.

Tawang became part of modern India when Tibetan leaders signed a treaty with British officials in 1914 that established the McMahon Line between Tibet and British-run India. Tawang fell south of the line. The treaty, the Simla Convention, is not recognized by China. "We recognize it because we agreed to it," said Samdhong Rinpoche, prime minister of the Tibetan government-in-exile. "If China agreed to it now, it would be a recognition of the power of the Tibetan government at that time."

Tawang's native population is almost entirely Buddhist. Its origin is obscure. It was a part of the kingdom of Tibet in medieval times although local tribal rulers have governed it from time to time. The British declared the area off-limits in 1873. India's independence from Britain severed it from Tibet. In 1962 Chinese troops conquered Tawang during the invasion of Tibet and for six months it was controlled by the Chinese. After their retreat, Tawang again came under Indian control.

India denied the Dalai Lama permission to visit Tawang the last time he requested to do so. This time it is playing the Dalai Lama card to the full. Officials in India's Ministry of External Affairs insist that "things are changing" and that India is getting more assertive. On Sept. 16, India's foreign minister, S.M. Krishna, rejected China's opposition to the visit.

In an interview on IBN7, the sister channel of India's CNN-IBN, Krishna said China's objections had no merit. While the government has not explicitly said the visit will be permitted, Krishna said: "Arunachal Pradesh is a part of India and the Dalai Lama is free to go anywhere in India. The only question is that he is not expected to comment on political developments." Analysts say the Tibetan leader's visit will reassert Arunachal's status as an Indian territory. "The timing of his trip [to Arunachal Pradesh] is significant. It comes while the debate over his visit to Taiwan is still hot," said Bhaskar Roy, a New Delhi-based China analyst. "Tibetans are as good at playing these games as the Chinese. They know such a visit will keep up the pressure on China."

In Dharamsala, Samdhong Rinpoche, Tibet's prime minister in exile, called Beijing's objections to the visit "absurd," adding that "Arunachal Pradesh and the Tawang region are an integral part of India. If the Dalai Lama, who has stayed in India for the last 50 years, is visiting any part of the country why does this bother China? If the Dalai Lama goes to Chinese territories it can raise objections but in this case has no business to interfere." The Arunachal Pradesh government is urging New Delhi to ignore the Chinese opposition. "Chinese claims over Arunachal Pradesh are simply baseless and not correct. Arunachal Pradesh is an integral part of India and would continue to be so," said Chief Minister Dorjee Khandu. "They [the Chinese] are opposed to everything that His Holiness does," said a spokesman for the Dalai Lama's private office in Dharamsala.

Tawang's strategic importance cannot be ruled out. The place provides the shortest route from Tibet into India. The Dalai Lama himself took this route to escape into India in 1959. Indian defence officials have already raised alarms declaring China and not Pakistan to be India's biggest threat. They believe that control over Sikkim and Arunachal Pradesh would enable Chinese forces to overrun the entire northeast border region. Chinese troops repeatedly have attempted to gain control of Sikkim's evocatively named Finger Area, a tiny but key strategic location where Beijing does not dispute the frontier.

In June this year, General J J Singh, governor of Arunachal Pradesh and former chief of army staff, announced the deployment of two army divisions of around 25,000 to 30,000 soldiers each along the Arunachal Pradesh border with China. The strength of India's Sukhoi fighter jet fleet in the Northeast is being increased. It remains to be seen if the Dalai Lama's visit will be the trigger that causes them to be used.

CHINA'S BORDER SPAT WITH INDIA

The recent meeting between India's National Security Adviser MK Narayanan and China's Vice-Foreign Minister Dai Banggio at Coonoor in Tamil Nadu was the continuation of a series of such meetings in the context of the border dispute between the two countries. While this is a good thing to go by, the main point is: what has been the actual progress in the matter? After every meeting, a standard joint communiqué is issued to the effect that the téte-a-téte was fruitful and the dialogue is being maintained in an atmosphere of friendship and mutual cooperation. Diplomatic jargon cannot be limitless; it must end somewhere.

Again, from time to time one hears of Chinese intrusion into Arunachal Pradesh, especially in the area of Sumdorong Chu Valley and the northern range of the Mishmi Hills. There is also the occasional media report that China claims this Northeastern state of ours on the grounds of a combination of history as well as geography.

India's drawback is that our foreign policy has always been linked to the vote bank. In fact it was a vote bank issue that created the border dispute with China in the first place way back in the late '50s and early '60s. The origin of this problem is worth discussing as this itself suggests the solution. Soon after China secured Tibet, Beijing sent a delegation to New Delhi under then Prime Minister Zhou en Lai with a proposal on Aksai Chin in northern Kashmir, adjacent to the Siachen Glacier. The delegation submitted to us that movement from Tibet to Sinkiang province was a huge problem because one had to traverse the inhospitable Kunlun Mountains en route. Hence it was suggested both countries could arrive at an understanding by which India could lease out Aksai Chin to China, as this would enable the latter to build an all-weather highway across this stretch of territory.

Thus movement from Tibet to Sinkiang would not then involve negotiating the Kunluns at all and India, too, could use this highway as a bonus. In any case, Aksai Chin was just an ice desert with an average height of 18,000-19,000 feet and nothing grew there, let alone having any human habitation. New Delhi reacted with its usual brash arrogance, thundering words to the effect that 'not an inch of our sacred motherland' would be given, et al. Zhou en Lai was shown the door gracelessly.

The Chinese delegation went back and decided to implement a tenet in Hindi conveying the meaning that if ghee cannot be taken out by a straight finger then a crooked finger would be used!

China militarily attacked India and physically captured Aksai Chin by force in late 1962 and built the desired highway through it. China is still very much in occupation of this area, cocking a snook at India now and then! On our part we bemoaned our fate, blamed Beijing for gerrymandering into our territory and generally made a political nuisance of ourselves. Nothing helped, of course.

During its attack on India, China had also deeply transgressed into what was earlier known as the North East Frontier Agency that later became Arunachal Pradesh. However, after delivering a crushing military-cum-political defeat on India, China moved back to its own side of the border in this area. This apart, China disputes an area along the Uttarkhand-Tibet border named Barahoti.

China has a strong army garrison in this area at a place called Taklakot that keeps a watching brief over Barahoti. India, therefore, has been well and truly boxed in by China, courtesy New Delhi's folly of riding the high horse with Zhou en Lai's delegation of yore. Diplomacy has never been a strong point with us and the country has suffered badly as a consequence. The science and art of statecraft continue to be subservient to the omnipotent vote bank as far as our leaders are concerned.

New Delhi, for reasons best known to itself, brought out a Lok Sabha resolution in 1994 wherein it was categorically stated that we would retake Aksai Chin by force. Obviously this resolution was nothing but a vote bank gimmick that our näive citizens — including many members of our intelligentsia — swallowed all the way. While firmly occupying Aksai Chin, China periodically needles India over Arunachal Pradesh and Barahoti. Normally, Barahoti remains dormant but Arunachal Pradesh makes news, sometimes with alarm. This has been the state of affairs since 1962. No government at New Delhi since that year has tried to accept the reality and taken any pragmatic steps to reconcile the border situation with China, notwithstanding the fact that currently our relations with China are improving virtually by the day.

The question is, what needs to be done in order to resolve the ongoing impasse? There is only one solution: India must formally accept Zhou en Lai's suggestion of yesteryear but cede Aksai Chin to China. It is doubtful whether China will accept the lease aspect now. The Chinese are a very proud race and will never climb down. In any event, China holds the aces in this matter, never mind the McMahon Line's relevancy to us. Truth to tell, this solution was hinted by China's previous regime under President Jiang Zemin through his then Foreign Minister Tang Jiaxuan during Prime Minister AB Vajpayee's tenure. While the Sikkim issue got reconciled, Aksai Chin could not be followed through due to the change of government in India in 2004.

China is not really interested in Barahoti and Arunachal Pradesh — Beijing uses these two as pressure points on New Delhi to see reason over the border dispute, a dispute that hinges purely on Aksai Chin. The sooner we come to terms with this, the better.

INDIANS THEMSELVES CONVINCED OF THE REASONABLENESS OF THEIR POSITION

To understand the Indian position we need to take account of the intense nationalism which underlies Indian politics. Even before 1959 Nehru was being strongly criticised for his apparent refusal to take a hard line with the Chinese over Tibet and the disputed border. After 1959, Nehru may have felt that he had no choice but to take an uncompromising stand towards China if he was to prevent the Indian Right-Wing from exploiting nationalist passions which had been aroused throughout the country. In addition, he had himself suffered a serious blow to his own prestige.

Thus it is possible to conclude that Indian behaviour throughout 1961-2 was influenced by a sense of wounded nationalism and wounded pride, which in turn were a reaction to the events of 1950. If, in fact, we can assume that Indian behaviour was emotionally based, we have a ready explanation of its seemingly unnecessary rigidity. To observers of Sino/Indian relations in the period prior to October 1962 (of which the author was one), it seemed highly likely that the Indian policy of military pressure along the disputed border, together with intransigence over the Aksai Chin and the Dho La strip, would inevitably provoke a Chinese military response in which the Indians could be the only losers.

That Nehru and his advisers had seriously misassessed the probable Chinese reaction to Indian policies and that this misassessment was at least partly a result of the emotional manner in which they had reacted to previous events, has been recently confirmed The former Commander of Indian Military Forces in the N.E.F.A., Lieutenant-General B. M. Kaul, in a book entitled The Untold Story and published in 1966, has given some of the background to events of 1962. Kaul states that Nehru believed the revolt in Tibet indicated a "break in the morale of the Chinese people and armed forces and that if India dealt with the Chinese it would get the better of them". * Kaul also states that the Indian Government decision to move against the Chinese in the Dho La strip was made on September 22, and by way of explanation adds: "Nehru and his Government were deeply concerned about public opinion which was worked up at the time". The decision was queried by the Army Chief, General Thapar, who on October 2 warned that the use of force against the Chinese was bound to have serious repercussions. Nehru assured Thapar that "he had good reasons to believe the Chinese would not take any strong action against us". Kaul adds that on October 11, nine days before the Chinese attack of October 20, he made an unsuccessful approach to the Government to establish "whether I should launch an attack on the Chinese despite their superiority and the possibility of a reverse".

What conclusion can be drawn from all this? Our original aim was to find out whether China had in fact followed a policy of active hostility towards India. If we accept that both sides appear to have been reacting defensively - the Chinese out of undue sensitivity over Tibet and fear of "imperialist" designs against their territory, the Indians out of a sense of wounded pride and nationalism - then it would seem that neither side has taken the initiative to promote hostility: that both sides would have preferred good relations. That both sides would in fact have preferred good relations seems clear from the record of Sino/Indian relations up until 1959.

Little of this has been accepted in the West, where China is widely condemned as the aggressive party in the dispute.

Explanations for Chinese behaviour range widely. The fact of Chinese withdrawal from the N.E.F.A. following defeat of the Indian forces there has not discouraged those who favour the "expansionist China" explanation. Others see the Chinese as wanting (a) to drive India into a pro-Western alignment in order to destroy her non-aligned image, despite the fact that a pro-Western Government on China's southern border means an increased danger to Chinese security, (b) to retard Indian economic growth which was said to be outstripping the Chinese rate of growth, despite the fact it costs China far more than India to maintain troops in the Himalayas and that foreign aid to India has sharply increased since 1962, (c) to overthrow Nehru's Government and replace it with a pro Chinese Government, despite the fact that the 1962 conflict was used as grounds for the imprisonment of the pro-Chinese communist opposition in India; and so on. If one consistent feature emerges from this catalogue of misunderstanding it is the Western refusal to examine impartially the Chinese case in a dispute involving relations with another country.

THE CHINA-INDIA BORDER ISSUE IN 2013: POINT AND COUNTER-POINT

On 15 April around thirty Chinese soldiers crossed an unguarded section of the China-India border – the Line of Actual Control (LAC) – and set up camp, reportedly nineteen kilometres inside territory India claims. In itself this was not an unheard of incident; one Indian newspaper reported that in 2012 there were 'over four hundred incursions', ninety per cent of which occurred in the Ladakh region, where the latest incident took place. This time, though, the Chinese troops set up a camp in the disputed territory, the first time they had done so since 1986.

A flag meeting was held by military representatives of the Indian and Chinese armies but to no avail. At subsequent meetings and through diplomatic channels, and amid much pressure from the mass media and the public, India asked China to withdraw to previously-held positions. China, in turn, asked India to remove the "fortified positions" its troops had constructed along the LAC.

The issue created a good deal of debate in China, India and the rest of the world, where it was reported upon and studied so as to deduce China's motivations for the "transgression" and India's strength and diplomatic maturity in how it dealt with it.

It is in this spirit of debate that Future Directions International presents this Associate Paper. Two noted analysts present the perspectives of China and India respectively. Dr Liu Zongyi is a visiting fellow at the Centre for Strategic and International Studies (CSIS) and a research fellow at the Shanghai Institutes for International Studies (SIIS). Acknowledging the complexity of the border issue, Dr Liu emphasises the symbiotic relationship between the two countries and observes India stands to gain more by allying with China rather than with the United States of America, with which country it is developing fast-growing ties.

Dr Jabin Jacob is the Assistant Director & Fellow, Institute of Chinese Studies, New Delhi. Whilst not denying the complexity of the border issue, Dr Jacob points out that incursions of this type will become the new norm and confidence-building measures will need to acknowledge this fact. He also notes that China, while acknowledging India's rise, appears to be unable to cast off its misgivings in relation to the growing India-US relationship.

TOWARDS MIDDLE POWER COALITIONS

So far these moves by Asian middle powers to look beyond their traditional approaches to security have been fairly tentative, limited to bilateral or at best trilateral arrangements. Middle powers are looking to one another and sensing the possibility of safety in numbers. So what might be their next move? A logical next step would be to begin building flexible middle power coalitions, to explore ways of harnessing the convergent interests and substantial capabilities of India, Australia, Japan, Indonesia and other nations in between.

Of course, the suggestion of a new coalition would immediately raise questions about whether Asia needs yet another security arrangement to add to its alphabet soup of underperforming organisations and initiatives. Talk of a middle power coalition would also raise questions about whether and why it should be an exclusive bloc: who is in, who is out? Moreover, certain middle powers would be more comfortable working with some than with others. So instead of a formal arrangement or a single all-encompassing initiative, the aim should be for regional powers to build on their recent bilateral achievements in security diplomacy and to move towards multiple defence cooperation arrangements involving three or more powers.

The idea is not to seek a single new forum that will replace either the alliances or the current ASEAN-led institutions. Rather, the model should be an array of overlapping coalitions that seek to improve the national security of their members through flexible partnerships defined by geography, capabilities, interests or shared functional objectives. These would be loose, self-selected 'minilateral' arrangements of capable middle players. Importantly, they would include neither China nor the United States.

These coalitions would not of themselves resolve the region's security dilemmas, but could be a valuable instrument to help participating countries advance and protect their interests while coping with change. They would provide an extra measure of insurance against some of the chief risks in the US-China relationship: potential US-China confrontation or conflict, Chinese hegemony, or an accommodation between Washington and Beijing at the expense of the rest of the region. Provided they were shaped intelligently, middle power coalitions could build regional resilience and insulation against the vagaries of the US-China relationship, without unduly provoking China or undermining US engagement.

It should be acknowledged that, initially at least, the United States would be more likely than China to see these developments as favourable to its interests. After all, the United States has encouraged greater regional security cooperation among its allies and non-aligned Asian partners. China is likely to be more suspicious, perhaps seeing such coalitions as an extension of US strategy rather than what they principally would be: prudent mutual help among regional states seeking to increase their ability to provide for their own and common security. This problem of perception is not a reason to abstain from careful coalition building;

rather, it is a risk that regional powers can manage. One way to address Chinese suspicions would be for these coalitions to present shared views to both Beijing and Washington on ways to reduce or manage security differences. At the same time, the coalitions could produce ready-made groupings of countries to engage with China in multilateral security activities, such as providing counter-piracy, search and rescue, and other public goods. Moreover, such coalitions could not be dismissed by China as 'containment', especially if they are not led by the United States. In this sense, middle power coalitions that do not include Washington could also help neutralise attitudes of reflexive anti-Americanism or Chinese-cultivated pan-Asianism within some regional countries.

Arguing for middle power coalitions is not the same as arguing for formal alliances among middle powers. It remains unrealistic at this stage to envisage coalition members taking on great strategic risk themselves to directly assist one another in a confrontation or conflict, such as a clash with China, in the absence of a lead role from the United States.

For instance, it is difficult to imagine India being willing to assist Japan with military force were it to find itself at war with China over disputed islands, given that India has its own border tensions and economic ties with China to worry about. For the foreseeable future, a coalition would be highly unlikely to have the political solidarity or resolve to balance against Chinese power in a conflict without the support of the United States. And even if such resolve could be found, the combined material capacities of a combination of regional powers minus the United States – say Japan and India plus several others – would not be a match for China.

What Would The Coalitions Do?

So far, the efforts of Indo-Pacific middle powers to build security relations with one another have been modest and bilateral, or managed in three-way partnerships involving the United States. A shift towards middle power coalitions, however informal, would be a step change. What, conceivably and realistically, could middle power coalitions do? Here are some possibilities.

Political consultations: This would occur first, including at leaders' level. Much of the current generation of regional leaders, notably three conservative leaders, Indian prime minister Narendra Modi, Japanese prime minister Shinzo Abe, and Australia prime minister Tony Abbott, have sufficient power domestically to be able to drive and sustain bold new foreign policy departures. They would be in a position to direct their diplomatic and defence establishments towards serious cooperation.

Diplomatic coordination: Next would come closer coordination by officials on emerging regional issues. An emphasis by these coalitions on the peaceful resolution of territorial disputes, respect for the Law of the Sea, and the right to secure freedom of navigation would help press ASEAN to be bolder and push the United States to remain purposeful against Chinese maritime assertiveness. At the same time, united diplomatic fronts by middle powers could help moderate China's behaviour by making it clear to Beijing – and domestic audiences in China – that their efforts reflect the will of the region rather than some American design. Visible diplomatic cooperation among Asian middle powers would counter Beijing's 'Asia for Asians' stratagem. The coordination activities could be expanded to include the creation of caucuses in regional and global meetings, from the East Asia Summit and other ASEAN-centric bodies to the G20 and United Nations forums, to mobilise on an issue-by-issue basis.

Intelligence exchanges: Given the vastness of the Indo-Pacific region, few if any regional intelligence establishments have a complete picture of its rapidly evolving geopolitical dynamics. Of special importance would be the exchange of military intelligence, especially in the maritime domain. Generating shared maritime domain awareness should be a major priority. This could begin in sub-regions, for instance India- Australia-Indonesia maritime surveillance cooperation in their contiguous waters of the north-eastern Indian Ocean, encompassing critical sea lanes. There may even be scope in time for some of the middle powers to share their intelligence-gathering capabilities or facilities, although this would need to factor in sensitivities about sharing of intelligence provided to some of these partners by the United States. Still, no one state

– including the United States – is in a position to monitor the vast Indo-Pacific littoral alone. So new cooperative endeavours in this field are worth exploring, and these could also help allay mistrust on intelligence issues among some middle powers, such as Australia and Indonesia.

Military exercises: India, Japan, Australia, Indonesia and Singapore already conduct a wide array of bilateral exercises with one another and other partners, from disaster relief through to some instances of high-end operational training. These could expand, both in scope and participation, as a step towards operational cooperation. These could be focused around the provision of regional 'public goods' through cooperation on counter-piracy activities, disaster relief, counter-terrorism, search and rescue, and the prevention of illegal activities at sea. India, Japan and Australia already participate in international peace and stability operations of various kinds. The three countries could do more to share their experiences and create an institutional framework for future cooperation in such operations. These three maritime powers could form an effective core for engaging with other partners on a case-by-case basis, including China as its navy becomes more active in the Indian Ocean.

Interoperability: As India encounters the projection of Chinese naval power, it will likely become more open to developing interoperability with partners, a concept it has traditionally resisted. If Indian wariness of working closely with the US Navy continues, it may be politically easier for it instead to build coalitions with such powers as Australia, Japan, Vietnam and Indonesia. India and its coalition partners could pursue agreements for logistical cooperation, replenishment access to each other's bases and island territories, and status of forces agreements that might better prepare all participants to respond to emerging maritime challenges. There are precedents. Despite India's strategic autonomy, Singapore for example has had access to Indian military facilities for over a decade.

Technology sharing and transfer: This might include the coordinated acquisition, production or maintenance of some military systems. Given the complexities of weapons procurement and development in each Indo-Pacific middle player – with India the most glaring example – this may seem unrealistically ambitious. But signs of change are evident. For example, India, Australia and Japan are all acquiring P-8 long-range maritime surveillance aircraft. India, which has long experience in operating Kilo Class submarines, is helping Vietnam to manage its acquisition of the same from Russia. India is negotiating the purchase and coproduction of US-2 amphibious aircraft from Japan. Canberra is reportedly showing an interest in Japanese submarine technology, and eventual Indian interest in this is also conceivable. In the short term, multi-nation collaboration on patrol boat production and purchases would be feasible, and partnerships in sonar technology development are another prospect worth investigating. The improving quality of defence production in Asia, particularly in Japan and South Korea, and those countries' increased interest in export potential provide a reason for partner states to consider diversifying beyond established European and US industry links. This dynamic will intensify with the expanding role of the private sector in India's defence industry, which is already well underway in shipbuilding.

Capacity building: Several of the proposed Indo-Pacific partners, notably Australia, India and Japan, have assisted other countries in the region improve their security capabilities, from maritime forces to counter-terrorism. Greater coordination of this work could reduce duplication and help states such as Indonesia, Vietnam and the Philippines improve their capacity to provide for their own security and become security providers in turn. Such capacity building could include training or the transfer of capabilities, such as a recent deal for Japan to provide patrol boats to Vietnam.

7

Sino-Indian Border Dispute and Their Competitive Symbiotic Relationship

Recently, the Sino-Indian border dispute once again became a focus of for the world's mass media. A "tent confrontation" between the Chinese and Indian armies took place and continued near the Line of Actual Control (LAC) for several days.

From the Indian point of view, the Chinese army invaded Indian territory, and this incident was "the most serious one in the past 25 years". Level-headed analysis will indicate, however, that China would not wish to provoke simultaneous conflicts with Japan and India, two major Asian powers. In fact, the Indian mass media's reports about Chinese incursions have been heard continually in recent years. Some reports that the Chinese have invaded India for more than 600 times in the past three years are ridiculous.

The Sino-Indian border issue is very complicated. It was left over from the time of British rule in India and has never been resolved. In the 1960s, a military conflict broke out between China and India over territorial boundaries. That conflict became the excuse for India to develop its armed forces vigorously, to get ready for battle, and to make nuclear weapons. The root reason cause of many of the "incursion" incidents reported by India is that the two sides have never reached a consensus on the position of the LAC since the boundary conflict in 1962. They have never delimited the LAC, let alone a formal border. It is therefore debatable to say the Chinese army invaded Indian territory.

Since 1993, however, China and India have signed two agreements and one protocol on the maintenance of peace and tranquillity and the establishment of confidence-building measures in the border areas. They have set up a working mechanism for consultation and coordination on border affairs. These efforts have helped ensure a durable peace and stability in the border areas. The possibility that China and India will come to serious conflict is very small.

Bilateral relations between China and India are very subtle; apart from the boundary problem, the issues of China-Pakistan relations, the Dalai Lama and water resources also hinder the promotion of China-India relations. These problems have given India a deep-seated distrust of China. Some Indians are gradually losing self-confidence as they observe the growing economic gap between China and India. The Indian mass media and some Indian strategic scholars frequently refer to a "Chinese incursion" and the "China threat" and propagate an attitude of no confidence in China's intentions. This situation provides opportunities for some Western countries to undermine Sino-India relations. With the US "rebalancing" toward the Asia-Pacific, the Sino-Indian relationship is undergoing subtle changes these days. Some Indian scholars promote an alliance under the US leadership to counterbalance China. For example, Harsh V. Pant, a professor of defence studies at King's College London, argues that India's strategic interests can only be realised by an Asia-Pacific arrangement in which the US retains its predominant status. The Indian Express columnist C. Raja Mohan similarly urges India to shift its policy of strategic autonomy and strategically cooperate with the US.

So far, India has concentrated on strengthening its "Look East" Policy to enhance strategic and security cooperation with countries such as Japan, South Korea, Malaysia and Vietnam. It has also taken a high profile in the South China Sea disputes. In December 2011, the first trilateral dialogue between the US, Japan and India was presided over by the US. One of the discussion topics was China's growing military and political global position.

It is no wonder that many think that India may abandon strategic autonomy to ally itself with the US and contain China.

Currently, Indian policymakers have a relatively clear view of Sino-Indian and India-US relations. India doesn't yet have the ability to directly confront China, and, as a country prioritising economic development, it is in need of a peaceful neighbouring environment. History shows that the US is not a reliable ally for India. Because of the effect of the economic crisis, the US is heavily burdened by its domestic economic problems, and there are doubts about how much money can be invested in counterbalancing China. The US anchors its hope on the strategy of "offshore balancing" to achieve balance with, or even contain, China by stirring up tensions between it and its Asian strategic partners. It is just taking advantage of India's strength to balance China, which, in effect, should kill two birds with one stone.

So, at present, we have the ironic spectacle of articles in both the US and Indian media trying to provoke each other into tensions with China. The Indian media highlights the idea that Uncle Sam is well-prepared to battle China, while the US media points out that India is engaging in military expansion in preparation for possible Sino-Indian boundary conflicts. India still maintains its status as a "swing state" in the international system. Although it has recently become more pro-US, since the US recognised India as a nuclear power despite it not being a signatory to the Nuclear Non-Proliferation Treaty (NPT), India will not abandon its strategic autonomy to ally with the US. Sino-Indian relationship is, in essence, a competitive symbiotic relationship. I say that for the following reasons: First of all, there really are some areas of competitions between China and India, mainly in geopolitics, trade and energy, etc. But that competition is not necessarily cutthroat and zero sum. China and India can cooperate if they have mutual trust. In fact, they do cooperate in fields such as energy and anti-terrorism.

In addition to the aspect of competition, the Sino-Indian symbiotic relationship can be divided into four areas: First, as two big powers that are rising simultaneously, China and India are in similar positions in the current international system. They are beneficiaries of that system, but at the same time, they are constrained by it and also suppressed by the dominant power in the system. They want to gradually advance the reform of this system. So, China and India have common interests on many global issues, such as the reform of the international financial system, climate change, and the WTO negotiations. China, India, Brazil and South Africa have organised the BRICS and BASIC groups, which promote the reform of the international order. If China, India and other countries cannot consolidate their views on these global issues, they could be crushed one by one by the dominant power in the system and lose forever the chance to rise again. Secondly, in the trilateral relations between China, India and the United States, India's status will benefit from China's rise. China's growth is a prerequisite for India's rise. If India really becomes embroiled in conflicts with China, it's hard to say whether the US will stretch out a hand to help it. But if India surpasses China, it will definitely replace its neighbour as the target of the US.

Thirdly, as two neighbouring powers in Asia, both China and India need a peaceful and stable periphery to develop their economies. Statesmen in both countries know clearly that development is their primary task, and that development needs stable circumstances. So, China and India have a common task to maintain the stability of the region. This is the determining factor that encourages China and India to keep their border areas stable for at least 10 years.

At least, the Chinese and Indian economies are complementary. Since they are in symbiosis, they could, theoretically, nourish and assist each other's survival and development. Sino-Indian bilateral trade has developed quickly in the past ten years, and the trade volume has risen 20 fold. Although India complains that there are some problems in the bilateral trade structure, and the Indian trade deficit is too large, it is evident that Chinese goods, which are of good quality and cheap, raise Indian people's living standards. China and India have ample room to cooperate, especially in infrastructure construction. China has large amounts of capital and extensive experience in the construction of infrastructure; India on the other hand needs to improve its infrastructure facilities, but lacks finance. Sino-Indian cooperation in this field will benefit both sides.

Within India, the so-called "China threat" is a trick of Indian political figures to pull the wool over the eyes of their people and Western countries. From the aspect of domestic politics, by making waves in relations with China, Indian politicians can obscure domestic contradictions, bolster up national morale, pull votes, and the military can get an increasing budget. From the aspect of international politics, India can obtain advanced weaponry and technologies from Western countries. In fact, the major direction of Indian military expansion is the Indian Ocean - the Navy received the largest part of India's rapidly growing defence budget. India's military strategy on land is defensive in nature but in the Indian Ocean, India has another competitor that is much stronger than China. The so-called "China threat" is just a cover.

The direction of Sino-Indian relations is determined for the medium-term at least, but the border issue is still a hindrance to bilateral relations. India did undertake some domestic reflection on the Sino-Indian conflict of 1962 and Nehru's policy towards China at that time, but no consensus was achieved. The Indian government never released publicly the Henderson-Brooks report that summarised the reasons why India was defeated. Taking a coherent view of this history will play a decisive role in the peaceful resolution of the Sino-Indian border problem. We should not neglect the negative role of the Indian multiparty system, in which foreign policy is often hijacked by domestic affairs. The role of the opposition parties and mass media in the Sino-Indian border conflict of 1962 is a case in point. It is necessary for the Indian government to reveal the truth about the Sino-Indian boundary conflict to the Indian people, and for Chinese and Indian scholars to conduct joint research projects on some historical problems, to alter the longstanding misconceptions held by both sides.

PERSECUTION OF CHINESE INDIANS

The state-perpetrated persecution of Chinese Indians was authorised by the Defence of India Act in late 1962. After the brief

Sino-Indian War, India incarcerated thousands of Chinese-Indians in an internment camp in Deoli, Rajasthan, where they were held for years without trial. The last internees were not released until 1967. Thousands more Chinese-Indians were forcibly deported or coerced to leave India. Nearly all internees had their properties sold off or looted.

Indian officials openly compare the internment of Chinese-Indians with the internment of Japanese-Americans during WWII. However, unlike the United States, the Indian government has not apologised or offered compensation to the internees.

The earliest recorded Chinese settlers in British India arrived in Calcutta in 1780. Because of the long history of tea cultivation in China, the British used "fair and unfair means" to lure experienced workers from China to work on the newly established tea plantations in Assam, starting in 1838. Other Chinese migrants were refugees from poverty, famine, and disasters in China. By the late 19th century, the people of Chinese origin had gained a reputation as craftsmen and traders in eastern India. During World War II and the ensuing Communist revolution in China, a large wave of Chinese war refugees settled in Calcutta, North Bengal, and Northeast India. Estimates of the ethnic Chinese population in 1962 varied from 20,000 to 60,000.

Following the independence of the Republic of India in 1947 and the founding of the People's Republic of China in 1949, the two countries enjoyed a period of friendly relationship, despite having unresolved border disputes in the areas of NEFA and Aksai Chin. The relationship deteriorated, however, after the construction of a Chinese highway in Aksai Chin in 1957, and India's support of the failed 1959 Tibetan uprising against Chinese rule. The hostilities culminated in the brief 1962 Sino-Indian War, resulting in a decisive Chinese victory but no change in the effective boundary between the two countries. The fighting lasted from 10 October to 20 November 1962. On 21 November, China declared ceasefire and withdrew from NEFA, the larger of the two disputed territories, but kept the smaller Aksai Chin.

After the outbreak of the war, the Indian government and some members of academia systematically portrayed the Chinese minority as untrustworthy and deceitful. The rising nationalism in India entailed brutal assaults on the ethnic Chinese, including Indian citizens and residents who had lived in India for generations. Many Chinese schools and media were shut down, and people of Chinese descent were assaulted by mainstream Indians; their property, restaurants, and shops damaged. The civil liberties of the ethnic Chinese were curtailed. People of Chinese descent were required to report to the authorities for "registration and classification", and it became harder for non-citizens to meet the residency requirements. The legal definition of foreigners was extended to include Indian citizens of Chinese descent.

Faced with widespread hostility, many Chinese-Indians expressed their support and loyalty for the Indian cause, condemned the Chinese government, and donated to India's defence funds. However, their expressions of support were met with suspicion and contempt.

After its defeat in the war, India passed the Defence of India Act in December 1962, permitting the "apprehension and detention in custody of any person [suspected] of being of hostile origin." The broad language of the act allowed for the arrest of any person simply for having a Chinese surname, a drop of Chinese blood, or a Chinese spouse. Under the draconian law, 10,000 people of Chinese origin were estimated to have been detained from all over India, including Calcutta, Bombay, Darjeeling, Kalimpong, Jamshedpur, and the Northeast. All of them were accused of being spies, but not a single charge has ever been proven. The internment of Chinese-Indians violated both the Constitution of India and the Universal Declaration of Human Rights, to which India was an original signatory.

Starting in November 1962, many ethnic Chinese were given the order to leave India within a month. About 7,500 people complied and left for various countries including China, Taiwan, Hong Kong, Pakistan, Japan, Australia, Britain, United States, and Canada. People who could not raise travel expenses or were unwilling to leave were imprisoned. While some were held in local prisons, thousands more were transported across India to the desert prison camp in Deoli, Rajasthan, built by the British in 1942 as a POW camp for Japanese, German, and Italian combatants during WWII. The camp housed 7,000 inmates, 60 per cent of whom were children or elderly people. Many internees, unaccustomed to the hot desert climate, died of heat stroke and related diseases.

In 1964, the Deoli prison authorities announced that all internees would be deported to China. The forcible deportations were arbitrary, resulting in the breakup of many families. In many cases parents were separated from their children and never heard from them again. The deportations stopped after a few months, and the government offered the remaining inmates the option to migrate to China. Some took the offer, but about 2,500 chose to stay and wait for the chance to return home.

In 1965, the Indian government began to release the internees. They were allowed to leave the camp in small batches. The last internees were released from Deoli in mid-1967, after four and half years of captivity. However, when the internees were transported to their old neighbourhoods, the local governments often did not know what to do with them and kept them in local prisons, in some cases for more than a year.

After the internees were freed after years of incarceration, many discovered that their properties had been sold off in their absence, but were only offered tiny sums for compensation. Almost all internees had their homes, shops, and factories looted or taken over by locals.

The Chinese population in Calcutta decreased by half, from 20,000 to 10,000. Those who remained were seen as enemies, and most could not hold any job except in the restaurant, tanning, and shoemaking businesses. Moreover, their movements were restricted. Until the mid-1980s, the Chinese-Indians were required to report to designated police stations once a month; until the mid-1990s, they had to apply for special permits to travel more than a few kilometres from their homes.

Indian officials openly compare the internment of Chinese-Indians with the internment of Japanese-Americans during WWII. However, unlike the United States, the Indian government has refused to apologise or offer compensation to the internees for their unjustified incarceration.

When asked about his opinion on the issue in 2008, Mao Siwei, China's consul general in Calcutta, replied that China would rather "look forward and not argue too much about the past for the time being". The Indian Chinese Association has been pressuring the Indian government to issue an apology, without success. The Association of India Deoli Camp Internees, a Canadian non-profit group, has written two open letters to Indian Prime Minister Manmohan Singh, but has not received a reply.

In 2004, Rafeeq Ellias recounted the appalling treatment of the Chinese residents in Calcutta in the documentary film *The Legend of Fat Mama*. The documentary won the Silver Lotus Award for best anthropological/ ethnographic film at the 52nd National Film Awards.

ACHIEVEMENTS IN THE BORDER NEGOTIATIONS

Since the 1980s, the China-India border talks have experienced three stages, with each stage covering roughly one decade. The first stage covered the 1980s culminated in Indian Prime Minister Rajiv Gandhi's visit toChina in December 1988. The second stage covered the 1990s ended with India's nuclear tests in 1998; and the third stage covered the past 10 years marked with Indian President Patil's China trip during the celebration of the 60th anniversary of the establishment of China-India diplomatic relations in May 2010.

The Eight-Round Border Talks in the 1980s

The eight-round border talks took place in the period from hostility to detente in the China-India-relations. The talks obviously eased the tensions in their bilateral relations and resulted in agreement on the disagreements. These talks relieved both governments of pressing too hard on matters of substance while procedural disagreement seemed to be employed as excuse for no-progress. This suggests that neither government found it urgent to resolve the border dispute in the 1980s. Both sides hoped to reduce tensions and stabilize and improve bilateral relations, but they realized it premature to proceed to resolve their border disputes.

The 1988 China-India summit was the first meeting of he top leaders of the two countries in the 28 years since premier Zhou Enlai's visit to India in 1960.

Rajiv gandi's Beijing trip in December 1988 ushered in a new era of China-India relationship. With the detente prevailed in the world during the last years of the Cold War, India's diplomacy has lost the fulcrum of Indo-Soviet strategic partnership while China's diplomacy has lost the pillar of Sino-US cooperation. China andIndia suddenly found that they needed to re-orient their foreign policies within the context of the changed world power structure. The five principles of peaceful co-existence again became the common basis of their foreign policy reorientation.

In his inaugural address on December 31, 1984, Rajiv Gandhi stressed the continuation of a non-alignment policy and expressed his desire to improve relations with neighboring countries.

Huang Hua's India's trip was marked by the agreement to open negotiations on the border dispute and the development of China-India relations. There followed eight rounds of China-India talks as an official channel of the China-India dialogue on the border dispute.

China's strategy on the eight-round border talks comprised two main aspects. One was to insist on a package deal, and the other was to develop their bilateral relations in other fields with the border dispute shelved. During his interview with Krishna Kumar, the editor of *Vikrant*, on June 21, 1980, Deng Xiaoping renewed the "package" approach on the border issue. He stated that China would be willing to accept the watershed principle in the eastern sector in exchange for India's renunciation of claims to Aksai Chin. In other words, both sides should agree to accept the present line of actual control as their boundary. During his meeting with Indian Prime Minister Atal Vajpayee in February 1979, Deng stated that " We shall seek common ground while reserving our differences. We can solve the boundary question through peaceful consultation. This question should not prevent us from improving our relations in other field.

India insisted on sector-by-sector negotiations and refused China's package deal and both sides failed to narrow their differences during the eight rounds of talks. However, all the principles and concerns put on the table by both sides constituted sme mutually acceptable principles for substantive discussions on the border question. Both sides cautiously inched forward without getting bogged down in differing interpretations.

At the eighth round held in New Delhi, on November 14-17, 1986, India gave up its position of "boundary settlement or nothing." China had accepted the approach of the sector-by-sector review within the framework of comprehensive settlement in 1984.

Both agreed that pending a settlement of the border issue, the two governments should develop friendly relations and strengthen cooperation in other fields. Both sides agreed that peace and tranquility should be maintained all along the border. Both sides are prepared for Rajiv Gandhi's Visit to China. Apparently, the stage as set for raising the border dialogue to the political level.

The eight rounds of the border talks in the 1980s showed that India's policy on the border talks changed first from non-negotiation to negotiation, and then from "boundary settlement or nothing" to overall development in all fields. China-India dialogue of the 1980s substituted China-India Detente for their enmity.

Rajiv's visited symbolized the general trend of transition from hostility and confrontation to detente and dialogue. The 1988 summit also marked a departure from the previous approach, political settlement approach substituted for the legalistic approach. Both sides reduced their stress on historical documents and focused instead on their respective security interests by attaching inpotance to mutual bargaining and mutual understanding.

A BRIEF REVIEW OF THE CHINA-INDIA BORDER DISPUTE

The entire China-India boundary has never been formally delimited by any mutually-accepted treaty. There has existed a boundary line of actual control between the two countries. It took shape on the basis of the extent of each other's administrative jurisdiction over a long course of time. The entire boundary has been traditionally divided into three sectors—the eastern sector, the middle sector, and the western sector with all in dispute. The western sector involves the dispute over the Aksai Chin area India claims as part of Latah andChina claims as part of Xinjiang. The middle sector involves a dispute over various points between the Tibet-Kashmir- Punjab border junction and the Nepal-Tibet-Uttar Pradesh border junction. The eastern sector involves a dispute over the area between the pre-1914 Outer Line and the McMahon Line.

In the eastern sector, the British–Indian government had observed the foothills of the Himalayas as the "Outer Line" of its administrative jurisdiction by 1914. Although the Chinese-Tibetan authorities had claimed the tribal areas beyond the British Outer Line within the Tibetan jurisdiction, their administrative jurisdiction actually covered only Tawang tract, the Walong area along the Lohit valley, and some other scattered enclaves in the tribal areas.

Today the line of actual control observed by both sides conforms to the McMahon Line. The disputed area between the pre-1914 Outer Line and the McMahon Line covers a total area of 90,000 square kilometers.

According to China, this area is composed of Tibet's three districts of Monyul, Loyul and lower Zayul. According to India, this area is its Arunachal Pradesh, formerly the North-East Frontier Agency of Assam State.

In the western sector, the line of actual control runs roughly along the Karakoram range, conforming to the Chinese claim. The Indian government claims that the boundary runs along the Kunlun range from theKarakoram Pass. The disputed Area is the Aksai Chin region between the two ranges, covering a total area of about 33,000 square kilometers. This area falls mainly in China's Xinjiang and part of it belongs to the Ari District of Tibet. India claims that it is part of its Ladakh area of the State of Jammu and Kashmir. This area, sparsely inhabited, serves as the traffic artery linking Xinjiang and Tibet.

Therefore, in terms of the general China-India border dispute, the McMahon Line in the eastern sector and Aksai Chin in the western sector have been central to the negotiations on the settlement of the border dispute.

The Mystery of the McMahan Line

After Russia successfully divided Mongolia into Outer and Inner Mogolia with the Outer Mongolia as a buffer zone between China and Russia, the British- Indian authorities dreamed the same dream and tried to divideTibet into Outer Tibet and Inner Tibet and made the Outer Tibet as a buffer zone between British India andChina. To achieve such a objective, the Simla conference was held in 1914,with British Henry McMahon, Chinese Chen Ivan, and Tibetan Lonchen shatra as representatives.

There were actually two parallel conferences at Simla, the tripartite conference focusing on the division ofTibet, and the other was the secret one, keeping Chen Ivan out of their negotiations on the Indian-Tibetan boundary. In early 1914, Henry McMahon and Lonchen Shatra secretly negotiated on the division of Tibet and the boundary between Assam and Tibet as a package deal. An agreement was reached through a secret exchange of notes in Delhi on March 24 and 25, 1914. This boundary line, later known as the McMahon line, was shown on a map in two sheets.

The tripartite conference focused on McMahon's proposal referring to China's suzerainty over Tibet and the outer-inner division of Tibet. On the map attached to the draft convention of the conference, two lines were drawn, one red and the other blue. The red line showed Tibet as a geographical and political unit, and the blue line divided Inner from Outer Tibet. In its southern extension, the red line curves around along the crest of theHimalayas, roughly conforming to the McMahon Line except in the Tawang tract where the McMahon Line reached short of the Tawang tract , implying that the Tawang tract remained part of Tibetan territory. On this map, the Tawang tract was not put within the British-Indian territory.

Without the consent of the Chinese government, Chen Ivan, under McMahon's threat and pressure, initiated the draft convention on April 27, 1914, but with the clear understanding that "to initial and to sign are two different actions," and that his initials would not bind his government, whose views he would immediately seek. The next day, the Chinese government instructed Chen Ivan that "The Chinese representative was forced to initial the draft convention. The Chinese government cannot accept it. You should declare it invalid." Since Chen Ivan refused to sign the draft convention, it was then amended and initialed by McMahon and Lonchen Shatra on July 3, 1914. On the map attached to the draft convention, the McMahon Line was marked just across the town of Tawang, indicating that the area to the north of Tawang would fall within the Tibetan territory.

The British-Indian government did not accept the Simla convention. Viceroy Hardinge forwarded McMahon's report on the Simla conference to London on July 23, 1914, stating that the Indian government recognized that a consideration of the northeastern frontier did not form part of the functions of the conference, and the views and proposal put forward might be regarded as personal to Henry McMahon, not carrying the endorsement of the Government of India.

Chen was also instructed to declare that the Chinese government "would not recognize any treaty or similar document that might now or hereafter be signed between Great Britain andTibet." The Tibetan authorities understood that without securing the Sino-Tibetan boundary, they could not accept the Indo-Tibetan boundary.

The Dalai Lama even recognized the logic relationship between the status of Tibet and the legality of the McMahon Line. In his 1959 address to the Indian Council of World Affairs, he contended that if Tibet had no sovereignty when the Simla convention laid down the McMahon Line, that line was invalid. He challenged Nehru that if you deny the sovereign status to Tibet, you deny the validity of the McMahon Line."

Three maps are related to the Simla conference. One is attached to the March 24 notes; one to the April 27 convention, and the third to the July 3 convention. As far as the Tawang Tract is concerned, the three maps show the McMahon line quite differently. On the first map, the McMahon Line was shown running alng south of the Thagla range far north of Tawang; on the second map, it is not shown in the Tawang tract; and on the third one, it is superimposed on the word " Tawang".

In 1936, Basil Gould, Political Officer in Sikkim, was dispatched to Lhasa and discussed the Tawang issue with the Tibetan government. The Tibetan attitude was Tawang had been Tibetan up to 1914 and they regarded the adjustment of the Tibet-Indian boundary as part and parcel of the general adjustment and determination of boundaries contemplated in the 1914 convention. If they could, with British help, secure a definite Sino-Tibetan boundary, they would observe the Indo-Tibetan border as defined in 1914.

In 1944, just before the British quit from India, basil Gould informed the Tibetan authorities that the Bitish-Indian government was willing to modify the McMahon Line soas to exclude Tawang from the territory it claimed. He also proposed that the Se La range should be a new boundary line. However, Thc Tibetan authorities did not accepted it and continued to collect revenues in the Tawang tract and remained administrative control over the Tawang tract.

It was in February1951 that the Indian government took over the Tawang tract by force before the PLA entered and liberated Tibet. The Tibetan authorities organized protest demonstrations in Tawang and Lhasaagainst India's occupation of the Tawang tract, but no avail.

As far as the objective of the Simla conference was concerned, it certainly aborted. The McMahon Line was not even accepted by the British-Indian government. After the Simla conference, from 1914 to 1935, on the official maps published by the Survey of India, the McMahon Line was not shown, but instead the Outer Line along the foothills of the Himalayas was shown. The Tibetan authorities continued to exercise administrative jurisdiction in the tribal areas as they did before. The Simla conference went down in history as an unaccomplished cause.

As to the Simla conference, the first official record appeared in Volume XIV of the 1929 edition of Aichison'sTreaties. It did not refer to the McMahon Line, but to the discussion on the Sino-

Tibetan frontier. It was stated that a tripartite convention was drawn up and initialed in 1914, but the Chinese government refused to permit its representative to proceed to full signature.

In 1935, Olaf Caroe, deputy secretary of the Foreign and Political Department of the British-Indian Government discovered the secret documents of the Simla conference in dealing with a case involving the illegal entry into Tibet through the Tawang tract. He realized that the northeastern frontier might be a matter of dispute with the Chinese in the future. He proposed to revise the official record of the Simla conference in the Aichison's Treaties and show the McMahon Line on the official maps. The British government approved his proposal.

This original 1929 edition was soon withdrawn from circulation and replaced by a spurious edition, actually printed in 1938, but with an imprint of 1929. However, at least three copies of the original 1929 edition survived, one in Peking Library, one in Harvard University library, and one in the India Office. In the revised edition, it was stated that the Simla conference negotiated an agreement on the status of Tibet and the boundary of Tibet with both China and India. Such a revision was nothing but scandalous diplomatic forgery. Then the McMahon Line began to appear o the Indian official maps. However, it was still marked as "Undemarcated Boundary."

The Puzzle of Aksai Chin

In the western sector of the China-India border, the dispute has centered on the Aksai Chin area. The British left Aksai Chin area as "undefined" at the time of their transfer of power in 1947.nehru himself once stated that " it is a matter of argument as to what art of it (Aksai Chin) belongs to us and what part of it belongs to somebody else.... The point is, there has never been any delimitation there in that area and it has been a challenged area."

Before the British left India, the British-Indian government had shown no boundary at all in that area on its official maps. In Volume XII of Aichison'd Treaties published in 1931, it was stated that"The northern as well as the eastern boundary of the Kashmir state is still undefined." The Survey of India maps published in the 190s and 1930s did not indicate any boundary alignment or show any color difference inthis are, and wide spaces between Kashmir and Xinjiang and between Kashmir and Tbet were shown blank. Louis Dane, Indian Foreign Secretry, stated clearly in a letter to the Indian office that Aksai Chin was I Chinese Xinjiag. The neighborhood of the Lanak Pass at the head of the Changchenmo valley was supposed to be the most northerly boundary point on the Kashmir-Tibet border.

In 1945, guided by Olaf Caroe, then foreign secretary of India, on new Survey of India maps the Aksai Chin area bgan to be shown by a color-wash with the words"Boundary Undefined" marked on it.

In 1947, the Indian Army in its "top secret" m submitted to thc British Cabinet Mission accepted the Karakoram range as the northern boundary of India in the western sector.

However, after the signing of the trade agreement concerning Tibet in 1954, following Nehru's instructions, new Survey of India maps began to show an international boundary in the western sector running along the crest of the Kunlun range, which for the first time placed the whole Aksai Chin area within the Indian territory. According to Sir H.A.F. Rumbold, an official in the Indian Office, the Simon Commission wished to include a map of India in Volume I of their report in 1929. Rumbold found nothing in the India office to justify the line on the Kunlun range shown on some maps. The Commission accordingly adopted a line roughly along the crest of the Karakoram range, excluding the Aksai Chin area. Nehru, even on August 28, 1959, stated in the Lok Sabha that "This was the boundary of the old Kashmir statewith Tibet and Chinese Turkestan. Nobody had marked it."

On the other hand, Chinese maps have shown the Karakoram range as its boundary in the western sector at least since the 1920s. There was no evidence that the British-Indian authorities ever disputed this with the Chinese government before they left India in 1947.

The widely accepted modern concept of boundary marking involes three steps: delimitation, delineation and demarcation.

Delimitation involves defining the boundary in written terms through treaties and agreements. Delineation involves sketching the boundary in maps through joint boundary surveys. Demarcation involves marking the boundary line on the ground through pillars, chains and other markers.

Reviewing the historic facts for the entire China-India border, such a China-India boundary has never existed, though each side has made its own territorial claims. Historical facts have also showed that, in the old days, wide desolate tracts in the remote high mountains between the two countries were physically inaccessible.

Therefore, the China-India border dispute has been the dispute on the "zone" rather than the " line" in the eastern and western sectors. Mutual understanding and recognition of such historical evolution of the China-India border should become the starting point for the future border deliberations.

LOOK BEYOND THE SINO-INDIAN BORDER DISPUTE

The Sino-Indian border dispute originated from the British and Russian expansion in Central Asia in the early 20th century. Since the 1950s, the border dispute has always shadowed the ebb and flow of the Sino-Indian relations. The simmering border dispute erupted after the revolt the Dalai Lama clique engineered in 1959. The CIA-supported revolt in Tibet, India-embraced the Dalai Lama, and India-hosted Tibetan Government-in-exile turned out to be one of the causes of the border war in 1962. Nehru's policy of no-dispute and no-negotiation and his forward policy became a direct cause of the border war. Then the China-India relationship dramatically moved toward hostility and confrontation from brotherhood and friendship and entered an era of cold war which lasted nearly two decades.

The Chinese and Indian governments have attempted to resolve the border dispute through diplomatic negotiations since the1980s. The border negotiations have been institutionalized and generated several meaningful documents. However, each other's position on the border disputes themselves has never been changed.

To accelerate and intensify the boundary negotiations, the two governments have agreed to appoint the two Special Representatives.

They have periodically met and conducted an in-depth exchange of views on resolving the boundary question. Both sides have agreed to press ahead with the framework negotiations in accordance with the agreed political parameters and guiding principles so as to seek for a fair and reasonable solution acceptable to both. Prior to that, both sides should work together to maintain peace and tranquility in the border areas. Although the border dispute remains unresolved in all the sectors, peace, stability, and tranquility have been maintained by the joint efforts of the two governments.

While we are cautiously optimistic about the steady improvement of the bilateral relations between the two rising Asian giants, we are increasingly concerned about the consequences of their geopolitical rhetoric and strategic suspicion originated primarily from the unresolved border dispute.

FACTS BEHIND CHINA-INDIA BORDER DISPUTE

If a general of the Chinese imperial government representing the Manchu dynasty had, by force of arms, pillage and plunder, succeeded in subjugating the North American continent and on that basis had artificially created a border line between the United States and Canada called, let us say, The Manchu Line, would a sovereign U.S. government abide by thus border line?

Let us suppose further that the boundary line demarcated by this general included, for the Canadian side, parts of Buffalo, Detroit, Seattle and Duluth. Let us suppose again that the treaty between Canada and the U.S. dictated by this general had never been accepted by any government of the United States, and that in truth the people of the U.S. regarded this treaty and its boundary line as illegal, null and void, and as the imposition of a foreign power at a time when the U.S. was weak, divided and under the domination of a foreign imperialist power.

All we have to do with this analogy is to just change the name – Canada to India, United States to China and China to Great

Britain — and the picture becomes immeasurably clearer than it is represented in the U.S. press.

The Mcmahon Line

It is the position of the Chinese People's Republic that the so-called McMahon Line — named after the British General McMahon — is illegal, null and void, and the result of a predatory, imperialist imposition of the British government in the year 1914.

No Chinese government ever accepted the McMahon Line. Neither did the Imperial Government of China in 1914, nor the Chiang Kai-Shek government ever agree to it. The very fact that even the Chiang Kai-Shek clique, which is nothing but a tool of U.S. imperialism, has not dared to dispute the Chinese People's Republic's position of the China-India border dispute, it in itself the most eloquent testimony to the correctness of the Chinese position.

Nevertheless, the Chinese People's Republic has made every effort to achieve a reasonable and just settlement of the territory in dispute. It has consistently shunned the use of arms.

Proposals For Negotiations

Although the border dispute is almost three years old now, and the Chinese have made innumerable other approaches to the Indian government to settle it on some amicable and acceptable basis the Nehru government has invariably turned them down. In the past two months alone the Chinese government made several proposals for negotiations.

It made a notable effort on August 4, and another one on September 13. In neither of these proposals did the Chinese government lay down any preconditions for the negotiations. Nor did the Chinese government resort to the type of language which could in any way be construed as a threat to India.

On the contrary, the diplomatic notes directed to the Indian government were couched in the most conciliatory language, and were calculated to effectuate a reasonable settlement which would safeguard the territorial integrity of China as well as India.

As a matter of fact, the London Times, certainly no friend of the Chinese revolutionary government, had to publicly admit on October 8 that if military operations were resumed on the Sino-Indian border, "onlookers will have to note that it was New Dehli.., that declined to embark upon them (talks)..."

The position of the London Times is of exceptional importance because it has always sided with India as against China. The London Times was obliged to make the above statement only after the Indian paper, Tribune, had reported that at a cabinet meeting the Indian government had decided to use armed force to deal with China.

Nehru's "Limited Offensive"

It was also reported in the world press on October 8, that Nehru had authorized India's new commander-in chief of the eastern border area to "fight a limited offensive operation."

These are the incontrovertible facts. As to what lies behind the aggressive attitude of the Nehru government, it must be borne in mind first of all that the imperialist world, particularly the U.S. would like nothing better than to see the two principal Asiatic powers, the two powers which hold the greatest revolutionary promise for mankind in the east, locked in military combat, shedding the blood of thousands, absorbing the resources and energies of millions of people, which should be used to construct a revolutionary way of life.

The efforts of the U.S. government, it must be noted, have been directed, insofar as India is concerned, not only to make it economically and financially dependent upon U.S. monopoly interests, but also to inflame the Indian bourgeoisie, particularly its right-wing extremist elements, against the Chinese People's Republic.

Four Billion U.S. Aid

According to The New York Times of October 22(1969), the U.S. has poured into India more than four billion dollars. A substantial section of this money has gone to line the pockets of Indian businessmen, government officials, and especially the extremist elements who are interested in diverting the mass discontent of the Indian peasants and workers into other channels. U.S. diplomats, State Department planners, and military figures in the Pentagon have for a long time felt that the biggest diversionary tactic that imperialism could employ to disrupt the revolutionary anti-imperialist front was to continually stir up, bribe and corrupt as many of the representatives of the Indian bourgeoisie as it could to fan the flames of an India-China war.

Nehru himself was subjected to unremitting pressure when he was in the U.S. More U.S. aid was used as bait to lure Nehru into the trap of a protracted India-China war, which can only result in further detriment to India, China and the cause of all oppressed people.

Since Nehru's Visit

Since the Indian Prime Minister left the shores of the U.S. there have been only rare intervals in which there has been a let up in the war fever fanned by the Indian bourgeoisie and its agent Nehru. For a long time Nehru played the role of moderator between left and right in the Indian-China border dispute, cautioning the extremist elements of the bourgeoisie in Parliament, and repudiating suggestions for offensive operations by his military advisers.

But his October 4 decision, taken after a cabinet meeting, made it clear beyond any shadow of a doubt that he had completely capitulated to the right wing on this issue and was kowtowing to U.S. imperialist interests. The present military efforts of the Chinese are merely a response to the offensive action taken after the Indian cabinet session.

A Defensive Battle

The Chinese government is fighting a defensive battle. It is only too well aware that U.S. imperialism is ready at all times to take advantage of any preoccupation that China may have with India to open another front against China wherever and whenever it finds it feasible, whether it be in the Pescadores, the Taiwan strait or new harassments over the air space of China. There are those who say China should give in — give up what belongs to China in the interest of peace. These are the people who are always ready to give, especially things that do not belong to them.

When to give — or whether to give — is a question which only the Chinese can decide, as it as *their* territory. Surely the Chinese, who have gone through hell and fire in the course of 22 years of civil war, in which they have had to trade many times — space for time — and in fact have endured many retreats, need no reminders on this score.

Solidarity of Asian People

The workers of the world and the progressive anti-imperialist countries in particular, are most deeply concerned in a speedy, reasonable and honorable settlement on the part of China and India. Such a settlement can only be arrived at if the ruling group in New Delhi accepts China's offer for the resumption of talks on a high level between the two governments without any pre conditions. A border settlement would remove a tremendous obstacle to the solidarity of the Asian people who are struggling for a new life, and would be a tremendous rebuff to imperialism and its servants and underlings.

8

India-China (Aksai Chin and Arunachal Pradesh)

In the 1962 Sino-Indian War, China seized a Switzerland-sized area, Aksai Chin (Aksayqin), and overran Arunachal Pradesh (an Indian state the size of Austria). There are also other, smaller pockets of disputed area. The PRC withdrew from virtually all of Arunachal Pradesh to the Line of Actual Control (LAC), which approximates the McMahon Line that is found in a 1914 agreement initialed by British, Tibetan, and Chinese representatives. Chinese and Indian forces clashed in the Sumdorong Chu valley of Arunachal Pradesh in 1986-87. Relations began to thaw in 1988.

On 7 September 1993, China and India signed an accord to reduce tensions along their border and to respect the LAC. During November 1996, China and India agreed to delimit the LAC and institute confidence-building measures (CBMs) along the frontier. The agreement pledged nonaggression, prior notification of large troop movements, a 10-km no-fly zone for combat aircraft, and exchange of maps to resolve disagreements about the precise location of the LAC. In August 1997 the sides ratified the CBM agreement. There seems to have been little substantive progress, except for a series of high-level visits. The most recent, on 27 April, was the first visit by a PRC Chief of Staff to India. However, two weeks before the visit the new Indian Defence Minister, George Fernandes, accused the PRC of repeated violations of Indian territory, including the construction of a helipad on "Indian" territory in the disputed zone, and of aiding Pakistan's nuclear and missile programs. On 3 May he publicly labelled China as India's number one threat and alleged that the PRC was stockpiling nuclear weapons in Tibet, expanding naval activity off the Burmese coast, and conducting surveillance against India from Burma's Coco Islands. After the visit of General Fu Quanyou and PRC protests, Fernandes said that his characterization of China as India's principal threat was a personal view, but he went on to pledge that the number of Indian troops along the frontier with China would not be reduced. Such a statement calls into question part of the agreed CBMs. (To view a map of this area click here.) China and India have yet to address their fundamental and very large land boundary disputes. Moreover, their bilateral relations are complicated by the issues of Tibet (Xizang), Sikkim, and Kashmir. India plays host to the Dalai Lama and a large number of Tibetan refugees. They present an implicit threat to Chinese control of Tibet, which it invaded in 1950. On its maps, the PRC continues to portray Sikkim, which was absorbed by India in 1974, as an independent country. In addition to the Aksai Chin, China and India dispute another section of Kashmir (the area west of Aksai Chin).

AKSAI CHIN

From the area's lowest point (on the Karakash River at about 14,000 feet (4,300 m) to the glaciated peaks up to 22,500 feet (6,900 m) above sea level, this is a desolate, largely uninhabited area. It covers an area of about 37,244 square kilometres (14,380 sq mi). The desolation of Aksai Chin meant that it had no significant human importance other than ancient trade routes crossing it, providing brief passage during summer for caravans of yaks from Xinjiang and Tibet.

One of the earliest treaties regarding the boundaries in the western sector was issued in 1842. The Sikh Confederacy of the Punjab region in India had annexed Ladakh into the state of Jammu in 1834. In 1841, they invaded Tibet with an army. Chinese forces defeated the Sikh army and in turn entered Ladakh and besieged Leh. After being checked by the Sikh forces, the Chinese and the Sikhs signed a treaty in September 1842, which stipulated no transgressions or interference in the other country's frontiers.

The British defeat of the Sikhs in 1846 resulted in transfer of sovereignty over Ladakh to the British, and British commissioners attempted to meet with Chinese officials to discuss the border they now shared. However, both sides were apparently sufficiently satisfied that a traditional border was recognised and defined by natural elements, and the border was not demarcated. The boundaries at the two extremities, Pangong Lakeand Karakoram Pass, were reasonably well-defined, but the Aksai Chin area in between lay largely undefined.

The Johnson Line

W. H. Johnson, a civil servant with the Survey of India proposed the "Johnson Line" in 1865, which put Aksai Chin in Jammu and Kashmir. This was the time of the Dungan revolt, when China did not control Xinjiang, so this line was never presented to the Chinese. Johnson presented this line to the Maharaja of Jammu and Kashmir, who then claimed the 18,000 square kilometres contained within his territory and by some accounts he claimed territory further north as far as the Sanju Pass in the Kun Lun Mountains. Johnson's work was severely criticised for gross inaccuracies, with description of his boundary as "patently absurd", and he was reprimanded by the British Government and resigned from the Survey. The Maharajah of Jammu and Kashmir apparently sent a few soldiers to man the abandoned fort at Shahidulla (modern-day Xaidulla) at one point, by the time most sources placed Shahidulla and the upper Karakash River firmly within the territory of Xinjiang. According toFrancis Younghusband, who explored the region in the late 1880s, there was only an abandoned fort and not one inhabited house at Shahidulla when he was there – it was just a convenient staging post and a convenient headquarters for the nomadic Kirghiz. The abandoned fort had apparently been built a few years earlier by the Dogras. In 1878 the Chinese had reconquered Xinjiang, and by 1890 they already had Shahidulla before the issue was decided. By 1892, China had erected boundary markers at Karakoram Pass.

In 1897 a British military officer, Sir John Ardagh, proposed a boundary line along the crest of the Kun Lun Mountainsnorth of the Yarkand River. At the time Britain was concerned at the danger of Russian expansion as China weakened, and Ardagh argued that his line was more defensible. The Ardagh line was effectively a modification of the Johnson line, and became known as the "Johnson-Ardagh Line".

The Macartney-Macdonald Line

In 1893, Hung Ta-chen, a senior Chinese official at Kashgar, handed a map of the boundary proposed by China toGeorge Macartney, the British consul-general at Kashgar. This boundary placed the Lingzi Tang plains, which are south of the Laktsang range, in India, and Aksai Chin proper, which is north of the Laktsang range, in China. Macartney agreed with the proposal and forwarded it to the British Indian government. This border, along theKarakoram Mountains, was proposed and supported by British officials for a number of reasons. The Karakoram Mountains formed a natural boundary, which would set the British borders up to the Indus River watershed while leaving the Tarim River watershed in Chinese control, and Chinese control of this tract would present a further obstacle to Russian advance in Central Asia. The British presented this line, known as the Macartney-MacDonald Line, to the Chinese in 1899 in a note by Sir Claude MacDonald. The Qing government did not respond to the note, and the British took that as Chinese acquiescence. Although no official boundary had ever been negotiated, China believed that this had been the accepted boundary.

1899 to 1947

Both the Johnson-Ardagh and the Macartney-MacDonald lines were used on British maps of India. Until at least 1908, the British took the Macdonald line to be the boundary, but in 1911, the Xinhai Revolution resulted in the collapse of central power in China, and by the end of World War I, the British officially used the Johnson Line. However they took no steps to establish outposts or assert actual control on the ground. In 1927, the line was adjusted again as the government of British India abandoned the Johnson line in favour of a line along the Karakoram range further south. However, the maps were not updated and still showed the Johnson Line.

From 1917 to 1933, the "Postal Atlas of China", published by the Government of China in Peking had shown the boundary in Aksai Chin as per the Johnson line, which runs along the Kunlun mountains. When British officials learned of Soviet officials surveying the Aksai Chin for Sheng Shicai, warlord of Xinjiang in 1940–1941, they again advocated the Johnson Line. At this point the British had still made no attempts to establish outposts or control over the Aksai Chin, nor was the issue ever discussed with the governments of China or Tibet, and the boundary remained undemarcated at India's independence.

Since 1947

Upon independence in 1947, the government of India used the Johnson Line as the basis for its official boundary in the west, encompassing Aksai Chin. However, India did not claim the northern areas nearShahidulla and Khotan, for including which in Indian territory, among other things, Johnson had been criticised. From the Karakoram Pass (which is not under dispute), the Indian claim line extends northeast of the Karakoram Mountains north of the salt flats of the Aksai Chin, to set a boundary at the Kunlun Mountains, and incorporating part of the Karakash River and Yarkand River watersheds. From there, it runs east along the Kunlun Mountains, before turning southwest through the Aksai Chin salt flats, through the Karakoram Mountains, and then to Pangong Lake.

On 1 July 1954 Prime Minister Nehru wrote a memo directing that the maps of India be revised to show definite boundaries on all frontiers. Up to this point, the boundary in the Aksai Chin sector, based on the Johnson Line, had been described as "undemarcated."

During the 1950s, the People's Republic of China built a 1,200 kilometres (750 mi) road connecting Xinjiang and western Tibet, of which 179 kilometres (111 mi) ran south of the Johnson Line through the Aksai Chin region claimed by India. Aksai Chin was easily accessible from China, but was more difficult for the Indians on the other side of the Karakorams to reach. The Indians did not learn of the existence of the road until 1957, which was confirmed when the road was shown in Chinese maps published in 1958. The Indian position, as stated by prime minister Jawaharlal Nehru, was that the Aksai Chin was "part of the Ladakh region of India for centuries" and that this northern border was a "firm and definite one which was not open to discussion with anybody".

The Chinese minister, Zhou Enlai argued that the western border had never been delimited, that the Macartney-MacDonald Line, which left the Aksai Chin within Chinese borders was the only line ever proposed to a Chinese government, and that the Aksai Chin was already under Chinese jurisdiction, and that negotiations should take into account the status quo.

In April 2013 India claimed, referencing their own perception of the Line of Actual Control (LAC) location, that Chinese troops had established a camp in the Daulat Beg Oldi sector, 10 km on their side of the Line of Actual Control. This figure was later revised to a 19 km claim. According to Indian media, the incursion included Chinese military helicopters entering Indian airspace to drop supplies to the troops. However, Chinese officials denied any trespassing having taken place. Soldiers from both countries briefly set up camps on the ill-defined frontier facing each other, but the tension was defused when both sides pulled back soldiers in early May.

Trans Karakoram Tract

The Johnson Line is not used west of the Karakoram Pass, where China adjoins Pakistan-administered Gilgit–Baltistan. On 13 October 1962, China and Pakistan began negotiations over the boundary west of the Karakoram Pass. In 1963, the two countries settled their boundaries largely on the basis of the Macartney-MacDonald Line, which left the Trans Karakoram Tract in China, although the agreement provided for renegotiation in the event of a settlement of the Kashmir dispute.

India does not recognise that Pakistan and China have a common border, and claims the tract as part of the domains of the pre-1947 state of Kashmir and Jammu. However, India's claim line in that area does not extend as far north of the Karakoram Mountains as the Johnson Line

CHINA'S CLAIM TO TIBET IS FACTOR IN BORDER DISPUTE

This is perhaps the most militarized Buddhist enclave in the world. Perched above 10,000 feet in the icy reaches of the eastern Himalayas, the town of Tawang is not only home to one of Tibetan Buddhism's most sacred monasteries but also the site of a massive Indian military buildup. Convoys of army trucks haul howitzers along rutted mountain roads. Soldiers drill in muddy fields. Military bases appear every half-mile in the countryside, with watchtowers rising behind concertina wire.

A road sign on the northern edge of town helps explain the reason for all the fear and the fury: The border with China is just 23 miles away; Lhasa, the Tibetan capital, 316 miles; and Beijing 2,676 miles. "The Chinese army has a big deployment at the border, at Bumla," said Madan Singh, a junior commissioned officer who sat with a half-dozen soldiers one afternoon sipping tea beside a fog-cloaked road. "That's why we're here." Though little known to the outside world, Tawang is a flashpoint in relations between the world's two most populous nations. It is the focus of China's most delicate land-border dispute, a conflict rooted in Chinese claims of sovereignty over all of historical Tibet.

In recent months, both countries have stepped up efforts to secure their rights over this rugged patch of land. China tried to block a $2.9 billion loan to India from the Asian Development Bank on the grounds that part of the loan was slated for water projects in Arunachal Pradesh, the state that includes Tawang. It was the first time China had sought to influence the territorial dispute through a multilateral institution. Then an Indian general announced that the Indian military was deploying extra troops and fighter jets in the area. The growing belligerence has soured relations between the two Asian giants and has prompted one Indian military leader to declare that China has replaced Pakistan as India's biggest threat.

Economic progress might be expected to bring the countries closer. China and India did $52 billion of trade last year, a 34 percent increase over 2007. But businesspeople say that border tensions have infused official deliberations over business deals, dampening the willingness of Chinese and Indian companies to invest in each other's countries. "Officials start taking more time, scrutinizing things more carefully, and all that means more delays and ultimately more denials," said Ravi Bhoothalingam, a former president of the Oberoi Group, the luxury hotel chain, and a member of the Institute of Chinese Studies in New Delhi. "That's not good for business."

The roots of the conflict go back to China's territorial claims to Tibet. Not only does the Dalai Lama, the exiled spiritual leader of the Tibetans, live in the foothills of the western Himalayas with the blessing of the Indian government, but China insists that this swath of northeast India has historically been part of Tibet, and thus should be part of China. Tawang is a thickly forested area of white stupas and steep, terraced hillsides that is home to the ethnic Monpa people, who practice Tibetan Buddhism, speak a language similar to Tibetan and once paid tribute to rulers in Lhasa. The 6th Dalai Lama was born here in the 17th century.

The Chinese army occupied Tawang briefly in 1962, during a war with India fought over this and other territories along the 2,521-mile border. More than 3,100 Indian soldiers and 700 Chinese soldiers were killed and thousands wounded in the border war. War memorials highlighting China's aggressions in Tawang here are big draws for Indian tourists. "The entire border is disputed," said Ma Jiali, an India scholar at the China Institutes of Contemporary International Relations, a government-supported think tank in Beijing. "This problem hasn't been solved, and it's a huge barrier to China-India relations."

In some ways, Tawang has become a proxy battleground, too, between China and the Dalai Lama, who passed through this valley when he fled into exile in 1959. From his home in the distant hill town of Dharamsala, he wields enormous influence over Tawang. He appoints the abbot of the powerful monastery and gives financial support to institutions throughout the area. Last year, the Dalai Lama announced for the first time that Tawang is a part of India, bolstering the Indian government's territorial claims and infuriating China.

Traditional Tibetan culture runs strong in Tawang. At the Tawang monastery, an important centre of Tibetan learning, monks express apprehension about China's rule over Tibet, which the Chinese army seized in 1951. "I hate the Chinese government," said Gombu Tsering, 70, a senior monk who watches over the monastery's museum. "Tibet wasn't even a part of China. Lhasa wasn't a part of China." Few expect China to try to forcefully annex Tawang, but military skirmishes are a real danger, analysts say. The Indian military recorded 270 border violations and nearly 2,300 instances of "aggressive border patrolling" by Chinese soldiers last year, said Brahma Chellaney, a professor of strategic studies at the Centre for Policy Research, a research organization in New Delhi. Mr. Chellaney has advised the Indian government's National Security Council.

"The India-China frontier has become more 'hot' than the India-Pakistan border," he said in an e-mail. China has grown increasingly hostile to the Dalai Lama after a severe outbreak of ethnic unrest in Tibet. This year, it turned its diplomatic guns on India. China moved in March to block a $2.9 billion loan to India from the Asian Development Bank, a multi-nation group based in Manila that has China on its board, because $60 million of the loan had been earmarked for flood-control projects in Arunachal Pradesh, the state that includes Tawang. The loan was approved in mid-June over China's heated objections.

Weeks after China first tried to block the loan, the chief of the Indian air force, now retired, told a prominent Indian newspaper that China posed a greater threat than Pakistan. Another official, J.J. Singh, the governor of Arunachal Pradesh and retired chief of the Indian army, said the next month that the Indian military was adding two divisions of troops, totalling 50,000 to 60,000 soldiers, to the border region over the next several years. Four Sukhoi fighter jets were immediately deployed to a nearby air base. Since 2005, when Chinese Prime Minister Wen Jiabao visited India, the two countries have gone through 13 rounds of bilateral negotiations over the issue. A last round was just held last month, with no results. Though China has actually resolved many of its border disputes in recent years, India remains a glaring exception.

The Government of Tibet in Exile

From July 20 to 23, 1994, Beijing staged the Third Forum on Work in Tibet which recommended the total destruction of an entire civilization flourishing on the Tibetan Plateau for thousands of years. This cultural "empire" once encompassed far-flung areas like Buryatia, Tuva and Kalmykia in Russia; Mongolia; Laddakh, Lahaul-Spiti, Sikkim, and Arunachal Pradesh in India; Mustang, Dolpo and Solo Khumbu in Nepal; Bhutan and parts of western China.

The policy formulated in 1994 in Beijing-and these days pursued with Cultural Revolutionary zeal in Tibet-will mean the annihilation of the spiritual homeland of this shared culture. Implementation of the Third Work Forum is thus having a crippling impact on the traditional culture of millions of non-Tibetans as the well-spring of their cultural inspiration is forcibly drained and there is nothing to replenish the continuous growth and development of this distinct and highly evolved civilization.

Losing Hearts and Minds

The decisions made at the Third Forum rest on two fundamental conclusions which Beijing drew. It realized it was losing out in two vital fields-ideology and propaganda. For a state whose existence is justified by its ideological superiority and the power of its propaganda to shape the thinking of the masses, the implications of this for the future was at best uncertain, at worst dangerous. Beijing concluded it was losing the ideological war because, despite the unrelenting assault on Tibetan Buddhism, Tibetans were as devoted to their traditional beliefs as ever. Beijing has succeeded in physically enslaving the country but it has not won over the hearts, minds and loyalty of the Tibetan populace.

Communist ideology, enforced by the military might of China, had failed to dent the heart of Buddhism. Added to this was the communist authorities' total bafflement at the non-violent policy underpinning the Middle Way Approach advocated by His Holiness the Dalai Lama to resolve the issue of Tibet's future status. For a regime which is based on Mao's dictum that political power grows out of the barrel of a gun, this supposedly eccentric philosophy which says victory lies in capturing the hearts and minds of people by the power of ideas rather than killing by the power of the gun comes as a bolt from the blue. Much of Beijing's knee-jerk reaction to, and its bafflement at, His Holiness the Dalai Lama's new policy of rapprochement lies at the heart of its new hardline policy.

Beijing considered it was losing the propaganda war because, for one reason or the other, the world's media and its pop culture considered-at least for the moment-Tibet and Tibetan Buddhism their very own cuddly pandas. Despite its financial might China found it extremely difficult to exterminate this image of Tibet and get its voice heard on the Tibetan issue in the court of the international media. In order to address these weaknesses the Third Forum concentrated on two issues. One was to focus on Tibet's economic development in the hope that this would keep Tibetan demonstrations off the streets. This was tantamount to bribing the Tibetans with promises of riches to come if they toed the party line. The other concern was to win the coming and new generations of Tibetans over to the Chinese viewpoint.

Beijing has given up on the present generation of Tibetans as a lost cause. If the coming generations of Tibetans were also lost to the 'Dalai Clique' this, the Chinese concluded, would have dangerous consequences for Chinese rule in Tibet. The 15-year-old Gyalwa Karmapa's dramatic escape from Tibet in January 2000 was a warning to the Beijing authorities of the erosion of loyalty to China. The Karmapa's flight, and the earlier escape of Agya Rinpoche, the abbot of Kumbum Monastery, came as a huge embarrassment for China, because retaining these high lamas gave China a degree of legitimacy for its rule in Tibet. This is the reason why Beijing is enforcing with greater strictness its 1993 instruction of recalling young Tibetans studying in schools and monasteries run by Dharmasala in India. This is also the rationale for Beijing closing down schools in Tibet which are privately run by Tibetans.

For these reasons Tibet today is in the throes of a second Cultural Revolution as the Chinese authorities step up their long-term strategy to exterminate Tibet's distinct cultural and ethnic identity. The authorities are pursuing a four-pronged strategy to achieve their final objective. They have stepped up repression while employing their huge propaganda machine to paint a rosy picture of Tibet. They have quickened the pace of economic development to dampen Tibetan nationalism and are simultaneously moving more Chinese settlers onto the Tibetan Plateau to change Tibet's demographic composition and to ease social unrest because of mounting unemployment back in China.

The Third Work Forum on Tibet was convened by the top Chinese leadership and was presided over by President Jiang Zemin. The authorities have now enshrined this Work Forum as the most "important strategic policy to rejuvenate Tibet" and have hailed its directives as the new manifesto for party work on the plateau. The significance of the Third Work Forum lies in the fact that it overturned the more liberal policies laid out for Tibet's "development" by the First and Second Work Forums held in 1980 and 1984.

The first two work forums were initiated by the late Hu Yaobang, then Secretary General of the Chinese Communist Party. This liberal and somewhat maverick leader is credited with masterminding a series of measures to improve the social, economic and political conditions in Tibet. The brief spell of liberalization markedly improved the living conditions of the majority of Tibetans and contributed to a more relaxed intellectual and social climate.

The Third Work Forum reversed these policies and reinstated hardline measures under which Tibet is still reeling today. The Tibetans in Tibet perceive the current repressive policies as a second Cultural Revolution. The question is why did China choose to jettison its earlier more liberal policies and adopt a manifesto which is leading to the systematic destruction of Tibet's distinct culture. The answer lies in domestic and international events which forced China to formulate a series of hardline policies on Tibet which eventually crystallized into the Third Work Forum for Tibet. The world which confronted China in the late 1980s and early 1990s was a frightening one.

Starting from 1987, Tibet was rocked by a string of protest demonstrations, which called for Tibetan independence. One of the largest demonstrations which erupted on March 5, 1989 in

Lhasa, forced the authorities to impose martial law on the city. These demonstrations are now seen to have been an inspiration behind the outburst of Chinese students' pro-democracy uprisings. The authorities saw the series of Tiananmen Square demonstrations as a sign of their Central Government losing control, and in an attempt to regain supremacy, the authorities slaughtered-perhaps hundreds if not thousands of students on June 4, 1989. These demonstrations were a chilling replay to the authorities of the May 4, 1919 student demonstrations in Beijing which signalled a political and cultural awakening across the erstwhile Middle Kingdom.

Bejing's fears of losing control were exacerbated by external events which saw the unraveling of the communist world. The Solidarity Movement in Poland, the fall of the Berlin Wall, and the implosion of the Soviet Union fed Beijing's paranoia over threats to the Chinese Communist Party hold on power. Official China's fears were further inflamed by the rapidly changing attitude of the broad masses as they turned back from communism to traditional beliefs like Confucionism, Buddhism, Islam, Christianity and indigenous folk cults. In the eyes of ordinary citizens communism was becoming totally discredited and this, more than anything else, was the biggest nightmare for China's leadership. The leadership's justification for staying in power was being disavowed by the masses. For a one-party dictatorship this historically indicates the first step along the slippery road to dissolution and removal of power.

For these reasons the Chinese leadership then reverted to its earlier view that traditional beliefs were its real enemy. In competing with Buddhism, Confucionism, Islam, Christianity and other isms, communism was losing out in terms of its ability to retain the loyalty and allegiance of the masses. The leadership revived the old aphorisms once served up to the Tibetan people to justify their policies to destroy Tibetan Buddhism during the Cultural Revolution. Bewildered Tibetans were then told that just as there cannot be two suns in the sky, so there cannot be both Buddhism and socialism in Tibet. Inevitably Buddhism then had to give way to socialism. And again, today, religion is being blatantly sublimated to Chinese state power. These were the fears of the Chinese leaders when they met in Beijing in 1994 to hammer out their new Tibet initiatives. For the Chinese authorities Tibet is an especially sensitive issue because of their conviction that hostile Western forces are using the issue of Tibet to "westernize" China and to lead to its territorial fragmentation. The third generation Chinese leaders came to the conclusion that stability in Tibet was vital to the stability of China as a whole. Earlier, Tibet was merely of peripheral concern to the vital interests of China's sprawling communist empire. Now, with the Third Work Forum, the authorities were saying, "We must clearly understand that we must do our work in Tibet not only for the sake our of own region's stability and development, not only for the interests of our people, but also for the sake of the whole nation's stability and development."

In Tibet, China faced peculiar problems because of the inherent strength of Tibetan Buddhism and the depth of devotion of the populace to His Holiness the Dalai Lama. The sustained burst of religious revival that followed in the wake of the brief spell of liberalization in Tibet confirmed the leadership's worst fears that decades of concerted assault on Tibetan culture and religion had not extinguished the people's traditional beliefs and values. From merely nuisance value, the Chinese leadership now viewed Tibetan Buddhism as a very real and imminent threat to the stability of Chinese rule in Tibet.

At the same time the Chinese leadership's attitude towards His Holiness the Dalai Lama changed. From being an uncertain ally in the peace process in Tibet, the current Chinese leadership now saw him as a full-blown "enemy". A top-level conclave held in Beijing on March 10, 1993 concluded that, "There are different factions within the Dalai Clique; they are, however, unanimous in their political nature and position. They differ from each other in ideological viewpoints and ways of expressing them. Different strategies must be adopted to use their differences, to deal with them differently in order to divide and destroy them."

Repeated statements by high-level officials describe the struggle against "splittism", the official term for Tibetan independence, as a "life-and-death struggle". At the 1994 annual meeting of the

"TAR" Communist Party Committee to brief members on the policy thrust of the Third Work Forum on Tibet, Raidi, deputy Secretary of the Committee said, "Up to now, his (the Dalai Lama's) standpoint on Tibet's independence has never changed, and we must reveal his double-faced true colour. The focal point in our region in the struggle against splittism is to oppose the Dalai Clique. As the saying goes, to kill a serpent, one must first cut off its head."

In short, the Third Work Forum decided that Beijing was in a position to solve the Tibet issue without the Dalai Lama's involvement. It abandoned the earlier liberal policy of including His Holiness the Dalai Lama in any future settlement of Tibet's status. His Holiness the Dalai Lama was clearly singled out as the cause of China's "Tibet problem".

The Third Work Forum also abandoned the policy of granting concessions to Tibet because of the plateau's "special characteristics". This policy had been the cornerstone of recommendations made by the First and Second Tibet Work Forums.

To carry out its new hardline policies in Tibet, Beijing appointed Chen Kuiyuan as the "TAR" Party Secretary in 1992. Chen Kuiyuan's appointment is significant because he had a track record for being a tough and ruthless administrator. He had already served as the First Secretary of the Chinese Communist Party in Inner Mongolia and is credited with repressing the rebellious Mongols, many of whom refer to him as "the butcher". Chen Kuiyuan was especially recommended to the post by Hu Jintao, the current Vice-President of China, who was then the First Secretary of the Chinese Communist Party in Tibet.

Tackling Tibetan Nationalism

The Third Work Forum policies chalked out for Tibet contained four key elements. China stepped up the scale of repression in Tibet. External propaganda work was escalated. The pace of economic development in Tibet-and its corollary of encouraging more Chinese settlers and businessmen to take advantage of the economic boom on the "roof of the world"-was also increased. In short, Beijing had decided to tackle Tibetan nationalism head-on and observers are still assessing the consequences on both Chinese rule in Tibet and on the populace.

Beijing remains convinced that these key components of its current policy will stabilize Chinese rule over Tibet and solve once and for all, the vexed problem of its negative image over the way Tibet has been handled. One main target of the current policy of repression is Tibetan Buddhism. Chinese leaders are increasingly alarmed by the proliferation of monasteries and temples which the period of liberalization spawned throughout Tibet: they are seen as the bastions of Tibetan nationalism. The authorities have set up "Democratic Management Committees" to control monasteries and nunneries and created "Work Inspection Teams" to supervise the "education" of monks and nuns.

A major thrust is underway to break the bond of loyalty between the clergy in Tibet and His Holiness the Dalai Lama in India. Campaigns like "Strike Hard" and "Patriotic Re-education", unleashed in 1996, are aimed at crippling the rise of Tibetan Buddhism which the authorities suspect is weaning the loyalty of the Tibetan people away from the communist party and towards His Holiness the Dalai Lama. One salient feature of the "Strike Hard" campaign is how differently it is interpreted in China and Tibet. China's "Strike Hard" campaign was started to weed out corruption. Tibet's version is used as a political tool to eliminate those whom the authorities label "splittists". In Tibet, rather than striking at corruption, the authorities turn a blind eye to this social disease in the hope that it will erode the traditional morality of Tibetans and undermine Tibetan Buddhism.

In fact, at a secret meeting held in December 1999 in Chengdu, capital of Sichuan province, Chen Kuiyuan, the hardline Party Secretary of "TAR" recommended to the Central Chinese Government that an all-out effort must be made to eradicate Tibetan Buddhism and culture from the face of the earth so that no memory of them will be left in the minds of coming generations of Tibetans-except as museum pieces.

Chen Kuiyuan stated that the main cause of instability is the existence of the Dalai Lama and his Government-in-Exile in

Dharamsala and these must be "uprooted". He recommended that Tibet, Tibetan people and Tibetan Buddhism-in other words the very name of Tibet-must be destroyed and the "Tibet Autonomous Region" be merged with provinces like Sichuan.

While treating Tibetans to boot-heel subjugation at home, internationally China was on an overdrive propaganda blitz. At a brainstorming conclave held on March 10, 1993, Zeng Jian-hui, Vice-Minister of the Propaganda Ministry, told participants, "The propaganda work on the question of Tibet is one of the focal points of the entire external propaganda work...With regard to attacks by the West and the Dalai Clique and their frequent activities, our external propaganda should launch offensive. We should expand our spheres of influence; in particular, we should infiltrate our propaganda into the mainstream life of the West.

"Firstly we should continue to send Tibetan scholars and Tibetan singing and dancing troupes abroad to lecture and perform.

Secondly, relevant embassies and consulates should aim at the public opinion and the activities of the Dalai Clique in the countries where they are stationed and utilize speeches, picture exhibitions, special articles and other forms to carry out propaganda work, so as to win over officials and people of those countries... We should reinforce the work of utilizing the power of foreign propaganda. A few years ago, in the light of the situation of that time, we made arrangements for foreign journalists to visit Tibet."

The September 3, 2000 edition of *People's Daily* carried a story headlined "Tibet Welcomes Foreign Journalists for Objective Reporting". It stated that "A senior Tibetan official said Sunday that Tibet welcomes foreign journalists to come for objective and just reporting, but not those who take distorted views.

Raidi, Deputy Secretary of the Tibet Autonomous Regional Committee of the Communist Party of China and Chairman of the Standing Committee of the Tibetan Autonomous Regional People's Congress, made the remarks at a meeting here with a press delegation of Thailand." In this context, it is interesting to note that N. Ram, the editor of India's *Frontline* magazine, devoted 36 pages of the September 15, 2000 issue to promote the Chinese line and recommended that the Indian Government expel the Central Tibetan Administration from Indian soil for being the main stumbling block to normal relations between India and China. It is difficult to assess to what extent the views contained in his stupendous reporting marathon are his own.

These editorial outbursts are in line with policy decisions outlined in the early nineties. During a two-day secret conclave in March 1993 in Chengdu, Vice-Minister Zeng Jian-hui, told participants, "All foreigners that we entertain and send to Tibet must have a relatively objective opinion of Tibet. We should use people from abroad to carry out the propaganda on Tibet for us, which is more powerful than if we do it."

Along with its external public relations strategy, China is presently carrying out a potentially much more dangerous policy of speeding up the pace of Tibet's economic development and its related drive to bring more Chinese settlers onto the Tibetan Plateau. Beijing's Western China Development Programme, which incorporates Tibet in its ambit, is devised to shift the focus of China's economic activities from Coastal China to the interior-both to narrow the imbalance in the level of economic development between the two regions and to ease population pressure on the coastal areas which attract millions of migrant workers.

The focus of Beijing's Western China Economic Development Programme in Tibet is to exploit the plateau's still untapped minerals and other natural resources and to upgrade Tibet's infrastructure-like roads and telecommunications-to facilitate transportation of these resources to China. The other purpose of the heightened level of economic activity is to divert the Tibetans' attention from their political fate to focus on their livelihood-thus undermining Tibetan nationalism. The Chinese authorities aim to manipulate the situation in Tibet still further by bringing in more Chinese settlers who would then demographically cement Chinese rule once and for all. These current hardline policies and their implementation in Tibet are impacting the stalled Sino-Tibetan Dialogue and will vitally affect the ability of Tibetans to survive as a distinct people and culture.

Beijing's Flawed Perceptions

The basic flaws in China's new policy in its search to resolve the problem of Tibet is thinking the solution can exclude the involvement of His Holiness the Dalai Lama. The other is in attempting to solve the problem over the heads of Tibet's citizens.

These two fundamental mistakes will exacerbate China's Tibet problem, not solve it. The reason lies in the history of Tibet and in the sentiments of the people.

The institution of the Dalai Lamas of Tibet is more than 600 years old, if we start from the birth of the first Dalai Lama in 1391. In the course of its growth and development, the very institution itself came to symbolize fundamental beliefs and the political destiny of the nation. The bond between the Dalai Lamas and the Tibetan people is fundamental and unbreakable; any attempt, however sustained, will never succeed in driving a wedge between the two.

Consequently, China's current policy of forcing Tibetans-especially monks and nuns-to denounce His Holiness the Dalai Lama and pledge loyalty to the Chinese Communist Party will prove counterproductive.

In view of this the Third Work Forum's basic assumption that in the case of Tibet time is on the side of China, and that Beijing can stall the problem of Tibet till the demise of the present Dalai Lama whereupon the issue of Tibet will solve itself, is fatally flawed-based as it is on a mistaken perception of the role played by the institution of the Dalai Lamas in the development of Tibetan history.

This assumption, if not reviewed, revised and abandoned, will prove catastrophic for the Chinese leadership and for those who chose to turn their whimsical personal analysis into state policy.

The reason is simple. The Chinese Communist Party was founded in the 1920s and came to power in 1949. Within this short span of time the masses have lost faith in communist ideology, and members of the party these days pay mere lip service to the ideological justifications of the party. Conversely, the institution of the Dalai Lamas as a political force is more than 300 years old. These days the Dalai Lama is recognized by Tibetans throughout the world as the heart of Tibetan nationalism. How can a party which has lost its soul outlast an institution which symbolizes the very soul of a people? For these reasons it is imperative for China to review and re-assess its current hardline stance towards Tibet. China must re-start its stalled peace process over Tibet and consider His Holiness the Dalai Lama as a vital and active partner in the procedures. If China does this it will have won a powerful ally and companion along the road to peace, stability and continued prosperity.

9

Sino-Indian Convergence: Bilateral and Global

Bilateral relations between India and the People's Republic of China (PRC) have indeed come a long way after they touched their nadir in the immediate aftermath of India's nuclear tests in May 1998. China had been singled out as the "number one" security threat for India by India's Defence Minister just before the nuclear tests. After the tests, the Indian Prime Minister wrote to the US President justifying Indian nuclear tests as a response to the threat posed by China. Unsurprisingly, China reacted strongly and diplomatic relations between the two countries plummeted to an all time low.

However, some six years later, the relations between the two countries seem to be on an upswing. The visit of the Indian External Affairs Minister to China in 1999 marked the resumption of high-level dialogue and the two sides declared that they were not threats to each other. A bilateral security dialogue was also initiated that has helped the two countries in openly expressing and sharing their security concerns with each other. India and China also decided to expedite the process of demarcation of the Line of Actual Control (LAC) and the Joint Working Group (JWG) on the boundary question, set up in 1988, has been meeting regularly. As a first step in this direction, the two countries exchanged border maps on the least controversial middle sector of the LAC.

The Indian Prime Minister visited China in June 2003, the first such visit in a decade. The joint declaration signed during the visit stated that China was not a threat to India. The two states appointed special representatives in order to impart momentum to border negotiations that have lasted twenty two years, with the Prime Minister's principal secretary becoming India's political-level negotiator, replacing the India-China JWG. India and China also decided to hold their first joint naval exercise later in the year and discussions on joint air exercise continue. India also acknowledged China's sovereignty over Tibet and pledged not to allow "anti-China" political activities in India. On its part, China has acknowledged India's 1975 annexation of the former monarchy of Sikkim by agreeing to open a trading post along the border with the former kingdom and later rectified official maps to include Sikkim as part of India.

India and China have found substantial convergence of interests at the international level. Both share similar concerns about the growing international dominance of the US, the threat of terrorism disguised as religious and ethnic movements and the need to accord primacy to economic development. India and China have both expressed concern about the US ' use of military power around the world and publicly opposed the war in Iraq. This was merely a continuation of the desire of both states to oppose the US *hyperpuissance* ever since the end of the Cold War.

Like other major powers in the international system, India and China favour a multi-polar world order where US unipolarity remains constrained by the other "poles" in the system. China and India zealously guard their national sovereignty and have been wary of US attempts to interfere in what they see as domestic affairs of other stares, be it Serbia, Kosovo or Iraq. Both took strong exception to the US air strikes on Iraq in 1998, the US-led air campaign against Yugoslavia in 1999, and more recently the US campaign against Saddam Hussein arguing that these violated the national sovereignty and undermined the authority of the United Nations system.

Both nations also favour more democratic international economic regimes. They have strongly resisted efforts by the US and other developed nations to link global trade to labour and environmental standards, realizing clearly that this would put them at a huge disadvantage vis-a-vis the developed world, thereby hampering their drive towards economic development, a top priority. Both have committed themselves to crafting joint Sino-Indian positions in the World Trade Organization (WTO) and global trade negotiations in the hope that this might provide them greater negotiating leverage over the developed states. They would like to see further liberalization of agricultural trade in the developed countries, tightening of the rules on anti-dumping measures and ensuring that non-trade related issues such as labour and environment are not allowed to come to the WTO.

In recent years, India and China have attempted to build their bilateral relationship on the basis of their larger worldview of international politics. As they have found a distinct convergence of their interests on world stage, they have used it to strengthen their bilateral relations. They have established and maintained regular reciprocal high-level visits between political leaders. There has been a sincere attempt to improve trade relations and to compartmentalize intractable issues that make it difficult for their bilateral relationship to move forward.

India and China have strengthened their bilateral relationship in areas as distinct as cultural and educational exchanges, military exchanges, and science and technology cooperation. Bilateral trade has recorded rapid growth from a trade volume of US $265 million in 1991 to US $3596 million in 2001.

In 2001, bilateral trade saw an increase of 23.4 percent over 2000. It is expected to rise to $10 billion this year. The two nations are even evaluating the possibility of signing a comprehensive economic cooperation agreement and a free trade agreement by the end of this year, thereby building on strong complementarities between the two. Both states are also taking steps to upgrade their military-related cooperation, leading to greater understanding on the bilateral military front, something that would have been unthinkable just a few years ago. As a first step in this direction, the Chinese and Indian navies carried out joint search and rescue operations off the Shanghai coast in November 2003. Both states are also seeking to cooperate on the nuclear front with China planning to import heavy water from India to be utilized in the pressurized heavy water reactors near Shanghai. Many observers have also pointed out a subtle shift in Beijing's stance on Pakistan vis-a-vis India. China's "neutral" position during the Kargil conflict and the intense Indo-Pak crisis following the terrorist attack on the India's Parliament is seen by many as a reflection of China's sincerity in its attempts to improve ties. In keeping with China's attempts to project itself as a responsible regional player, China is seen by some as supporting peace and anti-terrorist efforts in South Asia by cooperating with the US and India. China is also seen as playing a central role in encouraging Pakistan to negotiate with India by using its leverage over Pakistan. After assuming office Prime Minister Manmohan Singh's government made it clear that it favoured closer ties with China and would continue to work towards improving bilateral relations with China. In his first address to the nation, the Prime Minister, Manmohan Singh, also emphasized the carrying forward of the process of further development and diversification of Sino-Indian relations. The late J.N. Dixit, National Security Advisor in the current government, wrote that "the Congress will continue the process of normalizing, strengthening and expanding India's relations with China, which is the most important factor affecting Asian security and stability". One of the first foreign visits of the new Indian foreign minister, Natwar Singh, was to China to attend the Asia Cooperation Dialogue in Qingdao, in East China's Shandong province and apparently had "substantive discussions" with his Chinese counterpart.

All this reflects on India continuing to build its relations with China on the convergence of interests that the two nations have achieved in recent years. Aside from the positive developments, one should not ignore the enormous obstacles that confront this bilateral relationship. There has been a dominant tendency in the Indian foreign policy establishment to focus on the strengths of its bilateral relations with China while pretending that problems confronting the relationship would somehow take care of themselves. The challenges in the Sino-Indian relationship are by no means insignificant nor will China take care of Indian interests. It is for India to recognize them for what they are and evolve a coherent strategy to tackle them.

INDIA-CHINA RELATIONS: AN INDIAN PERSPECTIVE

There is a growing perception now that the global economic gravity has shifted to Asia and that India and China, the emerging economic powerhouses in the region, will shape the Twenty-first century. In making such feelings a reality however, the nature of the future dynamics of domestic conditions as well as external relations of the two nations appears a crucial factor; this article attempts to focus in particular on the future prospects for India-China ties on the premise that this, along with the roles of other Asian powers like Japan, is going to be important in the matter of guaranteeing the stability and prosperity of the region as well as rest of the world. The article tries to present the Chinese side with Indian perspectives of key developments. Chinese perspectives are already being made available in India in a similar manner. The writer feels that put together, such exchanges will facilitate creation of a better mutual understanding between the two sides, impacting favourably on the overall India-China relationship.

Growing Optimism

Broadly speaking, India-China ties at government levels remain stable at this juncture; New Delhi and Beijing have established a 'strategic and cooperative partnership for peace and prosperity' and signed a document on 'shared vision for the 21st century', signifying that the Sino-Indian ties have gone beyond the bilateral context and acquired a global character. Accordingly, India and China are cooperating on international issues related to the diversification of global energy mix, climate change, arms control and disarmament, non-traditional security threats, counter-terrorism, WTO, WMD, human rights and South-South Co-operation. Bilaterally, the two sides now aim at building 'a relationship of friendship and trust, based on equality, in which each is sensitive to the concerns and aspirations of the other'.

They are not viewing each other as a security threat and are by and large satisfactorily implementing confidence building measures in the disputed border, besides carrying out joint military exercises. Special Representatives of India and China have so far held thirteen rounds of border talks, though with no tangible results. Most important is that with an attitude of promoting ties looking beyond the unsolved and 'complex' border dispute, India and China are speeding up their trade and economic contacts. Bilateral trade is fast gathering momentum, with the volume to the tune of US$ 40 billion now and projections for US$ 60 billion by 2010.

China has emerged as India's largest trading partner, replacing the US, in April 2008- February 2009 period. Also significant is the ongoing momentum in their exchanges of high level visits reflecting the desire of each party to forge stronger ties, of which the recently concluded state visit of Indian President Ms Patil to China is a prominent example. Notwithstanding the encouraging picture brought out above, there are issues deeply dividing India and China; resolving them once for all is of utmost necessity, to further strengthen their relations. There are some talks in India about the past civilisational contacts helping resolution of the issues; they however lack substance. As modern nation states, the India and China have developed geo-political interests, which often tend to clash. What follows is a discussion on the conditions contributing to India-China frictions and the likely scenario in bilateral ties in future.

Problem Areas—Boundary Issue

As this writer sees, the boundary issue comes foremost in the list of problem areas. It is most sensitive one for both India and China as it relates closely to territorial integrity and sovereignty in respect of each side. It therefore needs to be handled carefully by the two nations. China's understanding of Indian perspectives on the boundary issue will remain incomplete if it does not take into account the traditional doubts prevailing in India on China having been territorially ambitious. Examples being quoted in India in this regard include Mao's description of China's 'palm' (Tibet) and 'five fingers' (Nepal, Sikkim, Bhutan, NEFA and Ladakh); references are also being made in India to the PRC's sense of 'historical loss' of territories expressed through their maps and atlas series, published in eighties. Such maps had even been seen claiming that India's Assam, even Andamans, were 'historically' parts of China.

Proceeding from 'doubts' to substantive points, it is being seen in India that the border positions of India and China are in conflict with each other and hence are difficult to solve. China's claims are based on its historical stand – all its borders, including with India, are as defined during the Qing dynasty period which ended in 1912.The root of the border problem with India lies in Beijing's position that a large chunk of its territory, especially the 90,000 Sq km area in the Eastern sector, were illegally taken away by the British India, after the 1914 Simla Convention and that India inherited the British legacy.

This has provided the rationale for Beijing in rejecting the McMahon line, a product of the Convention and in claiming the entire Arunachal Pradesh state of India as part of Chinese territory, called by it as 'Southern Tibet' Authoritative scholars in China have categorically stated that Beijing cannot recognize the McMahon line; if it did so, it would amount to Chinese admission of the 1962 conflict as a 'war of aggression' as well as an implicit acknowledgement that Tibet was once independent of China. On the other hand, for India, McMahon line remains the 'de facto' border with China.

The Sino-Indian border problem remains complicated with the Chinese claiming recently the 2.1 Sq km 'finger area' of Sikkim, the status of which as an Indian state has already been recognized by Beijing 'de facto'. On the current scenario, meriting attention are India's concerns arising from various factors – the reported Chinese intrusions, said to number 270 in 2008, into the Indian border, the adverse reaction of Beijing to the visit of the Indian Prime Minister Dr. Manmohan Singh to Arunachal Pradesh, China's bid to stop the loans for Arunachal Pradesh from the Asian Development Bank and strong Chinese state-controlled media criticisms of India's dispatch of additional troops to and positioning of advanced fighter aircraft in its Eastern border. Adding to India's discomfort has also been the rise in the level of Chinese media rhetoric against India, noticed in 2009; this has however subsided now.

Sino-Indian border talks, despite thirteen rounds of talks so far between two Special representatives, have not led to any tangible result in finalising a 'frame work' for a boundary settlement in accordance with the Agreement on Political Parameters, reached in 2005. While Beijing's stand is to approach the border issue in the spirit of 'mutual understanding and mutual accommodation', India wants 'ground realities' to be taken into account. About the reported Chinese claim over Tawang, an interesting argument is that besides strategic factors, the same has been due to the China's fears that Buddhist monasteries in the border including the one in Tawang have been centres of Tibetan resistance to the Chinese authority and as such, they should be taken over by it. Interestingly, the Chinese have introduced some new elements to the border question by questioning the already agreed position of keeping areas with settled populations out of the dispute. Is China ready for accommodation on the border issue? The statement made by the PRC Ambassador to India in November 2006 that both sides should make compromises on the 'disputed' Arunachal may be meaningful in this regard.

China's general stand is to 'shelve' the difficult border issues like the one with India and instead work for 'common development'. For e.g the PRC wants to 'shelve' the South China Sea territorial dispute, leave the Senkaku issue with Japan for 'future generations' to solve and 'put aside the Sino-Indian border dispute waiting for a suitable climate for solution' (Deng Xiaoping to the then Indian leader Vajpayee, Beijing, 1979). What is being noticed in India is that China never gives up its claims on sovereignty over disputed areas. An example is Japan-China settlement on exploring the disputed Chunxiao gas field in the East China Sea.

Though Beijing has agreed for joint development of the field, it has declared that China's sovereignty over the field is indisputable. The Chinese 'shelving' formula needs close scrutiny of India in particular. As this writer views, this formula has inherent flaws – for some at least, the projected completion of China's military modernization in 2050 may create new pressures on the leaders in Beijing at that time to become aggressive on all border issues. What are therefore needed are serious efforts from India and China at their border talks, leading to a 'compromise' based solution to the issue, much sooner than later.

Other Bilateral Issues —Tibet Issue

Tibet issue is prominent among other problems. It can be said that with India accepting the Tibet Autonomous Region as an integral part of China and standing firmly against any anti-China activity of the Dalai Lama from India's soil, this issue does not figure in Sino-Indian state to state relations. However, Beijing appears to be having reservations on India's motives with respect to the Dalai Lama.

The State-controlled media allegation, made on the eve of Manmohan Singh – Wen Jiabao meeting in Thailand, that the Dalai Lama is colluding with India whenever Sino-Indian border talks are held, along with the Chinese official view that the proposed visit to Arunachal Pradesh by the Dalai Lama in November 2009, 'further exposes the anti-China and separatist nature of the Dalai clique' and a subsequent authoritative comment that such visits cast a new shadow on Sino-Indian relations, firmly point to Beijing's approach linking the Dalai Lama factor with the Sino-Indian border question. China's fears need to be understood in the context of March 2008 unrest in Tibet, posing a challenge to China's sovereignty over that territory, even weakening Beijing's position in its border negotiations with India. Also, the question as to why India is tolerating the Tibetan Government in Exile in its soil, seems to be bothering China. Premier Wen Jiabao's description of the Tibet issue as a 'sensitive' one in relations with India, assumes significance in the context of what has been said above. The writer feels that Chinese suspicions on India-Dalai Lama relations are not going to disappear soon; the picture may change if talks between Beijing and the exiled spiritual leader succeed, but chances in this regard appear to be bleak at least for the moment.

China-Pakistan Nexus

China-Pakistan nexus is the next major bilateral issue. A better understanding is required in China about India's sensitivities on this account. The Chinese military, missiles and nuclear help to Pakistan continues, but Beijing is not in a position to give a guarantee to India that Pakistan will not leverage such support from China, to fight against India. Not surprisingly, New Delhi perceives that China's military assistance to Pakistan has direct implications for India.

China's Defence Modernisation

On the third issue of China's military modernization programme, India's concerns are being expressed through its important government documents, for e.g. the Defence Ministry's Annual Report (2008-2009) has said that the programme has implications for India's defence and security. Asking Beijing to show greater transparency in its defence policy and postures, particularly on the double-digit growth in defence spending in last two decades, it has observed that China's stated aim in its Defence White Paper for 2008 to develop missiles, space based assets and blue water naval capabilities will have an effect on the overall military environment in the neighbourhood of India. The Chinese side should properly address such concerns of India.

China's policy towards India's Neighbourhood

India's concerns also relate to China's attempts to establish a strategic presence in India's neighbourhood, for e.g port projects like Gwadar (Pakistan), Hambantota(Sri Lanka), Chittagong (Bangladesh). They are giving rise to fears in India of a Chinese encirclement of the country, under what has come to be known as a 'string of pearls strategy'. The PRC has taken care to officially repudiate such concerns, by asserting that it has no plans to try for domination of the shipping lanes in the Indian Ocean and has no intentions to establish a chain to encircle India. An India-China understanding on the issue is a must for further improving bilateral relations.

India-US Relations

Chinese critical positions on the India-US relations are also a matter of India's concern. The Chinese have welcomed the India-US Strategic Dialogue and are themselves promoting ties with the

US. Still, China seems to nurture fears about US-India collusion against it. Its official media description of India's policy as one 'befriending the far and attacking the near' is unmistakably an indirect, but strong criticism of the developing strategic relations between India and the US.

East Asia Integration

It would be necessary for China to pay attention to the Indian perception that it hesitates to accept India's leading role in the East Asian regional integration process on the plea that the process should only be based on ASEAN+3 (China, Japan and South Korea) cooperation, and that ' outsiders' like India, Australia and New Zealand have no place in it.

India's Defence Strategy

Reports in India about the country's defence strategy visualizing war on two fronts- Pakistan and China, have been commented upon in China.

A Chinese comment (China Youth Daily) has said that India's real target is China, not Pakistan. Indian strategic planners have only done a scenario building; war is not an option for India, which wants to settle its historic problems with its two neighbours peacefully. Under the strategy, both land and sea power are getting emphasis in India, which reflects a logical consideration of the country's geopolitical position.

How to Read Chinese Media?

The Indian public does not understand the reasons for appearance of hawkish views on India in some of China's strategic journals/websites. Global Times and writers like Colonel Dai Xu, have often given controversial views on India. How far such views reflect official thinking remains a question in India. Is the People's Liberation army (PLA) influencing China's foreign policy making? Even the US Defence Secretary Robert Gates has hinted to such possibilities (Shangrila Dialogue, Singapore, 2010).The answer to such misgivings may lie in the need for reporting transparency in China.

Economy

Questions are being asked in China on how India will use its economic power. They are similar to doubts in India and abroad about China's intentions once its modernization programme gets completed, say in 2050. China has announced peaceful development as its goal. India's objectives are on the same lines – enriching the entrepreneurial and economic potential of the country through a suitable reform strategy as well as integrating the country with the world's economic system under a new order. India's increasing role in G-20 mechanism speaks for the latter in particular. Another basic point relates to attempts to compare the development models of India and China. Which one is the better? A debate may be unending in this regard- generally, the Indian model based on democracy is being viewed favourably from a long term point of view than that of China which rests on a one-party system. The main difference is that while China has been following a model based on investment flow from abroad and exports. India has been giving a boost to entrepreneurship and free enterprise. In the opinion of the writer, the Indian superiority in the service sector notwithstanding, it will not be easy for India to catch up fast with China, which has already emerged as a manufacturing giant.

What will be India's global interests as an emerging power is another topic getting focus in China. As Dr Manmohan Singh, the Indian Prime Minister puts it, India's goal is to gain its rightful place in the comity of nations, making full use of the opportunities offered by a globalised world, operating on the frontiers of modern science and technology and using modern science and technology as important instruments of national economic and social development. The emerging India's partnerships with the US, China and other powers, India's role in the G-20 mechanism etc stand to explain its interests in the 21st century. Realising its responsibilities as a growing power, India is cooperating with other nations on addressing issues of global concern like terrorism, climate change, disarmament, world trade etc.

In conclusion, it can be said that there are mixed views on China in India; Indians are noticing the prevailing good atmosphere in bilateral relations at state levels, but their concerns are continuing on China's strategic intentions vis-à-vis India. More and more people to people contacts between the two sides can bring a beneficial change to such conditions.

SINO-INDIAN RELATIONS 1950-1959

The Sino-Indian relationship from 1950 to 1959 was particularly warm, and several reasons for these cordial relations existed. Arguably the most important was the hasty diplomatic recognition of the PRC in December 1949 by India, making them the second nation in the world after Burma to do so. This conferment of legitimacy was helpful in establishing a cooperative environment with China, as many nations chose instead to recognize the Republic of China (ROC) in Taiwan. Furthermore, India's existence as a socialist and not a capitalist state, allowed for greater cooperation with the PRC since they did not come into direct conflict with Maoist ideology like the U.S. This basis of diplomatic and ideological congruency led Prime Minister Nehru to attempt to revolutionize international affairs by producing the Panchsheel Agreement between China and India in 1954. The Panchsheel Agreement stressed five points; (1) mutual respect for each other's territorial integrity and sovereignty; (2) mutual non-aggression; (3) non-interference in each other's domestic affairs; (4) equality and mutual benefit, and finally; (5) peaceful coexistence. This agreement originates from Nehru's optimism that post-colonial nations could invalidate the precepts of a bipolar world, and that the regional powers of Asia can contradict the validity of traditional balance of power politics.

The diplomatic and ideological reasons for Sino-Indian cooperation are bolstered by shared historical experiences. Both China and India share a long and uninterrupted cultural and historical tradition. Both nations at one time were great powers. Most importantly though, both nations were invaded by Western imperialists and consummately humiliated and exploited. This occupation and exploitation by the West caused the growth of significant nationalist forces within India and China, and the desire to gain independence. The ROC received its independence in 1912, and the later consolidation of the PRC in 1949 ushered in a new era of Chinese sovereignty and independence from imperialism. Likewise, India achieved its independence from Britain in 1947.

Due to their history of Western occupation, China and India had additionally failed to develop independent industries. Their occupations meant that the Chinese and Indian economies were still largely agrarian, and dependent on the import of finished goods. This led the Indian government to implement a form of democratic socialism, while the PRC engaged in agrarian based communism, or Maoism. Regardless of their system's differences, both nations abhorred capitalism creating an ideological common ground. Their common historical experience produced a familiar perspective upon which Indian and Chinese policymakers could relate to one another.

This environment of common history and diplomatic cooperation producing positive relations would be challenged by the Chinese policy of taking back historical possessions. The 1950 invasion and takeover of Tibet by the PRC would begin to show strains in the relationship. Trepidation over Tibet's seizure by the PRC was based in the idea of a historical Indian-Tibetan relationship, but the Seventeen Points Agreement of May 1951 ironed out their differences with India recognizing China's historical sovereignty over Tibet while still preserving Indian economic and social interests in Tibet. The agreement appeared to settle a possible dispute over Tibet between the two powers, but right-wing elements in the Indian parliament expressed this viewpoint of the PRC invasion, "the final action of the Chinese, in my judgment, is a little short of perfidy". This underlying opinion of the Tibet invasion by the PRC would bring forward another issue heightening tension in the relationship.

This issue was the definition of China's border with India in the Northeast and Northwest. Maxwell argues that one of China's diplomatic priorities was defining diplomatically agreed boundaries, as "boundaries are one of the first expressions of a modern state" and the PRC sought this validation of modernity. However, to not endanger Sino-Indian relations over the border question, Nehru and Zhou Enlai agreed to leave the border issue between mid-level bureaucrats to be mediated at a later date paving the way for the 1954 Panchsheel Agreement. Thus, this issue remained on the back-burner of Indian foreign policy until the PRC began to make moves towards its historical conception of Sino-Indian boundaries south of the McMahon Line in 1957. Two years later Tibet rose up in a massive revolt against Chinese authority. China's People's Liberation Army (PLA) moved in to put down the rebellion by breaking popular will in the capital of Lhasa. March 31, 1959 the Dalai Lama fled from Tibet into India where he was granted political asylum. This course of events angered the Indian public as they saw it as a renunciation of Indian trade and cultural access to Tibet guaranteed in the Seventeen Points Agreement. PRC officials chaffed at India's meddling in their domestic affairs by granting asylum to the Dalai Lama and thereby violating the 1954 Panchsheel agreement. The Tibetan revolt combined with gradual Chinese assertion of borders in 1957 due to diplomatic impasse, are the primary factors contributing to a hostile Sino-Indian diplomatic relationship from 1959 to the outbreak of hostilities.

Important the Systems Theory

Now that a historical context for Sino-Indian relations during the 20th Century has been established, it is necessary to define the systemic level theory from which the case will be analyzed. A systemic level of analysis eschews the individualities of states and the impact of individual leaders on foreign policy outcomes. Instead it focuses on the structure of the international system, and how this structure forces states to conform to a set of probable responses regardless of their individual differences.

In Kenneth Waltz's seminal work, *Man the State and War,* he lays down the foundation for a levels-of-analysis framework for studying international relations. Waltz does not contend to have created this framework, but instead argues that different theories of international relations promote one or another level of analysis over the other. The basis of this assertion is in Waltz's take on how is politics best to be studied, "Can man in society best be understood by studying man or by studying society" ? If one believes that man in society can best be understood by studying man then you will focus on individuals and reject the influence of society on them, and vice versa. This idea is then refocused from the question of man and politics to the question of why states go to war.

Classical realists like Hans Morgenthau believe that war is driven essentially by the natural evilness of man. Essentially the "ubiquity of evil in human action arising from man's ineradicable lust for power and transforming churches into political organizations ...revolutions into dictatorships... love for country into imperialism". From this perspective, society and government are not influential forces in history, but instead magnifiers of mans collective malevolence when grouped into nations. From a classical model states cannot cooperate because "passion often obscures the true interests of states as of men," and not because "states are never honorable and peaceful". Waltzian neo-realism departs from these ideas by exploring the other half of the question. Believing that "Man is born and in his natural condition remains neither good nor bad," but is influenced by society to one extreme or the other, as states are influenced by a society of states (the international arena) to engage in war or not.

Neorealist systems theory is driven by one primary characteristic: in no matter what form the system is structured, the system is driven by the essential existence of anarchy. The source of this anarchy is the absence of an overarching international body with the power to force the conformity of the units of the structure (the states). As such the United Nations and other international organizations are not important and have no bearing on the system since they lack the capability of shaping the unit actors decisions. Acknowledging this, states are the only relevant actors, and the anarchic system leaves them with two realities. The first is that states are responsible for their own security, and secondly that threats to this security are unending.

Additionally, neo-realism departs from classical realism in that classical realists view power itself as the ultimate goal of the state, whereas neorealists view power as a means with the end being security. Peace in an anarchic system is fragile, and therefore each state must provide for its own security. However, providing for one's own security through military power or alliances often times undermines the security of neighboring states. This paradox where increasing a states security undermines the perception of security in another state is known as the "security dilemma," and is a major structural explanation for the outbreak of war. This is due to the fact that one can never be certain if additional security measures are defensive or offensive in the anarchic system. Another cause on the systemic level for the outbreak of war is the failure of deterrence. Deterrence strategy implies a buildup of military force adequate enough in perception or reality to prevent a state from threatening another states security. If any state misperceives the deterrent capability of another, or believes it has a greater offensive capability war is likely to break out.

In addition to these universal characteristics of the systemic structure is the variable concept of how power in the international system is actually divided. In the period of the Sino-Indian war the world was locked in a bipolar balance of power led by the U.S. and the Soviet Union. In a bipolar system states are rigidly aligned to either pole, but states in each camp have great flexibility of strategy. This was caused by the zero-sum nature of a bipolar system, in that the gain of one side is the loss of the other. As such, the leader of either faction is unwilling to allow client members to fail in policy endeavors. Finally, in a bipolar system states that refuse to join either faction drastically increase their security dilemma unless they have the power to challenge the international structure towards a multi-polar balance. Now that the neorealist systemic level theory is defined it shall be applied to explain the variables causing the outbreak of the Sino-Indian war.

Derivation and Events Leading to Border Dispute

The 1914 Simla Convention between Britain and Tibet established the McMahon Line as the official border between British India and China, denying the right of Chinese suzerainty over Tibet. However, the line's namesake McMahon, was ordered back to London in disgrace over the "chicanery" he exercised in border negotiations in which he presented a different map to the Chinese envoy, thus distancing Britain from the legitimacy of the negotiated border. Thirty years later British cartographers began drawing the McMahon Line as the border between British India and China, thus reviving the lines legal legitimacy.

When India gained its independence from Britain in 1947 it inherited all of the British territorial agreements, and as such inherited the McMahon Line as the border between it and China. Indian belief in the legitimacy of the McMahon line dated back to the Simla Convention of 1914, as well as to the numerous maps of British India with the line delineating its northern border.

As such Nehru shrugged off Chinese insistence in border negotiation during the 1954 agreement stating that "the McMahon line marked their border with China, where was the need" ? Despite India's view of the McMahon Line's legitimacy, China had not signed the Simla Convention and under no circumstances consented to any bilateral agreement between Tibet and Britain because it violated their sovereignty.

Indian intransigence on negotiating a border acceptable to both parties led the PRC to act independently in areas south of the McMahon line. The justification for this was that in the absence of mutually negotiated borders, the true national boundary was a line of actual control represented by the extent of either nation's ability to administrate the territory.

Practical assertion of this idea was first revealed to India in 1957 when an Indian patrol discovered an all-weather road which had been constructed in the Aksai-Chin Plain connecting Xinjiang and Tibet. The Indian government launched diplomatic protests asserting a violation of their territorial integrity; however the PRC "considered [Aksai-Chin] to have long been Chinese territory". This issue was not resolved as the Indian government refused to engage in territorial negotiations until Chinese forces completely withdrew from the Aksai-Chin Plain. The PRC refused to do so, and instead of a diplomatic solution India began to pursue a more confrontational approach to assert their territorial claims.

The rebellion in Tibet helped to drastically sour relations between the PRC and India, but the border dispute widened due to a change in Indian military strategy. This change in military strategy was to create forward-posts behind the Chinese claim line, and in strategic locations to flank Chinese military positions.

These posts were constructed to assert Indian territorial claims in the Ladakh region and to threaten the Xinjian-Tibet road in Aksai-Chin. By September, 1962 a similar series of forward posts had been built beyond the Chinese claim line in Tibet, and four such posts were built even beyond the McMahon Line. This resulted in an inability to claim that these posts were simply to defend Indian territorial integrity. The territorial dispute from India's perspective, coupled with the building of forward military posts by the Indian military caused the 1954 Panchsheel Agreement to not be renewed in 1961. Crossing both the claim and McMahon lines, both nations were in violation of each other's territorial conception, and India was now physically challenging Chinese sovereignty in Tibet.

FRESH PROGRESS OF SINO-INDIAN RELATIONS IN RECENT YEARS

China is now on of India's largest trade partners whereas India is China's largest trade partner in South Asia. According to statistics released by China's Ministry of Commerce, bilateral trade between the two countries reached $ 66.47 billion in 2012, China's export to India was $ 46.47 billion and China's import from India was $ 18.8 billion, falling by 10.1%, 5.7% and 19.6% respectively from the year before. India had a deficit of $ 28.87 billion in its trade with China with an increase of $ 1.79 billion from 2011. Chinese companies had signed contract projects to an accumulated amount of $ 60.131 billion with a turnover of business of $ 33.518 billion by the end of 2012. In two way investments, the Chinese Ministry of Commerce had approved or put on record $ 725 billion of direct investment from China in non-financial projects in India while Indian companies had actually invested $ 486 million in 800 non-financial projects in China by that time. This indicates that despite the negative impact of the overall international economic environment and growing trade frictions between the two sides, Sino-Indian trade and economic cooperation have continued to grow steadily as smooth progress of the contract projects portends enormous potentialities for mutual investment.

Tortuous Path of Security Cooperation

The Indian side unilaterally suspended military exchanges with China in 2009 when the Chinese side began to issue stapled visas to inhabitants residing in the Indian-controlled zone in Kashmir.

Nevertheless, after the Fifth Round Defense and Security consultation between the Ministries of National Defense of the two countries in January 2013, the two sides argued to resume defense cooperation and launch the third joint military exercise scheduled this year.

As the two countries' international roles grow, the maritime interaction between the two sides has become a focus of concern as they begun to explore for dialogue on maritime security as of 2012. It should be noted that the two countries are prepared to start "dialogue on the Tibetan issue" in the post-Dalai Lama time with a view to reducing the frictions over this issue left over from history.

In April 2010, the two sides signed the*Agreement between China and India on the Establishment of a Hotline between Prime Ministers of the Two Countries*. This is one of the latest actions taken by the two sides for enhancing mutual assurance. This will be an effective way of dispelling misunderstandings on both sides at a time of crisis and preventing the escalation of the crisis. Therefore, it is of great significance for an exchange of view on strategic issues between leaders of the two countries. Just recently, the two sides held the Sixth Round Consultation on Anti-terrorism in Beijing, during which the participants had in-depth discussions of international and regional developments against terrorism and bilateral cooperation in this area. By and large, the two sides have made progress in the negotiations over sensitive and complex security and strategic issues and slowly but effectively reduced the "deficit" in strategic mutual reassurance.

Border Areas under Effective Control

Given that no major breakthrough is in sight in a short time, the two sides are prepared to tighten their control over the border areas and prevent contingencies. For this purpose, the Special

Representatives' Meeting for boundary negotiations is charged with a wider scope of responsibilities and functions. Moreover, the two sides formally signed the*Agreement between the Government of the People's Republic of China and the Government of the Republic of India on the Establishment of a Working Mechanism for Consultation and Coordination on India-China Border Affairs*. This consultative body is comprised of diplomats and military officers from both sides, led by principals at the Director-General level of Ministries of Foreign Affairs.

It is mandated to handle all matters concerning peace and stability along the China-India borders and study how to carry out exchanges and cooperation between military personnel and agencies of the two countries in border areas so as to serve as a proper channel and platform for enhancing information exchange and better collaboration and ensure for handling border affairs through the diplomatic channel in a more timely and effective manner, thereby preparing good conditions for resolving the boundary question through negotiations and promoting better relations between the two countries. In April 2013 when "troops face-off at tents" occurred in the western sector of the Sino-Indian border, the two sides successfully prevented the escalation of the event, which might lead to the deterioration of the bilateral relationship through such a consultative and collaborative mechanism for boundary affairs and through timely diplomatic contact and meetings between frontier officers of both sides at the border.

The successful "soft-landing" of the troops face-off indicates that the two sides still have different views on and perceptions of the line of Actual Control. It also proves that the cooperative regimes and institutions for the boundary issue are truly helpful in crisis management. Generally speaking, border control is a kind of preventive measure of "negative assurance", but it is indispensable in the course of resolving the boundary questions between China and India, and serves as an important institutional guarantee which has prevented major military conflicts over the past several decades along the Sino-Indian border that has not been formally delineated to date.

Bilateral Cooperation

In recent years, as India plays an increasing salient role in the reshaping of international order, it has become one of the strategic partners China counts on. The two countries support each other in regional cooperation and made joint efforts to promote peace, stability and development in Asia.

China and India join hands in handling many global issues such as international trade and financial issues and sustainable development, energetically safe guarding the tights and interests of developing countries and new emerging powers and facilitating improvement and reshaping of the existing international economic order. All these are outstanding highlights for bilateral cooperation which provides a convincing footnote for Sino-Indian strategic partnership. The United States and some other western countries feel hard pressed by the common positions of China and India on energy security, climate change and some other global issues. The BRIC countries, G20 Summit and the East Asia Summit (EAS) have now become important venues for close interaction between leaders of the two countries in sustainable development of bilateral relations.

A Plus in Bilateral Relations

To commemorate the both anniversary of the establishment of diplomatic relations, China and India co-launched "India Year" and "China Year", an exchange program of culture activities in 2010. In 2011, the two sides hosted more people-to-people exchange programs under the auspices of "Sino-Indian Year of Exchanges". And in 2012—defined as "Sino-Indian Year OF Friendly Cooperation", the exchange programs in the field of humanities helped to reduce the negative memory of the border conflicts that had broken out 50years before.

Moreover, the exchange of visits of "hundred-member" youth delegations were well received in the host country. Indian audiences very much enjoyed the shows put up by Chinese artists' troupes on their commercial performance tours in India in recent years. India is now one of major tour destinations for Chinese cultural and theatrical troupes. This has injected new vitalities into cultural exchanges between the two countries and energetically promoted non-governmental exchanges and mutual understanding between the two peoples.

SINO-INDIAN RELATIONS IN CHANGING CIRCUMSTANCES

Having gone through a decade of exploratory efforts by the two sides in the new century, Sino-India relations at present display the following outstanding features:

Top leaders of both countries define Sino-Indian relations as one of the most important sets of bilateral relationships in their foreign relations and an increasing higher priority in their diplomatic agenda. As the two largest countries in Asia and the developing world as well as countries with an ancient civilization and major emerging market economies, China and India have great potentials for bilateral cooperation and more and more common interests and carry growing strategic weight in the restructuring of regional forces in Asia. Clearly, Sino-Indian relations have an increased impact on the international trading system, the international financial order, the global development agenda and regional cooperation in Asia and the Pacific. If one used to observe Sino-Indian relations by gradually shifting one's perspective from South Asia to the Asia and the Pacific at large five or six years ago. One should now shift one's focus from Asia and the Pacific to the world at large in analyzing Sino-Indian relations. Just as Indian Prime Minister Singh points out, "Today, both India and China are in the midst of rapid transformation. The development agenda has taken centre-stage in both our societies. Our systems are different, but people in both countries are united in their aspiration for a better future. When countries of the size of China and India, together accounting for 2.5 billion people begin to unshackle their creative energies, it impacts on the whole world."

Pragmatically and Rationally

Due to the lack of strategic mutual assurance in the past several decades, anything in the offing or any contingency might easily stir emotions on both sides. This has always been a major deficiency in the bilateral relations. In recent years, however, under the guidance of top leaders of both countries, Sino-Indian relations have again become more practical and rational. The manifestation of this are: 1) Leaders of the two countries have reiterated that the earth is a vast planet which allows for the rise of China and India as new emerging powers; 2) in 2012, the year that marks the fiftieth year after the border conflict, the mainstream view in the media and public opinion in both countries was that the two sides should reflect on and learn lessons from the past with a conclusion that the two countries should never fight again and work together for a better future; 3) Each side is more keen on discovering and learning from the strong points of the other, refraining from treating it emotionally or with preconceived ideas, and drawing on good experiences and valuable assets of the other side to the good of its own development. This is particularly the case in the areas of trade, economic cooperation and the mutual investment. Such changes have markedly highlighted the importance of cooperative Sino-Indian relations and facilitated the growth of friendship mass organizations and associations as a valuable asset in Sino-Indian relations.

Reserving or Solving Differences

In the past fifty years and more, an important principle governing Sino-Indian relations has always been to bear longer interests of bilateral relations in mind and seeking common ground while reserving differences. While "freezing", controlling and shelving major differences, the two sides taking store by the overall interests of bilateral relations, have been working hard for cooperation and common development in other areas so as to prepare conditions for resolving such differences and contradictions in the future. In recent years, both sides have realized that an important way of enhancing strategic mutual reassurance and future promoting bilateral relations as well as freezing Sino-Indian relations from interference of third parties is to iron out their disputes through better communication, dialogue and consultation. While continuing to find out and expand the convergence of interests, the two sides should proactively try to narrow down or resolve the differences. Despite the fact that the two sides are yet to prepare all necessary conditions for the resolution of the boundary dispute and that one has not seen a marked increase of favorable factors, they wish to talk and settle this issue and act accordingly with a deeper understanding of the importance of maintaining peace and stability in the border areas.

With this in mind, China and India have made progress on some "theory issues" in their relationship.

They have launched, or are ready to launch, talks on establishing new mechanisms for the border issue, strategic and economic dialogue, maritime security dialogue, dialogue on the Tibetan questions in addition to steady progress in the consultations on trans-border water resources, combating terrorism and mil-to-mil relations.

Bilateral Relationship

In the past ten years, China and India have gradually found out how to keep on good terms through properly handling their differences and disputes and making cooperative efforts for common development and better bilateral relations.

First, new ideas and suggestions for enhancing Sino-Indian relations have kept emerging, such as "new concept of China-India relationships", "2.0 edition of China-India relations", "Five Principles of Peaceful Coexistence", "How emerging powers should treat one another", etc. Of late, Mr. Sanjaya Baruÿformer Press Consultant of Prime Minister Singh has made a comparative analysis of President Xi Jinping's recent "Five –Point proposal" on Sino-Indian relations and Prime Minister Singh's five principles governing Indo-China relations. The fact that leaders of both countries are thinking of putting bilateral relations more on a theoretical basis indicates that Sino-Indian relations are becoming more and more important and that the bilateral relationship now stands at a critical juncture of reaching a new height.

Second, each side tends to take a more pragmatic and forbearing approach to the presence and activities of the other side in the region of its pivotal interests. The joint "China-Indo-Japan ship escorts" in the Gulf of Aiden and China-Indian consultation and collaboration at East Asia Summits point to the fact that the two countries have less "zero-sum mentality" and more cooperation and win-win in mind.

Third, the two sides are less on the alert and more accommodating towards each other in exchanges of views in multilateral fora. Cases in points are their collaboration in G20 events, BRIC meetings and UN conferences on climate change.

CHINA, INDIA, SOUTHEAST ASIA AND GLOBAL POLICY REFORM

The opening wide of China's door to trade and FDI has not occurred in isolation. Trade policy around the world has become progressively more liberal as part of wider packages of market-based reforms. A veritable trade policy revolution has spread across the developing world, especially since the early 1980s, though it has been patchy and uneven. The Asian financial crisis, followed by crises in Russia, Brazil and Argentina, raised strong doubts about further liberalisation. This has centred on financial liberalisation, especially of short-term capital flows, but it has had a knock-on effect on trade and FDI. Broadly speaking, previous liberalisation has not been reversed, but its forward momentum has slowed.

Southeast Asia fits this pattern. The real burst of trade-and-investment liberalisation took place in the 1980s and first half of the 1990s, particularly in Malaysia, Thailand and Indonesia. Singapore and the Philippines were exceptions: in the former, export-led industrialisation and the return to liberal trade policies took place earlier; in the latter, substantial trade-and-investment liberalisation had to wait until the 1990s. Vietnam started opening its borders as part of its transition from Plan to Market from the late 1980s. Cambodia has seen liberalising reforms only more recently. Laos remains largely closed; and Myanmar even more so. Tiny Brunei is a largely unreformed economy and polity based on oil-revenue windfalls.

The Asian crisis changed matters somewhat. True, trade, FDI and other liberalisation measures were not reversed. Indeed, Singapore, Thailand and Indonesia went further in a liberalising direction – in the latter two countries induced by IMF structural-adjustment programmes. But, with the exception of Singapore, government enthusiasm for further liberalisation declined markedly. This was reinforced by powerful interests keen to protect their markets against foreign competition, and a populist backlash of sorts against globalisation in general.

How does China fit in? Its first decade of reforms centred on internal liberalisation, especially in agriculture. Then followed a brief period of uncertainty and suspense after the Tienanmen massacre.

The last decade, however, has seen the biggest trade-and-investment liberalisation programme the world has ever seen. In short time, China has swung from extreme protection to rather liberal trade policies, indeed very liberal by developing-country standards. This was crowned by its accession to the WTO, with by far the strongest commitments of any developing country. The pace of internal and external liberalisation has not let up since.

This recent episode is all the more remarkable in that it has happened in the world's most populous country. In contrast, most episodes of radical external liberalisation have occurred in quite small countries (e.g. most of the east-Asian Tigers, Chile, and the east- European transition economies). While many others slowed down after the Asian crisis, China continued to race ahead.

India has had a rather different trajectory. Its retreat from the "licence raj" – its equivalent of Soviet-style central planning – began half-heartedly in the 1980s; but it was a foreign-exchange crisis in 1991 that provided the window of opportunity for more thoroughgoing market-based reforms. These were radical by Indian standards, though less so compared with policy reforms elsewhere. They covered macroeconomic stabilisation, trade liberalisation, relaxation of FDI restrictions, privatisation and, not least, the dismantling of domestic licensing arrangements that had governed most formal economic activity. Since the initial burst in 1991-93, reforms have proceeded in a stop-go manner. They have not been reversed; but they have moved ahead more slowly and fitfully compared with southeast Asia (pre-Asian crisis) and China (pre- and post-Asian crisis). Democratic politics, including the complications of multi-party governing coalitions and the federal division of powers between the Union government and the states, has made faster, more decisive reforms elusive.

The above account is admittedly impressionistic; the following sections will go into relevant detail on trade-policy developments. Before getting into that detail, it is worth flagging four big lessons from recent policy-reform experience.

First, there are sceptics who play down external liberalisation and its link to growth. In China, other parts of east Asia and India, liberalisation has been gradual, partial and controlled, they say, and it has been mixed judiciously with industrial-policy interventions and capital controls. That is (more or less) true. But, as Martin Wolf argues, "it mistakes the trees for the forest." Of course none of these countries has adopted full-blown free trade like Britain in the nineteenth century or Hong Kong in the twentieth century. Rather – this is the central point – they have, to varying degrees, moved in the direction of a market economy, with better protection of property rights, freer enterprise and competition in place of state ownership and planning, and more exposure to foreign trade and investment. To argue otherwise would be absurd.

Second, one is accustomed to dry social-scientific talk about liberalisation, followed by large numbers on growth and poverty reduction. That should not obscure the biggest boon of all. The market economy, not least through trade-policy reform, has opened up personal freedoms and life-chances that were unimaginable even a generation ago. That is the product of increasing wealth and the institutions that accompany it. In short, market-based reforms are about prosperity *and* economic freedom – though not necessarily civic and political freedom, at least in the short term.

Third, trade-policy reforms can only be understood as part of broad market-based reforms, and in conjunction with "second-generation" institutional reforms. External liberalisation delivers abundant, long-term gains only *in interaction with* the build-up of domestic market-supporting institutions. Opening to the world creates the spontaneous stimulus for institutional upgrading to better exploit trade-and-investment opportunities, e.g. through better currency and banking practices, and the development of ports and inland communications. Reciprocally, better enforcement of private-property rights and contracts, cleaner, more efficient public administration, and more investment in education and infrastructure, maximise the gains for importers, exporters, and domestic and foreign investors. Openness, therefore, is a *handmaiden* of growth, not a quick fix.

The link to institutions also points to big and enduring gaps in Chinese, Indian and southeast-Asian reforms. Liberalisation of tariffs and quotas at the border can be done relatively quickly and easily, in technical if not political terms. But trade-related institutional reforms "behind the border" are full of local particularities, technically complicated, administratively demanding, politically very sensitive and inevitably gradual. This applies to the legal system and public administration, and to domestic regulations concerning intellectual property, services, competition and investment rules, public procurement, customs administration, food-safety and other product- and process-related standards. Taken together, this involves nothing less than restructuring the state to make it support, not hinder, a complex, globally integrated market economy.

The World Bank and other sources now pay much more attention to the quality of institutions and how they shape the business climate. China and India do very badly on "investment-climate" indicators such as the number of legal and administrative procedures involved in starting a business, the time taken during this process, bankruptcy procedures, corruption and contract enforcement. Southeast Asia presents a mixed picture: Singapore regularly comes out at the top end of these indicators; the new ASEAN members include some of the worst-governed countries in the world; Indonesia and Philippines also do poorly; Malaysia and Thailand fare better, but still with much room for improvement.

Fourth, one cannot escape the link between economic-policy reform and political systems. In China, centralised authoritarian politics has maintained political stability and driven economic reforms at a frenetic pace. Decentralised democratic politics slows down Indian reforms. That widens the policy and performance gap with China. Southeast Asia again presents a mixed picture: pluralist democratic politics in Indonesia, Philippines and Thailand (all relatively recent developments) exists alongside authoritarian, semi-authoritarian and semi-democratic politics in other ASEAN countries.

The long-term picture might well look different. In China, there is bound to be increasing tension between centralised authoritarian politics and decentralised market-economy reforms. Widening economic freedoms and a burgeoning middle class will create new demands not just for better-quality governance, but also for civic and political freedoms. How that tension will be resolved remains to be seen; but it is a question mark hanging over the future of a sustainable, flourishing market economy in China.

As for India, while democratic politics slows things down in the short term, it is progressively *legitimating* market-based reforms along the way. A decentralised political and civic culture, with in-built checks and balances, allows for multiple experiments at state and local levels. It is no accident that the more innovative policy reforms tend to come less from the Union government and more from forward-looking state governments in the south and east of India. That sets up a demonstration effect for others to emulate. Finally, a free-breathing society is best suited to a sophisticated services-based market economy full of individualistic, risk-taking entrepreneurs. These are the "open-society" characteristics of the West, and particularly of the USA. India's open society – its combination of Western-style democracy, constitutional liberalism and supporting institutions — is its long-term insurance policy for a flourishing market economy. That is less the case in China or southeast Asia.

CHINA'S, INDIA'S AND SOUTHEAST ASIA'S TRADE-POLICY FRAMEWORKS

Trade-and-economic policy reforms

In China, since 1978, economic-policy reform has been incremental and ultra-pragmatic. The more comprehensive transformation of the Chinese economy and society belongs to the post-Tienanmen phase. A headline reform package was introduced in 1994, covering banking, finance, taxation, investment, foreign exchange and foreign trade. It included the unification of the exchange rate and a new Foreign Trade Law. Currency convertibility, privatisation, the formal recognition of private-property rights and a host of other market-based reforms have followed.

China's integration into the world economy, particularly through its trade reforms, is also more a product of the latter phase, following more gradual opening in earlier phases. Liberalisation has whittled down licensing coverage (down to 5 per cent of imports in 2000 from two-thirds of the total in 1988), and the use of plan prices (to less than 5 per cent of retail commodities by 2000). Even in agriculture, where state pricing is more important, over 80 per cent of sales are at market prices. The overall coverage of non-tariff barriers (NTBs) (licenses, quotas, tendering requirements, state trading and designated trading) had come down to 21.6 per cent of imports and less than 10 per cent of tariff lines by 2001. NTBs fell by about 80 per cent during the 1990s. At a rough estimate, the protective impact of NTBs has fallen from 9.3 per cent in the mid 1990s to 5 per cent today.

Tariffs have come down sharply in tandem with the decline in NTBs. The simple average statutory tariff was 43 per cent in 1992. Waves of tariff reform, particularly one in 1996, had brought it down to 17.5 per cent by 1998 and 16.6 per cent by 2001. Extensive duty exemptions almost completely liberalised imports of intermediate inputs and of investment goods used for export processing.

In sum, as Nicholas Lardy argues, China had undertaken enormous unilateral liberalisation of trade and FDI, and with it sweeping industrial and agricultural restructuring, in the decade *before* WTO accession. That still left significant knots of up-front protection: declining state-run industries; oil and sensitive agricultural commodities subject to monopolistic state-trading arrangements; high-tech industries targeted for industrial-policy promotion; and, most important, services sectors.

China's accession to the WTO and subsequent initiatives have taken reforms even further. That will be discussed later. But it is now clear that the main obstacles to doing business in China have less to do with formal border barriers and more with (formal and informal) non-border barriers. These concern the unpredictability and arbitrariness that come with large regulatory discretion; the lack of a rule of law in terms of impartial judicial oversight and enforcement of property rights and contracts; and the anti-competitive drag of state-owned industrial enterprises and state-owned banks. All this gets deep into domestic economic policies and institutions. It concerns the long-term restructuring of the Chinese state, away from pervasive interference and in the direction of a smaller, more limited operation that can perform fewer functions better. This is a vast trade-related reform agenda; but it has as much to do with the liberalisation of internal trade and the integration of domestic markets as with further external liberalisation. Growth and more widely shared prosperity can only improve if there is a better interaction between external openness and the internal market, mediated by market-supporting institutions.

Indian trade-policy reforms have not been as dramatic or breathtaking, but still considerable by Indian standards. In 1991, the average unweighted tariff was 125 per cent, with peak tariffs on agricultural products going up to 300 per cent. The tariff structure was extremely complicated, with high tariff escalation (higher tariffs on processed goods compared with semi-processed and unprocessed production inputs). This was accompanied by extremely high NTBs (quotas, licensing arrangements and outright bans). Inward investment was either banned or severely restricted. Exchange controls and the internal restrictions of the licence raj (almost) completed the picture.

Much has changed almost fifteen years on. Most border NTBs have been removed, as have internal licensing restrictions. Applied tariffs have come down to an average of about 20 per cent. The maximum tariff on manufactures was lowered to 20 per cent in 2004, and then to 15 per cent in the 2005 budget. Manufacturing tariffs will be rationalised into three bands (0-5-15 per cent); and the intention is to bring average tariffs down to ASEAN levels (around 10 per cent) soon. However, agricultural tariffs remain very high, averaging over 50 per cent. Most restrictions on manufacturing FDI have been removed. Executive orders are being used to relax FDI restrictions in services (given the difficulty of securing a parliamentary majority for such measures).

Hence Indian trade-policy reforms have come far, especially in manufactures. This leaves much to do on tariffs and NTBs in agriculture; and on FDI as well as domestic-regulatory restrictions on foreign services providers. These are much tougher nuts to crack, as are domestic labour-market regulations, privatisation of SOEs, domestic agricultural policies, and a bloated public administration.

What about southeast Asia? Overall, largely as a result of reforms in the 1980s and 90s (earlier in Singapore), the old ASEAN members have average tariffs in the 10-per-cent range or lower, with correspondingly low NTBs. FDI restrictions have been progressively lowered. Tariffs, NTBs and FDI restrictions are particularly low in manufacturing – hence in large part the integration of the region into east-Asian and global manufacturing supply chains, especially in IT products. But agricultural protection is much higher; tariff escalation is not insignificant; and services markets are subject to high FDI and domestic-regulatory restrictions. Dual-economy structures have resulted: relatively open and efficient manufacturing sectors driven by FDI and exposed to global competition coexist with protected, inefficient domestic sectors. The new ASEAN members, either stuck with planned economies or in transition from Plan to Market, have much higher tariff and especially non-tariff barriers.

Singapore is the regional exception. After Hong Kong, it has the world's most liberal trade policies and is the world's most globalised economy. It is a free port with zero tariffs on all imports except four tariff lines (on alcoholic beverages). It is fully open to FDI except for a few services sectors. Unilateral liberalisation and domestic regulatory reform, especially since the Asian crisis, have reduced protectionist barriers in some services sectors.

Malaysia is one of the world's most globalised economies with relatively liberal trade policies by developing-country standards. However, there are peak tariffs, tariff escalation and assorted NTBs in politically sensitive goods sectors; and protection in services remains high. Protection must also be seen in the context of *bumiputera* policies to discriminate in favour of the Malay majority.

Thailand retains relatively high protection by the standards of other old ASEAN members, but its average tariff has come down closer to their levels. However, it still has greater tariff dispersion and escalation; NTBs are not insignificant; and protectionism in services is considerable. No meaningful liberalisation of the economy has occurred under the present Thaksin administration.

Indonesian trade policies have swung from high protection to openness in a comparatively short period. Its average tariff has come down to under 10 per cent. The IMF Structural Adjustment Programme agreed with the Indonesian government in 1998 significantly accelerated trade-and-FDI liberalisation and domestic regulatory reform in goods and services sectors. However, there are higher tariffs and tariff escalation, particularly in agriculture. There is also recent evidence of creeping protectionism through higher NTBs, particularly on agricultural products, textiles and steel. Overall, government enthusiasm for further liberalisation has clearly waned in recent years.

The situation in the Philippines is rather similar to that in Indonesia. Trade policies have swung from high protection to openness in the past decade. The average tariff has come down to well under 10 per cent. But this coexists with peak tariffs and tariff escalation in sensitive sectors, particularly in agriculture. There is recent evidence of creeping protection through higher NTBs, again concentrated on agricultural products. Protectionism is much higher on FDI and trade in services than it is on trade in goods. Restrictions on foreign ownership written into the Philippine constitution remain the most visible market-access hurdle. Overall, the government has displayed little enthusiasm for further liberalisation since the Asian crisis, and domestic protectionist pressures have increased.

Vietnam's transition from Plan to Market has proceeded in stops and starts since 1986, but it has come far cumulatively – though not nearly as far as China. Liberalisation, including trade, has picked up since 2000, though domestic institutional reforms have lagged behind. Foreign trading rights have been liberalised extensively; quantitative restrictions and other NTBs have come down; and the average nominal tariff now stands at about 18 per cent, though the tariff structure contains higher tariffs on many products and high tariff dispersion. Protection in services remains very high. The government continues to discriminate heavily in favour of state-owned industrial enterprises and state-owned banks. Overall, Vietnamese protection in terms of tariffs, NTBs and FDI restrictions remains much higher than it is in the old ASEAN members. It also compares unfavourably with China, given the latter's huge external and internal liberalisation measures before and after WTO accession.

Cambodia has progressed with trade-policy reforms, crowned by its accession to the WTO in 2004. Laos and Myanmar are much further behind.

The foreign-policy dimension

Trade policy stands at the junction of domestic economic and foreign policies, with tight links to both. The imperatives of China's modern foreign policy are steady integration into the global economy and political stability in the east Asian neighbourhood. These objectives have driven fundamental change in China's relations with other major powers, and its participation in international institutions. The Beijing leadership sees China as an emerging great power, indeed part of a concert of great powers, with shared global interests and responsibilities. That is one new frame in which to view Chinese foreign policy.

"Constructive engagement" characterises China's key bilateral relationships, especially the central one with the USA, but also with the EU, India, ASEAN and others. The overriding objective is to forge stronger commercial bonds, contain protectionist pressures directed against Chinese exports, and prevent geopolitical tensions from getting out of hand.

Constructive engagement in international institutions proceeds alongside closer relations with major powers. China joined a host of international organisations through the 1980s. It has participated actively in the IMF, World Bank, WIPO and other international economic agencies, tapping into technical expertise and policy advice in addition to financial aid. It has also been active in the UN. In all these forums, China has acquired the good-citizenship credentials of a "system maintainer", not a "system wrecker". Its approach to international law is the same: it wants to join existing arrangements, make them work better, and play its part in future rule-making.

The rapid professionalisation of the leadership and higher levels of public administration reinforces these trends. Since the 1980s, a new technocratic and outward-looking generation of officials and diplomats has emerged, many with significant foreign exposure.

In sum, Chinese foreign policy has evolved a pragmatic mix of nurturing big-power relationships and active participation in international institutions. The former is a *Realpolitik* calculus; the latter an expression of multilateral credentials. The two approaches are seen as complementary. Their common denominator is much less confrontational, more flexible, sophisticated and nuanced diplomacy, low on megaphone rhetoric and high on patient, behind-the-scenes cooperation to achieve practical results. Trade diplomacy, multilaterally in the WTO and on bilateral and regional tracks, is perhaps the most visible sign of this foreign-policy transformation.

However, this foreign-policy story, on its own, would be Panglossian. Set against the very real trends mentioned above are occasional tendencies of aggressive nationalism. This seems to be directed at Taiwan and Japan, notwithstanding ever-closer commercial ties with them. Finally, the Chinese government seems happy to maintain cosy relations with some of the most repulsive regimes around the world. An optimist would argue that foreign policy will ultimately be swayed by the imperatives of global economic integration. Optimism, however, should always be tinged with realism.

India's foreign policy has undergone a parallel transformation since the end of the Cold War. It has switched from leadership of the "non-aligned" Third World and support for the Soviet Union to constructive engagement with other powers in the developed and developing worlds. Its relations with the USA are blossoming, both on the "high politics" of security and the "low politics" of commercial relations. It is trying to cement parallel alliances with China, ASEAN, Brazil and South Africa. It is playing a more forward-looking, system-maintaining rather than system-wrecking game in international institutions. However, this has not yet translated into much more pragmatic and flexible diplomacy in the WTO – one key difference with China.

Generalisations about ASEAN are difficult in that its members have different foreign policies with few common denominators, despite ASEAN rhetoric to the contrary. Hence there are substantial intra-ASEAN differences in bilateral relations with external powers; and ASEAN cooperation in international institutions, including the WTO, is lacking. However, security concerns and global economic integration have given ASEAN countries one common denominator: nearly all want to have good relations with the USA and the rising powers of China and India. But this is mostly a matter of bilateral (country-to-country) cooperation rather than cooperation involving ASEAN as a group.

THE INFLUENCE OF INDIA'S SECURITY CONCEPT ON ITS CHINA POLICY

Earlier sections of this book explain changes in India's post-Cold War security concept and adjustments to its China policy. In the process of this discussion, we have distinguished two phases of adjustment to both the post-Cold War India security concept and China policy, and established that these changes were more or less simultaneous. We have also found that India's China policy reflects its security concept; in other words that adjustments to the content of India's China policy correspond to continuities and discontinuities in India's security concept. It may be said that this consistency demonstrates the important influence India's security concept has had on its China policy. Policy-making, in any event, is the linking of concepts and policy; in other words, concepts, through government policy-making, crystallize into policy. Exploring the evolution of the Indian policy-making class and mechanisms, therefore, also benefits understanding of the manner in which security concepts of different eras and phases have influenced India's China policy.

India's foreign policy behaviour during the Cold War was largely determined by a few predominant personalities, both its foreign and security policies having long been dominated by Nehru and Indira Gandhi. The two leader's views on China had decisive influence on India's China policy. When considering India's defeat in the 1962 Sino–Indian Border Conflict and the open wound it represented to both the Nehru family and the INC, their adoption of an unyielding tack toward China was the sole political means of saving face. Sino–Indian relations consequently remained in stalemate for nearly 30 years. When Rajiv Gandhi replaced his mother in 1985, he seemed at first to follow her line on foreign policy. The rapidly changing international situation, however, forced him to veer from it, and specific improvements in Sino–Soviet relations compelled his adjustments to India's China policy. Soviet leader Mikhail Gorbachev urged Rajiv Gandhi during a visit to India in 1986 to improve relations with China, saying it would suit Soviet interests, and hinting at a press conference that the USSR would no longer be willing to provide support to India in the event of Sino–Indian conflict. In this situation, Rajiv Gandhi considered that India on its own would be powerless against a threat on two fronts. He was hence forced to change his preparations for a two-front war, as it was apparent that dispelling tensions along the eastern front through reconciliation with China would allow him to concentrate India's energies on the western front with Pakistan.

The Nehru family's stately bearing was absent after the Cold War, and the INC's power had declined. The insularity that had characterized India's foreign policy-making process since independence, however, did not change. The nation's foreign and security policy stayed in the hands of the prime minister and cabinet from 1991 to 1996, during which time the views of Prime Minister Rao and leaders of the INC government on security and foreign policy matters were decisive, and the influence of parliament, think tanks and academic institutions was negligible. It is notable, however, that Rao's background as home minister, defence minister and external affairs minister throughout the 1980s, as well as his status as the Congress Party's elder statesman, signified that he was a loyal adherent of Nehruvianism, and unrepresentative of any new type of thinking. The transformation of India's security concept during the Rao administration, therefore, can be understood as entirely the result of external forces.

As earlier mentioned, changes in the international and domestic situation compelled Rao to change his understanding of national strength. He began emphasizing the strategic influence of economic strength and promoting restoration of the economy as a matter of urgency in withstanding security threats in the aftermath of the Cold War. This passive reaction to a complex situation gave the impression of India's overall foreign policy as passive and defensive. India adopted a focused approach to diplomacy during this period, directing its energies towards restoring the economy but maintaining a low profile in international affairs, as expressed in its China policy. Rao continued and furthered Rajiv Gandhi's adjustments by focusing on stabilization of Sino–Indian political relations and establishing tranquil borders as means to ensuring the recovery of India's domestic economy.

Two major changes occurred in India's foreign policy-making process during 1998. The first was the BJP's assumption of office that ended the long-standing INC power monopoly, and established foundations for a clean break with the traditional security concept. Although the BJP's domestic policies had a relatively ideological slant and promoted a Hinduist revival, the party was pragmatic as regards foreign policy. In contrast to the Congress Party, it dared to confront history, criticise India's previous foreign policy and introduce new thinking. Jaswant Singh, successively the Vajpayee government's External Affairs Minister and Finance Minister, published early in 1999 a book entitled *Defending India* in which he systematically describes his new security concept. Various views were thereafter expressed in government-issued articles. The BJP was obviously preparing to move on from the passive security concept of the Rao era. The second major change was India's refinement of its foreign policy-making mechanism. The November 1998 establishment of the National Security Council symbolized India's casting off of the influence and control of personality-based policy-making in favour of scientific research, inquiry and decision-making, and comprehensive long-term planning. The introduction by National Security Advisory Board subordinated to the National Security Council of scholarly authorities, reporters and former government and military officials demonstrated how much more open India's foreign policy-making process had become.

The BJP differed in its approach to China policy from both that of the Cold War era Nehru family, with its 1962 complex, and the early 1990s Rao government, which had been wearied and bound hand and foot by domestic and international pressure. The BJP's seizing of this historic opportunity confirmed India's rise as the nation's long-term strategic goal and placed its relationship with China on the strategic level. In other words, the BJP saw the Sino–Indian relationship as an important influence on India's rise. Although the two nations would be dealing with historically significant problems, they could be seen as a starting point.

The gradual opening of India's foreign policy-making process, moreover, made way for a vibrant exchange of ideas regarding China policy, which fell roughly into three groups: the first held that Sino–Indian cooperation suits both sides' interests and that post-Cold War China has no intention of making an enemy of India, desiring instead friendly relations and strategic partnership; the second that China is a long-term strategic threat to India because China's strategic objectives lie in establishing hegemony over Asia, which necessitates India's containment and, therefore, limitation of Indian influence. India, therefore, should adopt diametrically opposed policies; and the third group, situated between the two, held that the two nations could simultaneously rise to become main Asian powers and that competition and cooperation could coexist. Discussions on how to evaluate and understand China by Indian scholars and strategic circles are ongoing. After frequent debates among Indian National Security Council groups, the third, middle-ground viewpoint seems to be gaining acceptance.

When the INC regained power in 2004, a variety of factors led the new government to carry on with the previous administration's security concept. The new INC government's China policy was its predecessor's legacy, because the rise of India's international status during the BJP coalition government left the INC powerless to dispute the success of the previous government's foreign policy. The INC's democratized and more youthful leadership team was also willing to jettison historical baggage and look to the future. Although the Nehru family's leadership role within the Congress Party remained uncontested, the influence of Prime Minister Manmohan Singh and Foreign Minister Mukherjee on foreign and security policy could not be disregarded. Moreover, the liberalization of India's foreign policy-making process was superimposed against a long-standing civil service system which ensured continuity of policy. In other words, many masterminds of BJP foreign policy still active in the external affairs ministry, defence ministry and other relevant functional departments under the INC, as well as in consultative committees, the media, think tanks and other non-functional departments, continued to exert influence.

Substantial changes occurred in India's China policy after the end of the Cold War whereby the nation's long-standing (1962–1988) antagonistic approach became one of reconciliation and engagement. These adjustments originated to a great extent in changes in the sub-continent's post-Cold War security concept, manifest in two major shifts which effected two major phases of adjustment in India's China policy. The new post-Cold War China policy nonetheless retained traces of the former, programme, imbuing it with a duality that reflected the overlap of India's old and new security concepts.

A change in India's security concept first became apparent during the period from the end of the Cold War to 1998. The first phase of adjustments this change triggered in India's China policy was evident in the sub-continent's extended concept of military might as national strength to one encompassing economic factors, and acknowledgement of the strategic value of economic strength in countering what it perceived as the looming threat of marginalization within the international community. Restoration of the domestic economy hence became a main measure through which to resist security threats in the post-Cold War era. Having made this shift in foreign policy objectives towards economic recovery, India set about creating a favourable environment within which to achieve this goal. Overall implementation of a China policy of preserving stable Sino–Indian relations by guaranteeing border tranquillity was vital to achieving this strategic objective. India consequently focused on the feasibility of reconciliation and, in view of China's reflective, inward-looking mood, no longer viewed China as an enemy. As regards India's specific policies, while focusing on the establishment of a progressive means to guaranteeing tranquil borders, thereby stabilizing Sino–Indian relations, India at the same time sought communication and cooperation in other areas. To avoid provoking China, the Indian government made tactical adjustments to its approach to Tibet from that of exploiting the issue and causing uproar to handling the matter in a low-key manner.

The new developments apparent in India's security concept in 1999 brought with it the second phase of adjustments to India's China policy. Indian leaders considered that the nation's security environment had improved to the extent that it constituted a strategic opportunity for India to rise to global-power status. This change in thinking and understanding caused the second shift of objective in India's foreign policy from that of improving the economy to the grand goal of global-power status. It corresponded to India's acknowledgement of the crucial nature of the Sino–Indian relationship and change of focus from border tranquillity and stable political relations to comprehensive considerations of how the two nations' relationship would strategically affect India's; rise. These insights compelled a shift of objective in India's China policy towards making China a positive factor in the sub-continent's rise; also recognition that this objective could be accomplished only by maintaining a stable basis for Sino–Indian relations. Official introduction during this phase of a comprehensive security concept signalled India's adoption of a more pragmatic, comprehensive handling of its relations with China. The specific steps it adopted were: increasing economic cooperation with China, thus benefiting India's economic development and stabilizing bilateral political relations; strengthening military communication and security dialogue, thus deepening understanding of China's strategic intentions towards India, increasing mutual trust, minimizing misunderstandings and avoiding conflict; and seeking Chinese support in its quest for a permanent seat on the UN Security Council, which would expand India's political power and international prestige.

In the course of research, however, it became apparent to the author that India's security concept did not undergo a thoroughgoing change after the Cold War ended, as elements of the Cold War approach remained in place. Although India's security concept extended after 1988 to include both military and economic security, the ultimate purpose of national defence as regards a fundamental guarantee of security nonetheless remained that of increased military strength to safeguard national unity and territorial integrity. India abandoned its strategy of pursuing security through alliances, yet still viewed parity and the principle of checks and balances as hallmarks of its national defence. Influenced as it was by traditional concepts, post-Cold War India's China policy was imbued with vigilance. Even though India did not perceive China as a threat in the short term, it was nevertheless concerned that the swing in balance of power between the two was not in its favour, and that China constituted a potential obstacle to India's rise. Indian leaders consequently embarked on a race against China to expand comprehensive national strength, particularly military force, including India's nuclear capability, as the means to a balance of power. India at the same time sought to offset Chinese influence both regionally and globally through development of strategic relationships with the United States, Japan and other nations. The sub-continent also remained vigilant in the long-standing issues of border disputes and Sino–Pakistani relations, and maintained pressure on China in this regard.

Changes in post-Cold War India's security concept were thus the result of both domestic and foreign factors. The first change during the early post-Cold War period was triggered by passive reactions to transformations in the nation's domestic and international situation that, in turn, prompted a passive transformation of thinking and understanding, manifest in passive defensiveness of India's foreign policy, specifically its China policy. The security concept that appeared during the late 1990s was comparatively proactive. The expanded strength of India's domestic economy and improvement of its external environment compelled a new understanding of security issues, as expressed in the proactive change in its security concept. This assertiveness was manifest in strategy and in an active, enterprising foreign policy. Seizing the historic opportunity to realize India's rise had become the common security objective of both major Indian political parties. Decentralization of political power and expanded openness of the foreign policy-making process, however, caused India's old and new security concepts to bind into one, and the resultant duality of India's hybrid security concept since the Cold War's end is reflected in its China policy. As India's dual security concept will continue into the foreseeable future, the duality of its China policy will be difficult to change.

CHINA AND INDIA : DIFFERENT APPROACHES, DIFFERENT OUTCOMES

What the above discussion of the divergence and convergence between Sino-Indian interests reveals is the success of China in attaining its foreign policy objectives and the failure of India to preserve its vital interests vis-à-vis China. This cannot simply be attributed to China's economic and military strength. While China is definitely the bigger player in the region and the world at large but its success vis-à-vis India owes as much to its power as to the way that power has been cultivated and used. While realizing fully well that it would take China decades to seriously compete with the US, it has focused strategic energy on Asia. Its foreign policy is aimed at enhancing its economic and military prowess to achieve hegemony in Asia. China's recent emphasis on projecting itself as peaceful power is merely aimed at allaying the concerns of neighbours lest they try to counterbalance it. China's readiness to negotiate with other regional states and to be an economically "responsible" nation is also a signal to other states that there are greater benefits in bandwagoning to China's growing regional weight rather than opposing its rise in any manner.

However, while declaring that it will be focusing on internal socio-economic development for the next decade or so, China has actively pursued policies of preventing the rise of other regional powers. In case of India, this manifests itself in its cultivation of Pakistan as a close ally. From supplying it nuclear and missile technologies to building its military infrastructure, China has done all it can to build Pakistan as a counterweight to India. This policy has largely succeeded as India no longer enjoys its earlier conventional superiority vis-à-vis Pakistan possession of nuclear weapons by both nations ensures that any step that India takes to strengthen its nuclear weapons profile is viewed by the international community as highly destabilizing in the context of the "nuclear flashpoint" that South Asia has become for the world at large. China has thereby been successful in emerging as a "responsible" global player, despite its abysmal nuclear and missile proliferation record while the international community rails at India for making the world much more dangerous.

China's attempts to increase its influence in Nepal, Bangladesh, and Myanmar, its persistent refusal to recognize parts of India such as Arunachal Pradesh, its lack of support for India's membership to the United Nations Security Council and other regional and global organizations, all point towards China's attempts at preventing the rise of India as a regional and global player of major import. It is this strategy that China has consistently and successfully pursued without any apologies. In fact, this strategy has been so successful that today China no longer believes that India can be a serious rival for Asian hegemony and some have pointed out, India is off of China's diplomatic radar.

In contrast to China's well-laid out policy vis-à-vis India, India has from time to time oscillated from one extreme to another. George Tanham has famously pointed out that India has shown little ability to think strategically on national security. In the case of India's China policy, it needs to be realized that there is nothing really sinister about China's attempts to expand its own influence and curtail India's. China is a rising power in Asia and the world and as such will do its utmost to prevent the rise of other power centres around its periphery like India that might in the future prevent it from taking its rightful place as a global player. This is not much different than the stated US policy of preventing the rise of other powers that might threaten its position as a global hegemon. Just as the US is working towards achieving its strategic objective, China is pursuing its own strategic agenda.

There is also nothing extraordinarily benign in China's attempts to improve its bilateral relations with India in recent times. After working to curtail India's influence in various ways, China would not like to see India coming close to the US in order to contain China. In this geopolitical chessboard, both the US and China are using India towards their own strategic ends.

India must resist the tendency of reacting to the actions of other. India's attempt to come up a coherent strategy towards China based on identified strategic objectives is of paramount importance. Prime Minister Manmohan Singh declared that it wants to have friendly relations with China, a reasonable foreign policy objective. However, without a clear articulation of India's national security objectives, pursuit of friendly relations with China should not become an end in itself. It should be a means towards achieving India's larger strategic objective of emerging as a major regional and global player.

India's China policy is also symptomatic of a larger misunderstanding in the Indian and political establishment with regard to a nation's foreign policy. For the left-liberal strand in the Indian polity, foreign policy is merely an extension of domestic policy.

As such since India is a secular, democratic, and peace-loving nation, India's pursuit of its relations with other states should merely be a reflection of these virtues. This has given rise to much of the moral rhetoric in foreign affairs. On the other hand, the Indian right, because of its preoccupation with establishing a "Hindu" nation and minority bashing, have extended its narrow sectarian view to foreign policy.

The consequence has been its obsession with Pakistan as evil incarnate in its foreign policy agenda and its inclination to view the world in black and white, friends and enemies, evil and noble.

Shaped by these forces, Indian foreign policy has merely been one of responding to events around it rather than anticipating them and evolving long-term strategies to deal with them. India's China policy is a casualty of this reactionary approach.

India needs to develop its economic and military might without being apologetic. It needs to clearly articulate its national interests and engage China on a host of issues, from the border problem to the alleged dumping of cheap Chinese goods in the Indian market. India needs to recognize that appeasing China is neither desirable nor necessary even as a direct confrontation with China is not something India can afford, at least in the near future. It must also be recognized that while for India, managing its relations with China is at the top of its foreign policy agenda, China does not view India as a significant global player and is largely indifferent to India's growing profile.

India is a rising power in Asia and there is nothing wrong in demanding its rightful place in the inter-state hierarchy. Simply put India and China are two major powers in Asia with global aspirations and some significant conflicting interests.

As a result, some amount of friction in their bilateral relationship is inevitable. The geopolitical reality of Asia makes sure that it will be extremely difficult, if not impossible, for *Hindi-Chini* to be *bhai-bhai* (brothers) in the foreseeable future.

This reality should be accepted by the Indian policy makers, rather than wished away. India should make a serious attempt to manage this friction by expanding the zone of cooperation with China even as it tries to steadfastly pursue its national interests. India should display the confidence to craft a foreign policy that best serves its national security interests without always looking over the shoulders to make sure that China is not displeased. Again, India can learn a lot by examining how China has managed its relationship with the US in the last few years.

While India certainly needs to engage China in an effort at reconciling security and political perspectives, it is naïve to assert, as many do, that India should first be sensitive to China's concerns, real or imaginary, before defining its foreign policy goals and strategic agenda. Does China consult India in its pursuit of its own strategic objectives? It does not and neither should India expect it to. In a similar vein, India should define its foreign policy agenda in view of its own national security imperatives.

But for this to happen, the government of India will have to formulate a clear China policy and, more importantly, a broader national security strategy. Ad-hocism just won't do. This should be the top foreign policy priority of the Indian government if it wants India to emerge as a global power of any reckoning. India should heed to Sun Tzu's advice and recognize that a merely tactical foreign policy approach without the backing of a sound strategy will only lead to nowhere.

10

Alternative Explanations of Border Conflict: Domestic Level Analysis

A valid criticism of a systemic level approach to explaining conflict is that it overlooks key variables and differences between states in the assumption that all states are equal due to constraints that the structure of the international system places upon them.

Singer argues that at this level of analysis "actors are characterized and their behaviour predicted in relatively gross and general terms".

To account for the generalization of state behaviour inherent in a systemic level analysis a brief domestic level analysis explaining the Sino-Indian war will be attempted. Based on Vertberger's literature review on the subject, my domestic level analysis will be limited to the most influential domestic variable driving China and India to war; ideological and political considerations.

Indian ideological and political causes for war centered on the belief in non-alignment as a viable alternative to the bipolar system. The source of Indian non-aligned thought was that the Cold War was a conflict between the imperialist Western nations, and therefore newly independent former colonies had no reason or interest in siding with their former masters.

The Indians by remaining non-aligned, hoped to establish a third pole of power in the international system organized by the nations of the Third World. This third bloc of nations would fight for issues that really mattered to them such as ending colonialism, racial discrimination, and raising living standards in the developing world. Nehru envisioned that this Third World bloc would act as an arbiter in the West's conflict, thereby gaining both moral authority and legitimacy.

In concert with the Bandung Conference in 1955 and the Sino-Indian Panchsheel Agreement, Nehru hoped to expand his concept of non-alignment into a full-blown pan-Asianism movement. This pan-Asianism was based in the common historical experience of colonialism that these nations shared, but Nehru failed to account for historical differences and regional rivalries.

Nehru asserted that, "the basic challenge in Southeast Asia is between India and China," but he forgot this reality in supporting an Asian solidarity bloc. Nehru, and India's conception of a non-aligned third world was based on not only its viability, but that India would be both the natural and unchallenged leader of such a group. Traditional Sino-Indian rivalry for influence in Asia challenged Indian thinking as China asserted its right to be the leader of such a group. The need to exert its regional great power status over China led to diplomatic intransigence on the issue of border negotiations. Thus, India saw Chinese dispute of border areas to be a political challenge to their right to lead Asia, and in turn pushed backed in order to show strength.

Chinese ideological and political causes for war centered on the belief that its Maoist interpretation of communist revolution was not only correct, but purer than the Soviet model. This dispute on the merits of Maoism over Leninism was focused squarely on the Soviet Union's insistence on backing the Indian position in the border dispute through political and military aid. The PRC challenged Soviet actions on three points; that their diplomatic position showed a lack of solidarity with a fellow communist nation, that Soviet support of a bourgeoisie regime in India would not forward the goal of communist revolution, and that India wasn't truly non-aligned but in fact in league with the imperialists.

Soviet military aid inflamed the PRC, especially in light of Soviet cuts to Chinese aid, because it appeared as if the Soviets were turning their backs on a Marxist brother. Furthermore, the PRC believed that only through struggle and challenge, not foreign aid, could they achieve the end of global Marxist revolution.

Finally, Indian overtures to the West for aid, and their assistance to the West in fomenting problems on China's border led the PRC on a quest to convince the Soviets that they were being used. The PRC concluded that superior PLA military forces and position in the region would force the Indians to rely on Western intervention to bail them out in the event of hostilities. This would both expose the Indians as true imperialists, and score an ideological victory against the Soviet Union in the enlarging diplomatic split.

The domestic level analysis contends that it is domestic differences between states that drive them towards conflict. Examining the most influential domestic factors (according to scholars on the subject) on Chinese and Indian decision making leading to the 1962 war, it seems as if ideology had differing levels of importance for each nation.

Indian ideology and their belief in leading a pan-Asian bloc nationalized tensions with China, creating a zero-sum game. If the Indian's backed down they would seem weak, and to avoid this they took a non-compromising stand on border issues.

In China, Maoist ideology was more so an issue with hierarchy within the Soviet bloc than with Indian recalcitrance on border issues. The PRC actively believed the Indians not to be non-aligned, but this was not important as ideologically they did not pose a threat to the Chinese communist system. As such, Chinese ideology was not as important in crafting policy, and Zhou Enlai was able to take a pragmatic stand. As Singer points out the overgeneralization of a systemic analysis, he also points out that a domestic analysis suffers from the same weakness but instead an undue focus on state differences.

The domestic analysis helps us better understand the importance of the border issue in each nation's context, but in this case it does not adequately explain the actions undertaken by either regime. Furthermore, only with a systemic level analysis can we explore the limitation on action caused by the international structure on each state. Ultimately, Chinese ideology does not explain why they did not take the offensive to oust India as imperialists, or why India decided to change its military policy towards an aggressive forward base strategy. Therefore, a systemic level analysis is more suited to explaining the actions leading to the Sino-Indian War.

While valid alternative theoretical models explaining the causes for war exist, a neorealist systems-level analysis best explains the factors leading India and China to war in 1962.

Keeping in mind the historical context of generally cordial Sino-Indian relations prior to 1959 it seems unlikely that solely ideological differences drove the two nations to war. If ideology was such an important motivator behind the militarization of the Sino-Indian border dispute, then it is unlikely conflict would have waited to develop until 1962.

Additionally, if Sino-Indian rivalry for dominance in Asia was so virulent why did India recognize PRC sovereignty in Tibet in 1951, and later agree to a mutual treaty of peaceful coexistence in 1954? A domestic level analysis cannot account for these otherwise amicable diplomatic relations.

What a systemic level analysis reveals is certain changes in national interests, geostrategic positions, and the anarchy of the international system brought both nations closer to the precipice of conflict. Various actions and reactions by both nations along the border created a security dilemma for each, and this brought the border dispute to the forefront of Sino-Indian relations. Furthermore, India believed they had the power to reshape the international system from a bipolar to multi-polar world. Their lack of either nuclear capability or significant conventional power exposed their status as simply a minor power of strategic importance in the international system. Thus either superpower was only motivated to preserve their security so long as it was in their interests to do so, and not as an ultimate necessity contrary to Indian belief.

The ultimate cause for war in 1962 was India's assertion that it was a major power in world affairs. China's incentive in limiting their defeat of the Indian military was motivated by their interest in de-legitimizing the McMahon Line and consolidating their sovereignty in Tibet. The systems level analysis reveals not only what urged each nation to war, but also explains how the anarchy of the system limited the extent of the fighting.

GLOBAL VARIABLES LEADING TO CONFLICT: CHINA

The systemic level variables motivating China towards conflict, like in India, revolved around Chinese national interests, the system's influence on Chinese behaviour through structural constraints, and the role of anarchy in the system. Because of the anarchic structure of the international system, China is no different than India and state security must be its prime end. China's membership in the communist bloc does not grant it any guarantee of protection, and therefore its national interests are calculated in ways of maximizing national security. As such we shall discuss the three main interests affected by the border dispute with India.

As in India's case, the delineation of official borders for the PRC was a prime interest in order to gain legitimacy in the international system. This legitimacy is rooted within the conventions of the Westphalian system, where borders are paramount as they define the extent of sovereignty and political self-determination. The PRC's inheritance of territory which was divided by Western imperialists had a strong legal and pragmatic interest in negotiating legitimate borders with its neighbours. The basis of Chinese territorial definition was on the extent of historical holdings, but the PRC had determined in 1950 to negotiate borders based off the alignments they had inherited. This meant that China would not bog itself down in unreasonable claims in Indochina or other areas of traditional imperial suzerainty. This mentality guided border settlement by peaceful means with Burma, Nepal, Pakistan, Afghanistan, Mongolia, Cambodia, and Laos. Peaceful settlement of the Sino-Indian border however, was not possible due to Indian unwillingness to negotiate based on the perceived legitimacy of the McMahon Line. A second national interest challenged by the border dispute with India was the Chinese right to non-intervention of foreigners in their domestic affairs. This principle of domestic sanctity from outside interference is also one of the rights of states in the Westphalian system. Chinese security was undermined by India's role in manipulating domestic events in both Tibet and in Ladakh. The Indian military's establishment of forward posts and patrols of the Ladakh region, beginning in 1960, was direct interference in Chinese domestic areas. While it was true China did not have legal sovereignty over the Ladakh area due to its position south of the McMahon Line, that argument remains moot as international boundaries must be agreed upon at least bilaterally, and the PRC gave it no such recognition. Furthermore, Ladakh, and more importantly the Aksai-Chin plain was a strategically important tract of land connecting Xinjiang and Tibet.

Indian interference in Tibet after the 1959 uprising was also taken as a direct violation of domestic sanctity, and a challenge to Chinese security and interests. The PRC became aware of Indian efforts to covertly aid the Dalai Lama and Tibetan separatists shortly after the PLA moved in to suppress the uprising. In fact, India had gone so far as to allow the CIA bases of operation along the border for a covert campaign in Tibet from 1957 to 1961. Furthermore, a series of four Indian military bases were constructed and manned in Tibet north of the McMahon Line. These actions illustrated India's desire to keep Tibet as a buffer state, and recognize Chinese suzerainty instead of sovereignty in the region, thus directly challenging China's security.

The Chinese interest of maintaining a secure border with India was also threatened by the border dispute. Reinforcement of Tibet after 1959, the Aksai-Chin road way, and Chinese military patrols of the border were an attempt to maintain their territorial integrity. This added military presence created a security dilemma for India, and they began building up and strengthening their own military capacity near contested areas. The adoption of a forward Indian military policy in 1960, coupled with Indian scouting patrols across the border and the construction of military posts around Ladakh and Tibet severely undermined Chinese border security. This led to the PLA "digging in" around contested border areas and effectively militarizing the border. China's response to the Indian military buildup as well as their covert programs in contested border areas was constrained by the structure of the international environment. A major constraining force on Chinese action was the geostrategic situation in Asia during the late 1950's. Beginning in 1950 with the Korean War, the major battles of the Cold War were fought in Asia in the West's effort to contain the communist bloc. The PRC had to contend with anti-Chinese forces in South Korea, a U.S. backed ROC in Taiwan, a U.S.-fortified Japan, and increasing U.S. involvement in Indochina by 1960. These numerous threats on China's Western front were significant, and severely limited their maneuverability in other areas of concern. Unbeknownst to the West, the PRC was increasingly unable to depend on the support of the communist bloc due to increasing belligerence from the U.S.S.R. on various diplomatic and territorial issues. The Soviets pressured the PRC to acknowledge Indian border claims, and Sino-Soviet relations strained under their own border issues.

Acknowledging the limiting effects of these security threats on Chinese military power, the PRC advocated a policy of peaceful border settlement. China used this policy to its advantage and scored a critical victory in neutralizing a potential Pakistani threat to their security interests by a warming of relations. The geostrategic environment in which the PRC found itself was one of being surrounded by a ring of hostile states. Indian diplomatic intransigence on border issues and known subversion in Tibet added another threat in that ring. Thus, the structure of the international environment drove the PRC to rely on diplomacy to achieve its interests against minor powers in order to preserve its military power for guarding its borders against larger threats. This situation explains a seemingly coincidental rapprochement in relations with Pakistan, India's arch-rival, while Sino-Indian relations simultaneously deteriorated in 1959.

This hostile geostrategic environment ruled out the option of using military force to settle the border dispute with India because of the potential pitfall of starting a two front war. Thus PRC actions along the Indian border were limited by the international structure to defensive posturing, deterrence, and entrenchment. This is illustrated by the numerous Chinese overtures to Indian representatives to keep patrols 20km behind each border. Rapprochement with Pakistan was pragmatic in the freedom of action the PRC gained by not needing to guard the Sino-Pakistani border heavily. Therefore, Chinese policy was constrained by the system to not initiate force against India in order to settle the border dispute, but instead to bolster its defenses. However, the PRC declared that "force would be met with force" on the border issue, and this is evidenced by the PLA counter offensives launched on October 20 and November 16, 1962.

Finally, the anarchy present in the international system played a significant role in the actions of the PRC on the border issue. Unlike their Indian counterparts, China properly assessed the international situation and never lost sight of the fact that only China could assure Chinese security. The emerging Sino-Soviet split was a key element in the PRC's unwillingness to rely on outside support for their interests. Not only did the Soviets urge China to a settlement counter to their interests, but they openly aided India in both the construction of a domestic MIG program and a pledge to help them develop nuclear energy. Simultaneously, Soviet aid to China was severely cut including assistance in developing a nuclear program. Clearly a common Soviet-Sino communist ideology was unimportant to their "allies," as they even ventured to grant India great power status through nuclear development.

In addition to the Soviet military aid was U.S. support of India in the form of agricultural assistance and millions in financial aid packages. Although India pledged neutrality, the PRC clearly believed that they were in the West's bloc. Indian based CIA operations into Tibet and India's role in the Korean War helped bolster this perception. Unable to rely on either superpower for protection or intervention on their behalf, the PRC assessed that any military movements in securing the border would have to be proportional, decisive, and most importantly retaliatory. This assessment was gained from a rational calculation of the potential geostrategic and political consequences of a PLA initiation of force. While neither the PRC nor India possessed nuclear weapons, they feared a PLA offensive into India would be interpreted by the West as communist advance and therefore provoke a nuclear response. In the wake of the Taiwan Straits Crisis, and keeping in mind Sino-Soviet agitation, China was unwilling to risk a potential nuclear strike from the West, especially without full Soviet support. This being the case, China resolved that its armed response to Indian aggression would be purely political. The PRC would paint itself as the victim of aggression, but would then unleash a massive but calculated counterattack to force diplomatic concessions by India on the border issue, thereby resolving the issue once and for all. While the systems level of analysis plainly explains both the motives and limitations of India and China leading to the Sino-Indian War, it is contended that the model overlooks key motivations of either state leading to conflict.

GLOBAL VARIABLES LEADING TO CONFLICT: INDIA

The three main variables motivating Indian behaviour towards conflict with China on the systemic level are: Indian national interests, the system's influence on Indian behaviour through structural constraints, and the relationship between Indian perception of the international structure and reality. To begin a systemic explanation of India's actions we must first identify its national interests, as it is what drives Indian action throughout the international structure. According to neorealist thought the primary end of all states is security. This being the case, not only is security the primary Indian national interest, but any issue relating to national security becomes a primary interest.

Official borders, and their enforcement is a primary interest of each state for obvious reasons. However, in the Indian case this issue takes on greater importance than it otherwise would for other nations. This can be attributed to two factors. The most prevalent factor was that India bordered a nation which not only questioned the legitimacy of the established border, but also violated it. The second factor is the modern international system is formed by the interaction of nation-states, which as defined by the Westphalian system are the only entities capable of legitimately exercising sovereignty.

A key component of nation-state status under the Westphalian system is the existence of demarcated and respected borders. These borders represent the extent of national sovereignty and define where each nation's authority begins and ends. The questioning of India's established border by China undermines both Indian sovereignty and security. Security is undermined first by the direct military and administrative challenge to Indian territory, and second by delegitimizing India's position as a nation-state. If India can neither defend nor define borders respected by other nations, other states may begin to question their position as a nation-state in the system and then their sovereignty. This was a chief concern for India as they regarded the Chinese threat to their border as one compromising their "independence, self-determination, and position as a great power in Asia".

Another issue of national security relating to Indian interests was defense of the McMahon Line. Two key issues aided the creation of security dilemma situation along the McMahon Line. The first was the discovery of the Chinese road connecting Xinjiang and Tibet through the Aksai-Chin area in 1957. The second was the imposition of martial law on Tibet in 1959 by the PLA. China argued that completion of the road southeast of the McMahon Line in Aksai-Chin was simply the reestablishment of a historical commerce route from Xinjiang to Tibet. This road not only represented a blatant Chinese violation of India's McMahon Line border, but it also caused armed tension in the region. Shortly after the roads discovery, PLA frontier guards began patrolling the Aksai-Chin region, but never more than 20km away from the road's location. The issue of the road in Aksai-Chin and the PLA's role in Tibet in 1959 became linked since the majority of Chinese troops entered Tibet via the road from Xinjiang. The surge of PLA soldiers into Tibet aroused suspicions of a forcible border assertion by the PRC. These tensions were heightened by the flight of the Dalai Lama from Lhasa, and the closure of Tibet to commercial and cultural access by India, guaranteed in the 1951 treaty. Defensive maneuvers or not, these activities created a security dilemma along the border as India felt that Tibet was "essential for mastery over South Asia, and the most economical method for guaranteeing India's security". Forced to account for increasing Chinese military power near or past the McMahon Line, India responded by deploying their military in forward positions along the border with China as early as 1960. Accounting for India's national interest with force posturing, they attempted to both affirm the legitimacy of the McMahon Line as a border and to account for the security dilemma created by the hardening of PLA positions in Tibet and Aksai-Chin.

The second way a systemic level analysis accounts for the 1962 war is the manner in which India's policy was defined by the structure of the international system. In looking at the geostrategic positioning of India within the system, it is immediately apparent that they attempted to remain neutral or unaligned in the bipolar structure. India remained a powerful enough state to deter the third world adventurism of either bloc within its territory, but weak enough to be challenged by hostile neighbours. An excellent example of this was the persistent threat of Pakistan on their Northwestern border. The poor relationship of Pakistan and India is rooted in domestic level variables, but a systemic level cause was a disputed claim over the sovereignty of Kashmir. Both sides claim the right to sovereignty over Kashmir, and this has resulted in a heavily armed border. Additionally, appearances of a Sino-Pakistani agreement to hem in India developed with Chinese diplomatic overtures to Pakistan for peaceful border settlement beginning in 1961. This forced India to take a hard-line stance in their border dispute with China out of fear that concessions would show weakness, and endanger their control of Kashmir in a Domino-Theory type logic train.

Another structural element of the international system was the existence of nuclear weapons. Nuclear weapons invalidated traditional calculations of deterrence, and thus the great powers were those whom possessed them. In India's regional calculations neither themselves, nor did any other surrounding nations possess nuclear weapons keeping intact the use of deterrence as a method of securing or defending interests. This being the case, the option of engaging in armed conflict with surrounding nations remained possible as long as in India's force calculations they were superior to their target. A prime example of India's employment of force to further interests was their invasion of Portuguese controlled Goa on December 17, 1961. This use of force to assert sovereignty over perceived territory is an excellent precedent for the October 9, 1962 offensive against the PLA in Ladakh. Force against PLA incursions remained off the table as long as the Indian military believed their strategic position and capabilities to be inferior to the Chinese. Returning from a 1960 diplomatic tour of the U.S., Nehru expressed the idea that due to Soviet and Western military aid, "the military balance had changed in favour of India". Thus in the absence of nuclear weapons, India disregarded the Chinese effort at deterrence and employed the use of force to settle their territorial claims.

Finally, it is necessary to point out how India's perception of the international system, which differed from reality, influenced their decision to employ force against the PRC. India perceived the international system as open to change from a bipolar to a multi-polar structure. This was based in their success of remaining unaligned to either bloc, while still receiving significant military and economic aid from both camps. Given India's strategic geographic position in the system, both superpowers sought to gain the allegiance of India to their side through the use of aid. Understanding this, India played both sides against each other, and assumed that either superpower would be willing to intervene on their behalf in the event of Sino-Indian hostilities for pragmatic and alliance building reasons. Thus, India viewed its use of force as a no lose situation. Either the force would succeed in attaining their national interests, or if Indian power proved to be inadequate, "the superpowers would intervene to prevent any large-scale war between India and China;" therefore, bailing out India from a potential catastrophe. This perception of Indian value to either superpower and the general misperception of the international system would cost them.

Ultimately the Indians failed to acknowledge that while the interests of the superpowers may partially depend on India's well being, the system is ultimately in anarchy and each nation is responsible for assuring their own security. Additionally, India had miscalculated both the willingness and ability of the superpowers to intervene on their behalf. In reality the Soviet Union could not exercise restraint on Chinese actions or compel them to drop the border issue. The Sino-Soviet split had not yet occurred, but its origin is in the late 1950's, and the attempt to restrain PRC actions towards India was a contributing factor in the decline of Soviet influence. Indian belief in U.S. intervention was based on a miscalculation of U.S. interests in Asia, as well as willingness to repel PRC advance based on the Domino Theory. While the U.S. intervened in Korea, Taiwan, and Indochina, India overlooked the essential element common to each. This element was the inability of each nation to resist communist advance on its own. In this case, the projected image of Indian power was a liability. The realities of the international system and its anarchic nature would ensure that their decision to use force would not be consequence free. Now the Chinese causes for war will be evaluated at the systemic level.

SECTORS OF SINO-INDIAN BORDER: WESTERN SECTOR, MIDDLE SECTOR AND EASTERN SECTOR

The Sino-Indian border is generally divided into three sectors namely: (i) the Western sector, (ii) the Middle sector, and (iii) the Eastern sector.

The Western Sector

This 2,152 km long sector of the Sino-Indian border separates Jammu and Kashmir State of India from the Sinkiang province of China.

The frontier between Sinkiang and Pakistan occupied Kashmir (PoK) is about 480 km long. The rest is boundary between Ladakh and Tibet.

The boundary in the western sector runs along the Muztagh Ata Range and the Aghil Mountain across the Karakoram Pass via Quara Tagh pass and along the main Kunlun Range to a point east of 80°E longitude and 40 km north of Hajit Langer.

It forms a physical boundary between Gilgit area and Sinkiang following the main Karakoram watershed separating the streams flowing into the Indus basin from those flowing into the Tarin basin.

Farther south-east the boundary runs along the watershed across Lanak La, Kone La and Kepsang La, then follows the Chemesang River across Pergyon Lake and the Kailash Range. Here the boundary constitutes the watershed between the Indus system in India and the Khotan system in China.

The western sector boundary is the outcome of the British policy towards the state of Jammu and Kashmir. These boundaries were defined by the treaties of 1665 and 1686 (known as Ladakh-Tibet agreements) and were confirmed by 1842 Dogra-Ladakh agreement among Kashmir, Tibet and China.

However, this boundary was never delimited precisely on maps and has led to several boundary disputes between China and India. The Chinese claim rests mainly on ethnic grounds, and on the assertion that the wastelands of the Aksai Chin in disputed territory were always linked more with Tibet and Sinkiang.

The Chinese claim that Aksai Chin is just an extension of Tibet with regard to language, religion and culture. But in Chinese documentation regarding the actual occupation of the area by Tibet in inconclusive.

The Indians, on the other hand, claim that the area has been historically administered by the state of Jammu and Kashmir since 1849, and that the Indo-Tibet Treaties of 1665, 1684 and 1842 confirmed the boundary between Tibet and Ladakh.

China claims the Aksai Chin district, the Changmo valley, Pangong Tso and the Sponggar Tso area of north-east Ladakh as well as a strip of about 5,000 sq km down the entire length of eastern Ladakh. China also claims a part of Huza-Gilgit area in North Kashmir (ceded to it in 1963 by Pakistan), although the whole territory has been effectively under the British sovereignty since 1895.

Since 1954, the Chinese have repeatedly violated the international border between India and China and penetrated deep into the Indian Territory in the western sector. China renewed aggression in 1959 and the Line of Actual Control (LoAC) become of series of positions occupied by the Chinese forces rather than a well defined border between the two countries.

In 1962, China waged a full scale war and its forces intruded far deeper into the Indian Territory. Currently the Chinese occupation line runs 16 to 240 km west of traditional line. China is in actual possession of about 54,000 sq km of the Indian Territory of which 37,555 sq km is in Ladakh area alone.

The Middle Sector

The middle sector boundary between China and India is 625 km long and runs along the watershed from Ladakh to Nepal. Two Indian states of Himachal Pradesh and Uttaranchal touch this border. The boundary of Himachal Pradesh follows the water parting between the Spiti and Para Chu rivers and continues along the watershed between the eastern and western tributaries of the Satluj. The Uttaranchal boundary is demarcated by the watershed between the Satluj on one hand and the Kali, the Alaknanda, and the Bhagirathi on the other. This boundary crosses the Satluj near the Shipki La on the Himachal-Tibet border.

Thereafter, it runs along the watershed passes of Mana, Niti, Kungri-Bingri, Dharma and Lipu Ladakh. It finally joins trijunction of China, India and Nepal. This part of the border was approved by the Tibetan and the British governments under the 1890 and 1919 treaties. Although there are not much serious territorial problems between the two countries, the Chinese lay claim on nearly 2,000 sq km area in this sector.

The Eastern Sector

The 1,140 km long boundary between India and China runs from the eastern limit of Bhutan to a point near Talu-Pass at the trijunction of India, Tibet and Myanmar. This line is usually referred to as the Me Mahon Line after Henry Me Mahon, a British representative who signed the 1913-14 Shimla Convention. This line normally runs along the crest of the Himalayas between Bhutan and Myanmar.

India has stressed that the Me Mahon Line is the international boundary between Tibet and India as was agreed to between the governments of India, China and Tibet. On the other hand China considers the Me Mahon line as illegal and unacceptable, claiming that Tibet had no right to sign the 1913-14 convention held in Shimla which delineated the Me Mahon Line on the map.

India challenges such a position, maintaining that Tibet was independent and in fact concluded several independent treaties which were considered valid by all parties, and were in operation for decades.

China declined the validity of the Me Mahon Line as an international boundary and laid claims to areas south of this line up to the foot of the Himalayan range in the Brahmaputra valley. The whole of Arunachal Pradesh, measuring over 88 thousand sq km has been claimed by China as the Chinese territory. This area has been administered by India since 1947.

Chinese government never formally questioned the validity of 1913-14 Shimla convention until 1959. India has been striking at the two crucial points. First, Britain and India had been exercising jurisdiction over the area since 1914 and 1947 respectively and second China never disputed the Indian control over the area until 1959.

Even in 1956 when the Chinese attention was drawn to certain maps drawn by China which showed these areas to be parts of China, the Chinese government promised to look into the 'cartographic errors' in their maps.

China's relations with India started taking a bad turn in 1950s when China started consolidating its position in Tibet and then in Ladakh. By 1956, China started intensifying its intrusions into the Indian Territory. India wishfully hoped that the insurmountable barrier of the Himalayas would prevent Chinese to attack Indian Territory. Indian apprehensions grew in 1956 when China built a road through Ladakh linking West Tibet with Sinkiang and quickly moved into Aksai Chin and eastern Ladakh. China also moved its forces into the North-East Frontier Agency (NEFA), the present Arunachal Pradesh.

Reported small-scale armed clashes between 1959 and 1962 escalated into a full-scale war in October, 1962 when China launched a major offensive in Ladakh in the western sector and NEFA in the eastern sector. Indian armed forces were not well trained to fight a modern war in a rough and rugged mountainous terrain. They were outnumbered and outgunned by the Chinese forces.

Following lessons have been learnt from Chinese aggression over India:

(i) The myth that the Himalayas were an effective defense barrier was exploded.

(ii) India's naive confidence in China's friendliness had dulled its perception regarding effective security measures in the Indo-China borderlands.

(iii) The prompt and positive response of western countries in rushing military supplies to the war zone helped improve the image of the West in Indian eyes.

(iv) India realised that posture of "non-alignment" was no substitute for defense preparedness.

Surprisingly, Chinese forces pulled back without annexing the disputed territory in the eastern sector. In the western sector, however, they did not pull out of most of Aksai Chin. Perhaps they did so due to the fear that their advance troops would have been cut off from supply bases in Tibet in winter of 1962 when the high passes in the Himalayas would have been closed by snow. The Chinese justified their withdrawal by stating that they had no further territorial ambitions.

The primary aim of Chinese invasion was to deprive India of its moral leadership in the world especially among the Afro-Asian countries, and to put pressure on it to join the socialist camp. China's collusion with Pakistan is a clear indication of this political ambition.

Perhaps China miscalculated its political power strategy. The support of the Western countries to India compelled China to rethink its strategy. India's unity in the face of Chinese aggression was another deterrent for China to achieve political mileage.

An uneasy truce had been prevailing for a long time since the October, 1962 war. Neither side made a serious effort to normalise the situation on the border. The Colombo powers, spearheaded by Ceylon (now Sri Lanka) and the erstwhile Soviet Union failed to bring about a respectable agreement between the two countries. Several countries condemned China as an aggressor. However, Cuba, Albania and Portugal supported the Chinese.

Of late, leaders of both the countries have engaged themselves in improving the bilateral relations. Several meetings have been held to resolve the problem of border issues. A major development took place in October, 2003 when China made a significant change in its official website. It removed the mention of Sikkim from its list of nations.

In May, 2004, China recognised Sikkim as a part of India for the first time. The world map in World Affairs Year Book 2003/ 2004 does not show Sikkim as separate country in Asia. It also does not mention Sikkim in its index of countries.

The move was significant since it involves recognition of Sikkim-China border which is a part of the Me Mahon Line. If things go as planned, the two nations should be able to work out the guide lines for transforming the Line of Actual Control (LoAC) into a mutually acceptable and internationally recognised boundary. However, China still insists that Arunachal Pradesh is a disputed territory.

China has also suggested a 'package deal'. It asked India to accept Chinese domination over Aksai Chin in return of China's acceptance of Me Mahon Line as the international boundary.

India, however, has advocated 'sector-by-sector' approach. Indian side is hopeful because China has settled border disputes with Russia and Vietnam.

BORDER CONFLICT AN OBSTACLE TO BUILDING TRUST BETWEEN CHINA AND INDIA

The then Indian chargé d'affaires Brajesh Mishra couldn't believe his ears at Chairman Mao Zedong's cue as they shook hands at a May Day parade on the Tiananmen rostrum in 1970. The wounds of the 1962 border war, in which India suffered a humiliating defeat, were still raw. Pointedly, Mishra was placed at the end of the line-up of diplomats arranged in order of precedence to meet Mao - after the British chargé d'affaires -

making the gesture all the more dramatic. Mishra immediately saw the opening Mao was creating for ties to resume, and was relieved it meshed with his own brief. Before he left for Beijing, then prime minister Indira Gandhi had laid it out for him in one sentence: "I am in a box so far as relations with China are concerned, and I want us to get out of that box." Despite this common yearning for détente, China and India would soon drift further apart - this time over the Bangladesh liberation war in 1971. While India backed the Bengali freedom fighters, Beijing threw its lot behind its "all-weather friend" Islamabad - a relationship that would dog Sino-Indian relations for decades. It wasn't until the 1990s that China and India would finally start a structured process of normalising ties. Economic relations have since gone from strength to strength, with China now India's largest trading partner. But as the recent three-week Himalayan stand-off brought home, the undercurrent of animosity still runs deep, and the possibility of unfriending each other all over again is never far away.

Arcing a curious trajectory, India and China's modern history would easily qualify for an "it's complicated" relationship status: active courting, followed by demonstrative friendship, violent break-up and now cautious reconciliation. It is this pull of a volatile past and the prospect of profitable cohabitation that Premier Li Keqiang will negotiate as he starts his India visit on Sunday. Li has already had a foretaste of the job at hand. His goodwill gesture of picking India as his first foreign destination on assuming power almost came undone with last month's border crisis. Even though both sides agreed to stand down, the episode will continue to hang heavy when Li lands in New Delhi.

According to Neville Maxwell, author of the seminal *India's China War*, such run-ins are natural as history shows an undefined border acts as a running sore between even the least bellicose of neighbours and can quickly turn malignant. "However much the neighbours may try to develop cordial relations in other aspects, the territorial dispute lurks in the background, making full trust unattainable," he says. Not that the "other aspects", notably economic engagement, are insignificant. Chinese goods have flooded Indian markets and Indian companies routinely raise yuan debt from Chinese banks. As the two sides have set a goal of US$100 billion trade by 2015, Li's visit is likely to see a raft of billion-dollar deals, with the attendant fanfare and boilerplate diplomatese on "strategic partnership".

But Professor Ma Jiali, executive deputy director of the Strategy Study Centre at the Beijing think tank China Reform Forum, points out: "The border dispute is the biggest obstacle to building strategic trust between China and India. It is directly related to the territorial sovereignty, core interests and national sentiment of the people of both countries." The dispute is over two separate territories, one in the western sector of the border and the other in the east. In the west, both China and India lay claim to 38,000 square kilometres of snowy wastelands known as Aksai Chin.

There is no demarcated border there, only a Line of Actual Control that fuzzily separates the territories controlled by them. And, each side has its own perception of where that line lies. It was in these icy heights that the recent stand-off took place. In the eastern sector, China claims some 90,000 square kilometres to the south of the McMahon Line, which was agreed to by Britain and Tibet in a secret deal in 1914 and not recognised by China. While China calls the region South Tibet, for India it is its Arunachal Pradesh state. The McMahon Line is the de facto border in this sector. Although China never accepted the McMahon Line, it was open to a land swap, under which India could keep what it claims on the eastern border while China would keep Aksai Chin in the west. Providing the best route into Tibet from the rest of China, Aksai Chin was non-negotiable for Beijing. For Delhi, both territories were off the table as inviolable flanks of national identity.

India and China have held 15 rounds of border talks at the special representative level since the mid-1990s but the gains have been limited. The border is remarkably well managed, with not a shot fired across it in over 20 years, but it's far from being settled, meaning the pre-1962 claims still hold for both sides. Half a century later, the border war today is seen largely as a dispute over land in the high mountains. But for a long time, India's first prime minister, Jawaharlal Nehru, who invested, and lost, substantial political capital in a policy of friendship with China (embodied in the early 1950s Indian slogan of*Hindi-Chini bhai bhai*, or India and China are brothers), would describe Aksai Chin as a place "where not a blade of grass grows".

And, in the course of the 1962 war, Chinese troops swept towards the plains as Indian forces retreated. Rather than holding on to their gains, China called a ceasefire and the troops returned to their old positions. Land was not the only thing the war was about. Far deeper factors were at play. The war coincided with the Sino-Soviet split. Declassified documents show Soviet leader Nikita Krushchev's irritation with China's handling of the border tension, and the Chinese leadership's anger at the Soviet backing of Nehru. For China, showing India its place was also a loaded message for the Soviet Union.

In India, Nehru was being squeezed between a rising left movement and the ascent of the right. In China, Mao was trying to reassert power within the party as the voices against the Great Leap Forward grew louder. And then there was Tibet. Nehru, while accepting China's sovereignty over Tibet, sought greater autonomy for it to act as a buffer between the two Asian giants. For him, Sino-Indian friendship was the cornerstone of Asia's rise, and for the relationship to work, China and India needed some space. Tibet would give them that space and guarantee the two armies would never come face to face. But for China, as Ma puts it, Tibet is a "core national interest". It is just as central to China's national pride as the border lands are for India's, with or without grass.

Dibyesh Anand, an associate professor at London's Westminster University, says: "There is a nationalist-security dissonance at the heart of how China and India approach Tibet and the border dispute. For China, Tibet is a nationalist issue and the border is a strategic issue, while for India, Tibet is a strategic issue and the border is a nationalist issue. The difference is, you can bargain over a strategic issue but not over a nationalist one." In *Protracted Contest: Sino-Indian Rivalry in the Twentieth Century*, sinologist John Garver notes the "brief period of Sino-India friendship from 1954 to 1958 coincided with a limited but genuine degree of Tibetan autonomy". India interpreted a 1954 pact signed with China on

Tibetan border trade as an implicit guarantee of Tibet's relative autonomy while China read it as India's promise to keep its hands off Tibet. The honeymoon ended when they started blaming each other for breaking the deal.

Things came to a head when the Dalai Lama fled to India following the Lhasa revolt of March 1959. China was furious that India provided him refuge and allowed him to set up a government-in-exile. Nehru was peeved that China wasn't cutting him any slack on Tibet, weakening his position at home. Mao was convinced India was colluding with the Americans to incite Tibetan refugees and India started patrolling the far-flung borders more aggressively under a "forward policy". From there on, war was but a matter of time. Many of the anxieties of 1962 linger. China still feels encircled by hostile powers and is as insecure over Tibet. "India uses the special status of Dalai to allow Tibetan refugees to launch separatist activities for creating trouble to resolve the border problem in the future. Indian politicians also interact with officials of the government-in-exile and Dalai," complains Ma. But Professor Susan Shirk, author of *China: Fragile Superpower*, believes that for the Chinese, it should be possible to shelve the territorial dispute. "This is because the media and the nationalist public don't pay much attention to it," says Shirk.

China sees India as one of the possible sources of trouble. For India, China*is* the trouble. India's sense of betrayal, at what it sees as a sudden and unwarranted land grab by a trusted friend, has festered with time, with China's rise and its proximity to Pakistan only fuelling its own fears of encirclement. "Tibet and the border dispute can take them back to a 1962-like situation. Economic interdependence should not be seen as replacing political negotiation," warns Anand. Unless, of course, they find a way to live with their differences and yet profit from each other.

Mishra, the chargé d'affaires in Beijing who went on to become India's national security adviser, would later recall in *Across the Himalayan Gap* that during his stint in China, he would attend the regulation diplomatic banquets but never actually got to eat anything. This was because the speeches would start during the second course and since the Chinese hosts would invariably lay into India and praise Pakistan, Mishra and his wife would have to walk out in protest. This went on for a while until Mishra noticed the speeches weren't starting until after the cakes and ice cream came out. A Pakistani diplomat told him the Chinese had noticed the Mishras were missing out on the food and decided to hold the speeches until after dessert.

ENDLESS ROUND OF BORDER DISPUTE NEGOTIATIONS BY CHINA

Endless rounds of border dispute negotiations have taken place between China and India. These have taken place at two levels, namely:

Joint Working Group (JWG) discussions which commenced in 1988

Special Representatives talks at the level of India's National Security Advisers and Chinese Vice Minister level since June 2003. The JWG has already completed over fifteen rounds of discussions. The Special Representatives held Seventh Round of talks in March 2006. The standard responses after each round have been of the type that was stated in March 2006: "The two Special Representative continued their discussions for an agreed framework for the resolution of the boundary question in a constructive and friendly atmosphere". Chinese leaders on visits to India come out with the oft-repeated statement that the boundary dispute should be left to future generations to resolve and meanwhile China-India relations in other fields should move forward. This is just an excuse to keep alive the border dispute as a strategic pressure point against India.

This leads to the question whether China is really serious about resolution of the China-India border dispute? The endless round of negotiations does not suggest so. It is best exemplified by an Indian media news report that no meetings have been scheduled between Indian and Chinese Special Representatives for talks on the boundary dispute before the visit of Chinese President Hu Jintao on November 20 "as India doesn't expect any substantive progress on the border issue in the near future." Symbolically, China's reluctance can be read as dissatisfaction with growing US-India strategic relationship and keeping alive the border dispute as a strategic pressure point against India. Obviously China is actively involved in delays and prolonging the resolution of the boundary disputes for strategic reasons.

Strategic Reluctance on Boundary Settlement with India by China

Veiled references in the past were made by Indian official spokesmen that progress could not be made as China was constantly pressurizing India to accept a swap by India of Tawang in lieu of Aksai-Chin. China has now come out in the open to demand and advocate this proposal. An Indian news-report covering the closed door meeting organized between Chinese distinguished experts and Indian academics by China's Institute of Asia-Pacific Studies, which is part of the giant official Chinese Academy of Social Sciences had this to report:

Chinese experts said that China would be magnanimous on the issue of Aksai Chin area if India agreed to give up Tawang. The high-level Chinese experts which included former Chinese Ambassador to India Chen Rui Sheng made it clear that the border dispute could be solved if India handed over Tawang to China.

The Strategic Significance of Tawang for India

At the outset it must be made clear that for the Chinese, Tawang is not just the Tawang Monastery region. For them Tawang implies the whole of India's Arunachal Pradesh. So as not to dilute their claim, they officially will not call it that Arunachal Pradesh should be returned to them. Coming to the strategic importance of Arunachal Pradesh or Tawang in Chinese parlance the following need to be recognized: Arunachal Pradesh provides strategic depth to India's Brahmaputra Valley and India's other North Eastern states. Arunachal Pradesh provides security to Bhutan on it entire Eastern flank by geographical contiguity.

Bhutan would be then be in a pincer group of China on both it flanks if Tawang is given away. This would be detrimental to India's security. China's borders would then rest on the plains of Assam; India might as well write off its other North Eastern states.

The Chinese obsession with the Tawang Region is totally strategic in its aims. In any future conflict with China and if India singly or in coalition with some other power develops offensive capabilities against China, this region offers the shortest cut to China proper and to Tibet. India's communications infrastructure in this region developed in World War II for US military aid to China is existent and can be further improved.

Arunachal Pradesh offers all-wealthier lines of communication to India for military needs to the Tibet border as compared to Aksai-Chin. In terms of any air operations by China in this region, Arunachal Pradesh would provide multilayered air defence deployments on the ground as deterrence. The region is rich in terms of mineral and natural resources prospects. There are many more reasons that one can state but the major ones should be enough. Arunachal Pradesh is of vital strategic importance for the territorial integrity and defence of India's North East states and should be non-negotiable.

China would be politically naive of it perceives that in the 21st Century, a powerfully rising India would accept the bait of a Chinese strategic barter of Aksai-Chin in lieu of Tawang India would be more politically naive than China if it thinks that China would concede the area of Aksai-Chin through which passes its lifelines to keep Xinjiang under Chinese control. Both in Aksai Chin and in the Arunachal Pradesh area, the strategic interests of China and India clash in the most intense manner. It would be a magical wonder if China can turn around to be strategically accommodative of India's strategic sensitivities. China's strategic reluctances to solve the border dispute with India can therefore be expected to bedevil China-India relations for a long time to come.

ADJUSTMENTS TO INDIA'S CHINA POLICY SINCE THE END OF THE COLD WAR

Certain scholars believe that India's China policy has undergone three major phases of adjustment since the end of the Cold War: the pre-1998 phase policy of reconciliation; the 1998–2000 phase policy of hostility; and the 2000 to present phase policy of engagement. The second phase around the time of the 1998 nuclear tests featured harangues from the Indian government regarding the 'China threat' and a brief deadlock in Sino–Indian relations. The author, however, believes that two, rather than three, phases of adjustment are applicable to an explanation of the state of bilateral relations between China and India in the post-Cold War era.

When considering India's overall strategic aims at the time of the 1998 nuclear tests and the implications and specific actions of its subsequent China policy, it is difficult to pinpoint two 180 degree-policy shifts in the course of just two years. Facts demonstrate that India named China as a threat at the time of the 1998 tests as a matter of expedience to acquiesce in the anti-China stance of certain parties in the United States and other Western nations; it was a ploy whose purpose was to divert attention from and rationalize the nuclear tests, thereby dispelling any notion of sanctions.

It should be borne in mind, however, that India's understanding of comprehensive national strength deepened after the Cold War, as did its leaders' belief that nuclear arms and credible nuclear deterrence were hallmarks of a superpower. Entering the nuclear club was consequently a stride towards achieving one of the sub-continent's greatest national aspirations. The Rao government, which pursued a China policy of reconciliation and engagement, had made preparations for nuclear tests but stopped short of carrying them out for fear of the potential burden on the newly recovered economy of international sanctions.

Prime Minister Vajpayee and other political leaders repeatedly and publicly expressed soon after the 1998 tests that India had no wish to hold China as an enemy or a threat, stating, to the contrary, their desire for reinforced friendly relations. At no point during this period did diplomatic engagement between India and China cease. Indian External Affairs Minister Jaswant Singh's visit to China in June 1999 demonstrated that the Sino–Indian relationship had recovered in the space of a year from any damage that the nuclear tests had inflicted upon it. That becoming a nuclear power while maintaining stable relations with China were post-Cold War

India's strategic goals was also implied by the sub-continent's explicit moves towards repairing its relationship with China. The 1998 nuclear tests constituted no fundamental change to India's China policy and should, within the scope of Sino–Indian relations, be regarded as a minor episode. Moreover, the shift of India's China policy in 1988 was not prompted by any change of security concept; Prime Minister Rajiv Gandhi's trip to China that year was motivated by the fact of Sino–Soviet reconciliation. Changes in security concept explicitly propelled India's; post-Cold War China policy adjustments. This book, therefore, primarily examines developments and changes in India's China policy after the Cold War. It holds that a substantive change indeed occurred; specifically from one of hostility and antagonism during the Cold War (especially 1962–1988) to reconciliation and engagement thereafter. This policy change, however, was by no means instantaneous but characterized by gradual, phased development. Two, rather than three, phases of adjustment tally with changes in India's post-Cold War security concept.

India's China Policy from the End of the Cold War to 1998

Indian leaders believed after 1962 that hostilities between China and India were inevitable, and viewed China as a major enemy. Prime Minister Indira Gandhi considered Sino–Indian antagonism as going far beyond border disputes, and that China was pursuing the more 'complex' policy of pressing India on all fronts and, moreover, displacing the sub-continent by establishing its own dominant position in the Asian power hierarchy. The goal of India's China policy during this period, therefore, was to ensure its supremacy over China in Asia and, in the event of armed conflict, to avoid repeating mistakes that had led to its defeat in the 1962 Sino–Indian conflict. India's policy at the time can be so summarized: strengthen military capability and deployment; seek aid from major powers, respectively, the United States, United Kingdom and USSR; and support Chinese separatist forces. After the Cold War ended, however, changes in India's domestic and international situation brought tremendous challenges, and its position as regards China and its related policy goals showed clear adjustments. India considered China as a nation going through a reflective, 'inward looking' period and, as such, had no intention of attacking the sub-continent. In the short-term, therefore, it constituted no threat. The goal of India's new China policy was to maintain stability in Sino–Indian relations, ensure peaceful borders and create conditions suitable for India to gather its resources and restore economic and military strength. The specific policy adjustments were as follows.

Achieve Simultaneous Progress in Solving Border Disputes

For almost two decades after 1962, India made resolution of border disputes a pre-condition for normalizing relations with China. Its insistence in this regard was the main reason for the longstanding chill in Sino–Indian relations. Although the two nations restored ambassadorial-level diplomatic relations in 1976, and in 1981 agreed to begin talks on the border issue, this principled standpoint did not change. Upon meeting with visiting then-External Affairs Minister Vajpayee early in 1979, Comrade Deng Xiaoping proposed an agreement that would provide 'a package solution' for relevant border disputes.

He said that if it were not possible completely to resolve border disputes at an early date, he would consider cooperation in other areas. But it was not until 1988 during Rajiv Gandhi's trip to China that the Indian government accepted this suggestion and formally initiated the process of normalizing bilateral relations which the successive Indian governments pursued and implemented after the Cold War ended. It is notable that during the time the two sides promoted negotiations on border issues they also exchanged high-level visits in which the two nations signed cooperative agreements in such areas as trade, technology, education and culture, and that cooperation between them grew ever greater in depth and breadth.

Shift Strategies on Border Talks

As India needed a peaceful, stable environment in which to concentrate on economic recovery, securing Sino–Indian borders was its primary goal in the early 1990s. Because of India's; pre-1988 insistence on not normalizing Sino–Indian relations until the border issues were settled, there were suspicions that the sub-continent was 'taking improvements in bilateral relations as a bargaining chip through which to force China to yield in border disputes'. India consequently insisted in the talks that began in 1981 on its own position as regards a segmented solution to the issue. India's objective understanding of the complexity of the Sino–Indian border dispute after the Cold War and of realistic strategic considerations and needs prompted an adjusted strategy for these talks. This was manifest in its suggestion of a gradual solution to border disputes: the first step would be to stabilize the Line of Actual Control (LAC) situation and eliminate disagreements over its demarcation; the second to reach agreement on preserving peace and tranquillity along the LAC; and the third to take measures to establish mutual trust along the LAC.

This accomplished, the two nations could then address substantive problems in their border dispute. This tentative plan enabled India and China to approach a consistent position whereby the two sides worked to achieve a solution to Sino–Indian border disputes and create an atmosphere of reasonableness and peace. The two nations made progress, signing in 1993 the Agreement on Maintenance of Peace and Tranquillity along the Line of Actual Control in the Sino– Indian Border Areas, and in 1996 the Agreement Between the Government of the Republic of India and the Government of the People's Republic of China on Confidence-Building Measures in the Military Field Along the Line of Actual Control in the India–China Border Areas. India saw these two agreements as on the one hand ensuring the two sides could resolve border disputes peacefully without resorting to violence, and on the other that border disputes would not inhibit the development of their bilateral relations.

Tibetan Issue and do not Provoke China

Leaders of India's independence movement had at the time of the British Raj followed the British colonialist concept of Tibet as a 'buffer region' between India and China. After winning independence, therefore, the Indian government supported from the very beginning the so-called 'Tibetan independence movement'. At around the time of the founding of the People's Republic of

China, India seized the opportunity offered by China's political upheaval to promote the international standing of the local Tibetan government and thwart China's liberation of Tibet. New Delhi continued unremittingly in its efforts to convince China's central government, even during the 1950s heyday of Sino–Indian amity, to give Tibet substantial autonomy and to reduce to the greatest extent possible the size of its garrison there. After the insurrection of 1959 the Indian government was more overt in its support of Tibet, giving asylum to fugitive rebels and propping up the so-called 'Tibetan Government in Exile' established by the Dalai Lama in 1960 in the Indian city of Dharamsala. India further incited and encouraged Tibetan independence activities after the Sino–Indian conflict of 1962.

In truth, Indian leaders considered their support for exiled Tibetans' separatist activities as an effective containment against China. But when Prime Minister Rajiv Gandhi visited China in 1988 he issued the statement: 'The Indian side reiterates the long-standing and consistent policy of the Government of India that Tibet is an autonomous region of China and that anti-China political activities by Tibetan elements are not permitted on Indian soil,' which implied India's change of approach from that of support for Tibetan independence. Indian leaders reiterated this pledge after the Cold War ended and imposed limits on Tibetan fugitives' anti-China political activities. For instance, Indian officials would generally contact the Dalai Lama and leaders of the so-called Tibetan government in exile before a visit by Chinese leaders to India, requesting that they refrain from Tibetan protests, demonstrations or other anti-Chinese behaviour.

Yet, differences still exist between China and India on the issue of Tibetan autonomy. Although, proceeding from the requirement of preserving stable Sino–Indian relations, the post-Cold War Indian government has been low-key in its support of the Dalai Lama and other Tibetan fugitives, this does not signify a substantial change in its strategic treatment of the Tibetan issue.

Changes in India's China Policy from 1999 to Present

Achieving recovery, contending for the status of global power had been India's ambition for decades. The growth of the subcontinent's comprehensive strength and improvements in the international environment in the late 1990s presented to it a real possibility of realizing this ambition, as well as a number of other unprecedented strategic opportunities. Against this backdrop, reconciliation with China and the unchanged overall direction of the relationship produced several new adjustments to the positions and goals of India's China policy. At this stage, India saw China neither as enemy nor friend, believing that cooperation could coexist with competition between the two nations. India still considered China as constituting no threat in the short term, but began focusing on long-term trends in the balance of power. The emphasis of the goals of its new China policy are on ensuring that future Sino–Indian relations are of benefit to India by making China a positive factor in the process of its rise. Maintaining the stability of Sino–Indian relations remains fundamental. The new policy adjustments are as follows.

Expand Economic Cooperation with China

Trade between the two nations ceased after the 1962 Sino–Indian Border Conflict, and did not resume until 1977. The volume of trade between the two sides in the 1980s wavered at around roughly Us." million. But after the Cold War ended, Sino–Indian trade experienced a seemingly spontaneous phase of rapid development. The trade volume between China and India increased from $264 million in 1991 to $1.988 billion in 1999—a yearly average of 31.2%—or an increase factor of 6.5 over eight years. Indian leaders' concerns about India's economic recovery nonetheless maintained at this point the China policy focus on stabilizing political relations and establishing tranquil borders. Indian leaders' understanding of economic strength and security having becoming more profound since 1999, their enthusiasm for developing bilateral trade soared. As China and India were the world's two most rapidly developing nations, Indian leaders could see the obvious potential for trade between them and that strengthening bilateral trade would be of great mutual benefit. Also that close economic ties could have a stabilizing influence on their political relationship. Statistics show that bilateral trade since 1999 has entered into a new period of growth. The average yearly growth to 2006 was 44.4%—a rate which exceeded that of the preceeding period and which is being achieved on an ever-stronger numerical foundation. The volume of Sino–Indian trade reached US$24.8 billion in 2006, having increased by a factor of 11.5 over 1999 and one of 93 over 1991. China became India's second largest trading partner in 2006, and India China's tenth largest. It may be said that the role of Sino–Indian trade has grown from one unworthy of mention to a decisive aspect of the overall bilateral relationship.

CHALLENGES AND IMPLICATIONS FOR DOMESTIC POLICY REFORM

The challenges facing China and India for sustaining rapid economic growth and meeting the MDGs are similar in nature. First there is the matter of continuing to reduce poverty and hunger and maintain food security. Two other serious issues concern the widening rural-urban income gap and the degradation of the environment. Also of concern is the need to restructure agriculture and markets to meet more diversified consumer and export market food demand, and the need to adopt policies that enable both countries to maintain comparative advantage in commodity production. How these challenges are addressed will determine to a large degree the success in meeting the MDGs, the ability to sustain growth and the role that these economies will play in world markets.

Food Security and Poverty

Two important questions related to achieving the MDGs of poverty and hunger reduction need to be answered. How does the growth in agriculture and in the non-agricultural economy affect poverty alleviation? What can we learn from the experience of China and India?

Ravallion and Chen (2004) for China and Ravallion and Datt (1996) for India conclude that there is a strong link between poverty reduction and increased agricultural productivity. However, Besley *et al.* (2004) argues on the basis of an enormously rich data set and very sophisticated econometrics that agriculture has played a minimal role at best in India's reduction of poverty (Timmer 2005). The China case study provides several interesting results on key factors that have determined the changes in rural poverty in China. Overall economic growth has been a key primary source of rural poverty reduction. But while economic growth is an essential and necessary condition for nationwide poverty reduction, it is not a sufficient condition. As incomes have grown the impact and effectiveness of general economic growth on poverty reduction has weakened. Fan *et al.* (2002) for China and Fan *et al.* for India (2002) examine the poverty impact of various agricultural investments and subsidies. Their work suggests that there are important multipliers at work and that the impact of these multipliers changes over time. In addressing the question of poverty impact of agriculture *per se* we need to look at the links between the agricultural and non-agricultural economy including rural non-farm employment.

Taking the aforesaid views into consideration, we observe in China that the TVEs provided a strong link between agricultural and non-agricultural economy which undoubtedly accounted for the sharp drop in poverty. Also fostering poverty alleviation has been the egalitarian nature of the reforms under the HRS. By contrast, the links between the agricultural and non-agricultural economy have been less strong in India and have been hampered by a host of regulations which have slowed the development of both agriculture and industry. Overall growth in the GDP is increasing in India while growth in agricultural GDP has been declining which does not speak well for reducing rural poverty.

Based on projections using the GTAP model both country studies conclude that they can meet domestic cereal grain demands without reliance on significant imports. Since the food shortages of the mid-1960s, foodgrain self-sufficiency has been a dominant feature of Indian agricultural policy. China also sets a high priority on foodgrain self-sufficiency. However, maintaining self-sufficiency in wheat production will almost certainly require improved management of water resources in the Punjab and neighbouring states and in the North China Plain.

Foodgrain self-sufficiency at the national level does not ensure food security at the regional or household level. It is a paradox that with more than 260 million people below the official poverty line in 1999-2000, India is one of the leading exporters of rice. Poverty incidence is expected to continue to fall in India from 26.1 percent in 1999-2000, reaching 8 percent in 2015 well beyond the MDG. But achieving this goal would appear to depend on the success of the reforms which target the growth in agriculture to rise from the sluggish 1.5 percent to 4 percent*per annum.*

From the experience of both China and India, the policy implications seem clear. Attention must be given to raising agricultural productivity and incomes in those areas that have thus far not benefited from new technologies or trade liberalization. At the same time emphasis should be on creating jobs in the non-farm sector, whether rural or urban based. For China this will require continuing reform of state-owned enterprises (SOEs) and encouragement of labour-intensive private industry. India's continuing reforms should foster growth in employment in both the manufacturing and service sectors.

The Widening Income Gap

In addition to the rural-urban income gap, especially that between agriculture and new, dynamic industries, there are regional disparities such as between the coastal and the central and western provinces in China or between the Punjab and Haryana and the states of Eastern India. Further within regions there is the disparity between those that have become commercialized, for example through contract farming and those that follow traditional practices. Disparity in India exists between the more commercialized farmers in the Punjab and Haryana as opposed to those in Bihar and Orissa. The issue here is not necessarily absolute poverty, but what Hayami (2005) describes as relative poverty. The less favourable areas need better education and health services and equal access to social services. Gulati *et al.* (2005) argue to this end that China and India should accelerate growth, improve efficiency and at the same time ensure that growth is both equitable and sustainable. To improve efficiency, India should phase out subsidies and efforts should be focused on developing infrastructure and new technologies. However, for many the path out of poverty lies not in agriculture but in non-farm opportunities. Both countries are experiencing rapid migration from rural to urban areas. But too little attention is paid to facilitating migration of rural workers to urban jobs where investments in the rural economy have a low payoff.

Both China and India are committed to addressing the income gap, but the approaches will be very different. China recently approved a 15 percent increase in the money earmarked for agricultural development, and rural services. Also China has initiated the "Five Balanced Development Strategies: balanced development between rural and urban, between economic growth and social progress, among regions, between human intervention and environmental conservation, and between internal and external economies." The proposed strategies and reforms are bold but there are many barriers to achieving the lofty goals of the programme.

The UPA Government came to power in India in May 2004 and the National Common Minimum Programme forms the bedrock of economic policy with the highest priority for agriculture and a holistic approach to agriculture and rural development.

But India faces a different set of policy and institutional constraints. Rationalizing subsidies and extending reforms that liberalized industry to agriculture through the removal of regulations and restrictions to trade seem to be crucial. India also must address the problem of a high variability in income and livelihood among regions and states.

Bibliography

Ajey Lele: *Strategic Technologies for the Military : Breaking New Frontiers*, Sage, Delhi, 2009.

Allen Carlson, *Unifying China, Integrating with the World: Securing Chinese Sovereignty in the Reform Era*, Stanford: Stanford University Press, 2005.

Amitabh Sikdar: *India and China : Strategic Energy Management and Security*, Manas, Delhi, 2009.

Anderson, M. and Bort, E.: *Boundaries and Identities: The Eastern Frontier of the Asia*, Edinburgh: International Social Sciences Institute, University of Edinburgh, 1996.

Anil, K.C.: *Military and Democracy in South Asia : Challenges, Politics and Power*, Sumit Enterprises, Delhi, 2009.

Asha Gupta: *Military Rule and Democratization : Changing Perspectives*, Deep & Deep, Delhi, 2003.

Bhat, T.P. : *India and China : Trade Complementarities and Competitiveness*, Bookwell, Delhi, 2008.

Cheek, Timothy: *Mao Zedong and China's Revolutions: A Brief History with Documents*. Boston: Bedford/St. Martin's, 2002.

Deepak, B R : *India and China : 1904-2004 : A Century of Peace and Conflict*, Manak, Delhi, 2005.

Dietmar Rothermund. *A History of India*. Totowa, New Jersey: Barnes and Noble, 1986.

Digumarti Bhaskara Rao: *Military Conversion : Impact on Science and Technology*, Discovery, Delhi, 2003.

Ellis, F. 2000. *Rural Livelihoods and Diversity in Developing Countries*. New York: Oxford University Press.

Evelyn Goh, *Meeting the China Challenge: The U.S. in Southeast Asian Regional Security Strategies*, DC: East-West Center, 2005.

Friedman, G.: *The Future of War of Cyber Crimes*, N.Y., Random House, 1996.

Gao, Mobo: *The Battle for China's Past: Mao and the Cultural Revolution*, London, Pluto Press, 2008.

George Mathew: *Grass Roots Democracy in India and China : The Right to Participate*, Sage, Delhi, 2007.

Gupta, S.: *Disrupted Borders: An Intervention in Definitions of Boundaries*, London: River Oram Press, 1993.

Huntington, S.P.: *The China Defence Modernisation Military and the State*, N.Y., Vintage Books, 1964.

Jagannath P. Panda: *China's Path to Power : Party, Military and the Politics of State Transition*, Pentagon, Delhi, 2010.

Kapur, C.K. : *Chinese Military Modernisation*, Manas, Delhi, 2003.

Kumar, Satish. *Rana Polity in Nepal: Origin and Growth*. New York: Asia, 1967.

Major Donovan: *Air Defence Power*. Sampson Low. London, 1940.

Narendra K Dash : *Buddhism in Indian Literature*, Aryan Books International, 2007.

Nayyar, K K : *National Security : Military Aspects*, Rupa, Delhi, 2003.

Posen, B.R.: *The Sources of Military Doctrine*, Ithaca, 1984, Cornell Univ. Press.

Prabir De: *India and China in an Era of Globalisation : Essays on Economic Cooperation*, Bookwell, Delhi, 2005.

Radhakrishna: *Military Ethics: Guidelines for Peace and War*, Sumit Enterprises, Delhi, 2009.

Rosen, P.: *Societies and Military Power: India and its Armies*, Ithaca, Cornell University Press, 1996.

Thapar, Romila. *A History of India*. New York: Penguin, 1966.

Theodore, William : *The Buddhist Tradition in India, China and Japan*, New York: Vintage Books, 1972.

Wilson, T. M.: *New Borders for a Changing: Cross-border Cooperation and Governance*, London: Frank Cass, 2003.

Index

P

S

W

❑❑❑